# Psychopathology at School

*Psychopathology at School* provides a timely response to concerns about the rising numbers of children whose behaviour is recognized and understood as a medicalized condition, rather than simply as poor behaviour caused by other factors. It is the first scholarly analysis of psychopathology which draws on the philosophers Foucault, Deleuze, Guattari and Arendt to examine the processes whereby children's behaviour is pathologized. The heightened attention to mental disorders is contrasted with education practices in the early and mid-to-late twentieth century, and the emergence of a new conceptualization of childhood is explored.

Taking education as a central component of the contemporary experience of growing up, the book charts the ways in which mental disorders have become commonplace in childhood and youth, from birth through to college and university, but also offers examples of where professionals have refused to pathologize children's behaviour. The book examines the extent of the influence of psychopathology on the lives of children and young people, as well as the practices that infiltrate education and the possibilities for alternative educational responses that negate the diagnosis of mental disorder.

*Psychopathology at School* is a must read for anyone concerned about the growing influence of psychopathology in education and will be of particular interest to educated readers and to scholars, students and professionals in education, psychiatry, psychology, child studies, youth studies, nursing, social work and sociology.

**Valerie Harwood** is a Future Fellow with the Australian Research Council and Associate Professor of Sociology of Education at the University of Wollongong, Australia.

**Julie Allan** is Professor of Equity and Inclusion at the University of Birmingham, UK, and Visiting Professor of Education at the University of Borås, Sweden.

# Theorizing Education Series

Series Editors

Gert Biesta
University of Luxembourg, Luxembourg

Julie Allan
University of Birmingham, UK

Richard Edwards
University of Stirling, UK

*Theorizing Education* brings together innovative work from a wide range of contexts and traditions which explicitly focuses on the roles of theory in educational research and educational practice. The series includes contextual and socio-historical analyses of existing traditions of theory and theorizing, exemplary use of theory, and empirical work where theory has been used in innovative ways. The distinctive focus for the series is the engagement with educational questions, articulating what explicitly educational function the work of particular forms of theorizing supports.

Books in this series:

**Making a Difference in Theory**
The theory question in education and the education question in theory
*Eds. Gert Biesta, Julie Allan and Richard Edwards*

**Forgotten Connections**
On culture and upbringing
*Klaus Mollenhauer*
*Translated by Norm Friesen*

**Psychopathology at School**
Theorizing mental disorders in education
*Valerie Harwood and Julie Allan*

# Psychopathology at School

Theorizing mental disorders in education

Valerie Harwood and Julie Allan

Routledge
Taylor & Francis Group

LONDON AND NEW YORK

First published 2014
by Routledge
2 Park Square, Milton Park, Abingdon, Oxon OX14 4RN

and by Routledge
711 Third Avenue, New York, NY 10017

Routledge is an imprint of the Taylor & Francis Group, an informa business

British Library Cataloguing in Publication Data
A catalogue record for this book is available from the British Library

Library of Congress Cataloging in Publication Data
Harwood, Valerie, 1967–
Psychopathology at school : theorizing mental disorders in education /
Valerie Harwood, Julie Allan.
pages cm. – (Theorizing education)
1. Children with mental disabilities—Education. 2. Youth with mental
disabilities—Education. 3. Psychopathology. I. Allan, Julie (Julie E.)
II. Title.
LC4601.H35 2014
371.9—dc23
2013040225

ISBN: 978-0-415-81042-5 (hbk)
ISBN: 978-0-203-07100-7 (ebk)

Typeset in Bembo
by Swales & Willis Ltd, Exeter, Devon, UK

# Contents

*List of illustrations*                                          vi
*Series editors' preface*                                       vii
*Acknowledgements*                                               ix

1   Introduction                                                  1

2   A brief history of mental disorders in school                17

3   The risk factors? 'Race', social class and gender            46

4   From the cradle to the crèche                                67

5   Primary school                                               86

6   Secondary school                                            103

7   Colleges and universities                                   120

8   Professionals' interruptions                                144

9   Conclusion: learning, teaching and the thrill of pedagogy   157

*List of legislation cited*                                     173
*References*                                                    174
*Index*                                                         200

# Illustrations

## Figures

| | | |
|---|---|---:|
| 2.1 | Observation and description of facts: hand postures indicative of brain function | 19 |
| 2.2 | Photographs of college students, depicting bad (top) and good (bottom) practices of mental hygiene | 37 |
| 2.3 | Apparatus used in psychological and psychoeducational clinics | 41 |
| 3.1 | *Après la saisie* by Jean Louis Forain, *c.* 1870–1900 | 58 |
| 7.1 | *Melancholia I* by Albrecht Dürer (1514) | 129 |
| 7.2 | *Cho Seung Hui Comics 3* by Carlos Latuff (2007) | 134 |

## Table

| | | |
|---|---|---:|
| 4.1 | Domains to be assessed in the comprehensive psychiatric assessment of a young child | 82 |

# Series editors' preface

This is the third volume in the *Theorizing Education* series. Drawing upon a number of empirical studies from Australia, the UK and USA, Valerie Harwood and Julie Allan highlight the important educational issue of the increased diagnosis of children and young people with medical conditions to be treated by drugs. In this, they are pointing both to the increasing scope of what they refer to as the psychopathologizing of education and the increased use of drug treatments by pupils and students in education. Through examining which groups are most prone to be subjected to these practices of psychopathologizing, they also point to the reproduction of inequalities in education. It is those from minority ethnic backgrounds, those from poor backgrounds and boys who are most likely to be diagnosed and treated with drugs and other therapies. They are particularly concerned that education is not simply a site for psychopathologizing, but is also actively engaged in its enactments.

From one angle, the increasing diagnosis of people with conditions to be treated might be argued to be a good thing, as it helps to explain 'bad' behaviour and under-achievement in education. On this reading, treatment should enable people to learn. However, Harwood and Allan argue that the range and extent of such treatments point to the displacement of education by medicine and the reproduction of exclusion and inequality. They argue for a critical and pedagogic response from educators. It is a powerful and provocative discussion.

The pertinence of this volume to the series is threefold. First, there is the question of the nature of knowledge informing educational practices. The latter are traversed and enacted by a diverse network of professional and disciplinary discourses, especially as increased emphasis in many countries is placed on education as part of children's services as the need for inter-professional working to support the development of the whole child/young person. Care, medicine and policing, as well as educational knowledge, enact the child in different and not always complementary ways. In examining the practices of psychopathologizing, Harwood and Allan are suggesting that certain types of medical knowledge and practices have become influential at the expense of the educational. While no one would deny the importance of the legitimate treatment of medical conditions, the ways in which 'disorders' and 'syndromes' are proliferating is a rightful area of concern.

Second, their argument points to the importance of theorizing in relation to empirical issues in education. Empirically, we can identify the increased diagnosis and treatment of conditions among pupils and students. We can ask and address important empirical questions about who is and is not being treated, how and with what consequences. But to address the issue of why such trends may be significant and in what ways requires a broader theoretical framing of the empirical phenomena. Framing the empirical through psychopathology is one way of highlighting the educational significance of these trends and educational responses to them.

This brings us to the third reason this volume is an important contribution to the series. To theorize is necessary, but then there is the question of which theories are most pertinent. We suggested in the first volume of the series that theorizing can attempt to explain, understand and emancipate. One of the reasons for the power and influence of medical discourses is that they seek to explain. Both rhetorically and practically this can be attractive in providing a 'clear' view of what the issue is and what is to be done. A lot of educational knowledge focuses more on understanding and emancipation. Its capacity to influence is often normative and less clear cut. Harwood and Allan draw upon the works of Foucault, Deleuze and Guatarri, and Arendt to frame their notion of the psychopathology and its work. They provide a powerful understanding of the nature and extent of how medicine intervenes in and becomes part of educational practices and make the case for a critical and pedagogical response.

The reproduction of wider inequalities within educational institutions is not a new phenomenon or point of commentary. What Harwood and Allan are highlighting are some of the new ways in which these are manifest through the extension of practices of diagnosis and treatment, which may pacify rather than educate. Whether the attempt to provide a better understanding of these practices and generate critical educational responses to them can counter the power of explanation, however problematic the latter may be, will depend upon our own responses and practices and those of many other educators.

Richard Edwards
Gert Biesta

# Acknowledgements

This work has been supported by two grants: The Australian Research Council Discovery Projects (Harwood, DP110104704) and the Academy of the Social Sciences in Australia International Science Linkages Bilateral Program (Harwood & Allan).

Parts of this work and some the ideas developed in it have been published elsewhere, and we thank the publishers for their permission to use this material. These publications are:

Allan, J. and Harwood, V. (2013). 'Medicus interruptus in the behaviour of children in disadvantaged contexts in Scotland', *British Journal of Sociology of Education*. DOI:10.1080/01425692.2013.776933.

Harwood, V. (2011). 'Connecting the dots: threat assessment, depression and the troubled student', *Curriculum Inquiry*, 41(5): 586–609.

## Illustrations

We wish to thank Carlos Latuff for permission to use *Cho Seung Hui comics 3* and the Trustees of the British Museum for permission to use *Melancholia* by Albrecht Dürer and *Après la saisie* by Jean Louis Forain. We also wish to acknowledge the following:

'Observation and description of facts: Hand postures indicative of brain function' from Warner, F. (1890) *A Course of Lectures on the Growth and Means of Training the Mental Faculty. Delivered in the University of Cambridge*, Cambridge: At the University Press (Cambridge).

'Photographs of college students, depicting bad (top) and good (bottom) practices of mental hygiene' from McKinney, F. (1947) *The Psychology of Personal Adjustment*, New York: John Wiley & Sons.

'Apparatus used in psychological and psychoeducational clinics' from Wallin, J.E.W. (1927) *Clinical and Abnormal Psychology. A textbook for educators, psychologists and mental hygiene workers*, London: George G. Harrap & Company.

Finally, our thanks go to Dr Samantha McMahon, who assisted with the production of the manuscript.

# Chapter 1

# Introduction

> My mate Liam he got discriminated just because he's in a special class and he doesn't want to learn. He just wants people to leave him alone. He has the same *thing* as me; I go crazy on them.
>
> (Tony, 13 years old, IUE Tasmania, Australia, emphasis added)[1]

When asked about discrimination this young person's immediate response was to tell a story about schooling. It is a story involving himself, his friend Liam, his former primary school and, significantly, the experience of having a 'thing'. Liam had experienced discrimination in primary school because he was in the 'special class' and, as Tony reveals, both he and Liam shared the same *thing*. This 'thing', as we will explore in this book, is psychopathology.

Psychopathology is a phenomenon that is firmly entrenched, if not ubiquitous, in schooling. We use the term psychopathology to refer to the range of mental disorders used in schools and education and to the discourses and practices tied to psychopathology that allow significant proportions of children and young people to be identified and treated as mentally ill. We are concerned with how psychopathology is marked out in concrete ways via designations of mental disorder, what we might term the archetypal diagnosis and what Tony called the *thing*. The presence of psychopathology in schools, however, occurs in other more complex ways, the most obvious of which is the medication of children and young people. As a practice in schools, medicating can occur in very public forms, with the lines of children in primary schools awaiting their medication observed and remarked upon by children and staff (Harwood 2006). This type of practice has effects that not only circulate local school knowledge about the children with the *thing*, but create opportunities for the production of knowledge about psychopathology. Schools are sites of significance in the contemporary production of psychopathology. The consequences of psychopathology for the children and young people who are 'captured' in the diagnostic gaze and pronounced mentally ill are both profound and far-reaching. Principally, the recourse to medical diagnosis takes the place of considerations of the education of these children. We seek, in this book, to show how this displacement takes place and to explore the possibilities for recovering pedagogy over pathology.

It is difficult to dismiss the degree to which mental disorders have become part of the mechanism for interpreting children and explaining their educational failure. Problems such as too much activity or too little, fighting, problems making friends, or failure to meet developmental milestones can be candidates for speculation about mental disorder. Phrases such as 'he's ADHD' or 'that's so ADHD' are popular metaphors for 'hyperactivity' and bring the language of mental disorders into everyday colloquial vocabulary. As we will maintain, these ways of talking about children have effects on how children are understood and contribute to the medicalization of children.

The cited rates of child mental disorders not only reveal the numbers that have mental disorders (or might be expected to have them); they reveal those most diagnosed, and at times identify those who are more likely to have mental problems. In the United States mental disorders are considered to affect 'one in five children in their lifetime' (Science Daily 2010), in the United Kingdom 10 per cent of children are estimated to have mental health issues (Mental Health Foundation 2012) and there are reports that 'one in five children worldwide has a mental disorder' (J. Smith 2011). Behavioural disorders such as ADHD are considered to be the most prevalent, with global estimates of this mental disorder across developed and developing countries placing rates as high as 5.29 per cent and contending that geographic location has limited impact (Polanczyk et al. 2007). Claims of worldwide or global prevalence are under dispute by some who maintain that geographic and cultural contexts are significant to interpretations of child behaviour and mental health (Amaral 2007; Alban-Metcalfe, Cheng-Lai and Ma 2002).

From the well-known ADHD to disorders such as bipolar disorder, learning disorder, depression and obsessive–compulsive disorder, mental disorders have become part of the common parlance of childhood. Increasing reliance on the medicines for mental disorders has brought the medicalization of children into focus and is the medium that has generated the most controversy. Children are now medicated at earlier ages than ever before and there are proliferating numbers of college and university students on depression-related medication. A recent opinion piece in the *New York Times* reports that three million children in the United States are using medication for ADHD (Sroufe 2012). Pills for childhood problems are a strong image of this medicalization and it is not surprising that there are considerable debates about uses of medication, especially with very young children.

Yet there are many outcomes of diagnosis that can slip under the radar when attention is emotively aroused by medication. One of these, as we outline in this book, is the fundamental change occurring in how children are understood. Developmental stages, for instance, now include navigating a narrow passage through the increasing proliferation of mental disorders. From this perspective, psychopathology at school further narrows the normalization of schooling and children (Baker 2002; J. Ryan 1991).

While developmentalism has had a discursive hold over how children 'progress' across childhood stages (Walkerdine 1984), we suggest that mental disorders contribute something more. Mental disorders create a radical shake-up of the influential discourses of developmental trajectories. This is because they are wildcards in the lexicon of childhood. The theories and practices that support mental disorders enable them to become manifest in ways that were once the domain of adulthood. For example, diagnoses such as bipolar disorder now affect children with regularity. In the United States some reports have cited bipolar disorder in children as reaching epidemic rates, with 800,000 diagnoses (Carmichael 2008).

## Children and medication

Medication is one of the most prominent topics in discussions about children and mental disorders. Tony, and numerous other young men and boys (and it is becoming more common with young women and girls) can be counted among the young people who are taking medication as an alleged means to continue with schooling. Such is the attention to medication that pharmaceuticals figure prominently in discussions concerning children and medicalization. The attention to medication is readily apparent in the number of news media stories published about child behaviour. So, too, is the attention given to schools and medication. This interplay is evident in the news media excerpt below, taken from *The Times* newspaper in the UK:

### New school year gives Shire Sales a boost

An unusually strong 'back to school' season helped Shire Pharmaceuticals to achieve a jump in sales of its drugs that help hyperactive children to concentrate in the classroom . . .

'The nature of these kinds of psychiatric diseases is that people are always trying to see if they can get better control,' Angus Russell, the chief executive, said. 'When they're not at school, some paediatric patients actually take a rest. They don't need the same focus or concentration during a vacation period. When they're back, for us, it's a good opportunity to have patients try Vyvanse for the first time.'

(A. Clark 2011)

This news media story describes the increases in pharmaceutical sales, portraying children as paediatric patients. Yet while attention is placed on increased use of medication, very little is mentioned about the substantial changes that have occurred as mental disorders become part and parcel of schooling. Responding to this silence is one of our objectives in writing this book.

It is not unusual for children to have long school holidays or for colleges and universities to have breaks of several months. Neither is it, according to the news media story cited above, unusual for paediatric patients to not require consistency in medication levels over holidays and school terms. Describing the increase in prescriptions at school, this article from *The Times* quotes a pharmaceutical executive's account of the logic for 'paediatric patients' to 'take a rest . . . on the vacation period' (A. Clark 2011). Once the holidays are over and school begins, medication rates greatly increase. So much so that Vyvanse, a new medication for attention deficit hyperactivity disorder (ADHD) produced by this UK-based pharmaceutical company, 'rose by 32 per cent to US$ 199 million' (A. Clark 2011). Booms in sales of school stationery or clothing might have been the expected markers of the seasonal change of children returning to school in earlier periods; with these newly available drugs, the return to school is signalled by increases in pharmaceutical sales.

In the new pharmacological time, the seasonality of schooling can be flagged by shifts in sales patterns of children's 'school' drugs. In this instance, the pharmaceutical company is reported to have 'enjoyed a 28 per cent surge in quarterly revenue to US$1.02 billion (£637 million), aided by patients trying new dosage regimes for its attention deficit hyper-activity disorder drugs at the start of the school year' (A. Clark 2011).

School holiday periods, however, have not always been seen in this light. More than a hundred years ago Charles F. Thwing was so concerned by long vacations that he published an article on the subject in the literary magazine *The North American Review*. The article, lamenting the problems long vacations can stir up, was titled 'A too-long vacation' and included appraisal of the negative effects on the young person:

> The vacation becomes dissipation – moral, intellectual. Forces that are needed in college are not recruited. Hardihood, endurance, concentration, pluck, grit, are not nursed through so long a period of inactivity. Laziness is the direct result of summer listlessness.
>
> (Thwing 1892: 761)

From this perspective, and quite at odds with the effect of holidays on paediatric patients, who need rest, long vacations were simply not good. Extended periods created 'dissipation' and contributed to 'summer listlessness'; holidays produced rest, and rest is a cause of problems. Inactivity is the destroyer of the good 'force' of concentration, the virtue needed for schooling.

It is worthwhile considering why in the contemporary context a change in medication usage over vacation periods does not raise particular kinds of questions. It doesn't, for instance, prompt queries about the status of the paediatric patient. Nor do changes in the need for medication raise doubts about the school. Rather, change is purely symptomatic of the disorder itself. What appears to happen is that the psychopathology that occurs within the school setting remains within the child. In this view the child has a mental disorder, with the spike in medication rates on returning to school confirming the existence of mental disorder.

The intersection between the school and the ending of holidays, where medication can be seen as naturally resuming, is a pertinent example of how the ideas of mental disorder have become mixed into schooling. While the contrast created by the historical example highlights differences that are characteristic of the time (such as between the ethos of work and leisure) (Harwood 2011), it draws attention to the anomaly of the current situation in schools in many countries. Indeed one of the defining characteristics of the intensification of psychopathology in schools is the way it remains effective in spite of such anomalies.

Characteristic of the rapidly expanding influence of psychopathology in schools, anomalies occur and yet psychopathology retains influence over how children and young people are understood. In the case of Shire Pharmaceuticals, it seems individuals with the mental disorder can seamlessly move as paediatric patients from school to long holidays and back to school again, with their status as subjects (here paediatric patients) remaining consistent. Because of this, the surge of medication as school resumes signals nothing more than the cessation of rest.

This capacity of mental disorder to be maintained across sites and within children is an example of the dominance of psychopathology in school settings. This is a dominance that has considerable effects. Significantly, it makes it possible for children to remain paediatric patients because they *are identified as having mental disorders in school settings*. Schools thus have a significant function not only as sites where mental disorders occur, but also as sites involved in the diagnosis of mental disorder. To grasp the influence of psychopathology on the contemporary lives of children and young people it is therefore imperative to look to the new practices infiltrating education.

One of the central arguments put forward in this book is that the schools have a significant bearing on the culture of mental disorder. Importantly, these ways of understanding are influential on how notions of normal/non-normal children are perceived. To better understand this phenomenon, our objective is to map the extent of psychopathology in schools as well as to outline the accompanying knowledge and practices that are deployed by the range of services affiliated with education. Our work in this regard is mindful of Appadurai's (2009) challenge of being conscious of history as well as looking to the future. Acknowledging this challenge, we aim to provide an extended analysis of how knowledge of psychopathology has become part of, and continues to exert influence upon, education.

## More than ADHD

As the most well known of the childhood mental disorders, ADHD has been named by some as a 'global issue' that could become, 'the leading childhood disorder treated with medications across the globe' (Scheffler *et al.* 2007). High diagnostic rates are cited across many countries, and, not surprisingly, it is the most debated of the childhood disorders. There have been calls for government investigation of ADHD, especially in relation to the spiralling use of medications. In the UK an inquiry was called into ADHD diagnosis and treatment (Lords Hansard 2007), and proposals for national ADHD guidelines by Australia's National Health and Medical Research Council met with fierce debate.

While ADHD receives a great deal of attention, there is much more to psychopathology at school than ADHD. Indeed, the focus on ADHD as a dominant knowledge (Foucault 1980a) obscures the complex interplay of discourses that make psychopathology both a legitimate and desirable explanation applied to children and young people in educational contexts. For example, McMahon (2013) describes a kindergarten teacher, in NSW Australia, who strongly advocated diagnoses for children in her class as a means of acquiring resources to support their learning. Her class went from zero to ten different behaviour disorder diagnoses in as many months – additionally, another child in her class was being assessed for early onset schizophrenia. This teacher (together with the school principal) explicitly instructed parents at kindergarten orientation interviews to get behaviour or mental disorder diagnoses for their children before they start school so she could organize timely funding and support for them. This demonstrates that ADHD is only one of many childhood mental disorders; there are many others that children are being diagnosed with and some, such as bipolar disorders, are described as increasing in prevalence. One of the problems with the focus on ADHD is that other mental disorders can be overlooked. This is a problem because it can result in less critique of these mental disorders, especially of changes in diagnostic rates or treatments.

The mental disorders used for children and young people include the behavioural disorders (to which ADHD belongs). This group includes oppositional defiant disorder (ODD) and conduct disorder (CD). Other types of mental disorders include personality disorders, depressive disorders, bipolar disorder, emotional disorders, learning disorders and reading disorders (American Psychiatric Association 2013a) and this can occur from an early age, for example McMahon's (2013) report on an Australian study which found diagnoses being sought for children in kindergarten, including disorders such as 'early onset schizophrenia'. Asperger's syndrome and autism are relatively well known and also firmly part of the range of childhood mental disorders. These mental disorders are defined in the *Diagnostic and Statistical Manual of Mental Disorders (DSM)* (American Psychiatric Association 2013a), and have the status of psychiatric disorders.

As well as psychiatric categories, there are other approaches for defining mental problems. In some countries or regions, problems with children are not always defined using the *DSM*, and the International Classification of Diseases (ICD) may be used (World Health Organization 2003). Approaches may also lean toward psychological constructs and associated assessments. Language can vary and children can be described as having behavioural difficulties or emotional difficulties. Such difficulties and problems can be defined using psychological tests and assessments, which might be used in tandem with the psychiatric categories of the *DSM*. Variation between the definitions is often due to differences in preferences between countries and within regions, as well as the type of service with which the child is engaged. In some instances this can also be down to the diagnostic preference of professionals (Allan and Harwood 2013).

At seeming odds with their specificity, mental disorders have effects on a broad societal and cultural scale. Descriptions of mental disorders are relied upon in many areas of society, such as in schools, as well as in government-funded services such as social security, child, family and community welfare, juvenile justice and disability services. These descriptions are not restricted to the public domain. Private sector companies such as insurance services, as well as employers, are linked to this network of diagnosis. For instance, this can occur via requirements such as for proof for childcare leave. In such scenarios parents or caregivers may be required to secure a diagnosis in order to get leave approval. This type of influence, together with its scale, is how the use of psychopathology contributes to the psychopathologization of children and young people.

## Psychopathologization of children

In this book we acknowledge the value of the critical work that has been developed in relation to medicalization, and draw on this literature to develop the concept of psychopathologization. According to Conrad (2007: 4), a key writer in the field, medicalization can be understood as a process 'by which nonmedical problems become defined and treated as medical problems, usually in terms of illness and disorders'. Questions of the medicalization of behaviour have been raised, especially in response to the spiralling diagnostic rates of mental disorders in children and young people, especially those of ADHD (Fife-Yeomans 2007; Williams 2007). Claims that child behaviour is being medicalized join critiques of medicalization such as debate concerning the medicalization of sleep (Seale et al. 2007), childbirth (Arney 1982) and obesity (Throsby 2012).

Distinguishing psychopathology and medicalization is useful because it helps to identify the knowledges and practices that produce the conditions of possibility (Foucault 1970) for psychopathology at school. This distinction is also important for identifying psychopathology at school as a phenomenon. Psychopathology marks out subjects as either having or being at risk of mental disorders. For instance, framing the movements of children as manifestations of mental disorder (such as not sitting still) is an example of psychopathologization in practice within the school environment.

The suggestion that behaviour is being psychopathologized gives pause to ask about the consequences of the application of mental disorders in schooling contexts. It is useful to question what is happening when, for example, a boy's activity is interpreted by a teacher as being 'ADHD'. In this instance is it the case that the activity is a non-psychopathological problem or is it a problem of psychopathology? When the interpretation invokes mental disorders such as

ADHD, the behaviour becomes one of psychopathology. The question then can be raised about when child behaviour becomes a problem of psychopathology. Because of the way it influences the conceptualization of problems, psychopathology almost inevitably contributes to how a child or children is or are understood.

One of the reasons why psychopathologizing in schools is an issue is because the process extends beyond the specific problem at hand. In many instances when behaviours are psychopathologized this conceptual view reaches across many areas of children's lives. An apposite example is the way psychopathologization can supersede cultural contexts. Interpreting the problems presented by an Australian Indigenous child demands cultural competency (Walker and Sonn 2010), and the risk with the recourse to psychopathology is that this can be overshadowed. One of the reasons for this is the attendant meanings that are brought to bear when the *thing* is named; there are, as we will discuss, a raft of expectations brought to bear on the individual with the *thing* or deemed to be at risk of it. Significant meaning can be conveyed about the future prospects of the child or young person, with psychiatric research reporting the risks associated with a diagnosis of behaviour disorder, including predictions of future criminality and mental health problems (American Psychiatric Association 1994). In this sense, much more than a label results when a problem is psychopathologized; it is a powerful association that evokes links to other mental disorders and predicts many societal problems.

## Schools and psychopathology

Although there is considerable international debate on the rise of the mental disorders of children and especially those pertaining to children's behaviour, schooling receives less attention as a site in the psychopathologization of children's behaviour. This is remarkable given that schools are integral to how children's and young people's behaviours are conceived. As well as being the pivotal location for inclusion in contemporary society (Marmot 2004) schools have a significant role in exclusion (Allan 2008). In this book we make the case that schools play a key part in the psychopathologization of behaviour.

The increasing rate at which psychopathology has entered the landscape of education has, we maintain, altered the normalization of the work that schools do. For example, ADHD is entrenched in many teachers' understandings of behaviour, especially pre-service teachers and recent graduates (McMahon 2012). This informs views on normal child behaviour and hyperactivity and influences how teachers respond to children. Although debate on mental disorders and children can include discussion of schools, schools are not often considered as a psychopathologizing force. In this book we take the stance that schools are more than a site which psychopathologization has reached – schools are part of how the psychopathologization of children and young people occurs.

In taking up this stance we are mindful of the effects of location and culture on patterns of psychopathology in schools. These geo-cultural and geo-social characteristics are evident in the different rates of mental disorders in schools. There is compelling evidence that schools located in disadvantaged communities have more children with mental disorders. Australian research has revealed that disadvantaged communities are more likely to have large numbers of young people with ADHD and behaviour disorders and have elevated rates of prescriptions for ADHD medications (Harwood 2010; Prosser and Reid 2009). Similar problems have been reported in Scotland (National Health Service 2007), particularly in areas marked by serious disadvantage (Lloyd *et al.* 2006). The reported high numbers of socio-economically disadvantaged children and youth prescribed ADHD medications has been flagged as a concern for paediatricians, who are at risk of 'medicating for social disadvantage' (Isaacs 2006). Research from the United States and other countries has likewise pointed to the relationship between disadvantage, poverty and higher diagnostic rates of mental disorders in children (Barnes *et al.* 2010).

One of the issues with higher rates in disadvantaged communities is that psychopathologies intrude on education. Here again the issue of psychopathologization looms large precisely because more than one problem is understood as psychopathology. Pathologies of poverty become pronounced (Schram 2000), with children living in disadvantaged communities at greater risk of a type of psychopathologization linked to social class. These issues with children and mental disorders in the context of education have escalated, especially in relation to the roles of teachers and schools in medicating children.

Incursion into the school connects schooling into the infrastructure of diagnosis in multiple ways. This ranges from the clear-cut instance whereby teacher referral and assessment is used for diagnosis by health care clinicians to more subtle ways that link children and young people into mental health. Exclusion from schooling is but one example of the way that schooling exerts considerable influence over how a child is conceptualized. The excluded child is, for example, very easily caught up in discourses of behaviour that are invariably inflected with, if not dominated by, a point of view imbued with the spectre of psychopathology.

## Theoretical perspective

In this book we draw on the work of Foucault to make our argument that psychopathology has become instrumental in schools and that schools play an instrumental role in expanding the new psychopathologies of children and young people. Foucault's emphasis on truth, power and the constitution of the subject (Foucault 1983, 1997a, 2000) is especially useful to our analysis as it allows us to think through the ways in which psychopathology at school is produced and has productive effects. To this end Foucault's (1983) conceptualization of power as productive is generative for grasping how schools can indeed be instrumental in a field that, on first glance, appears to be the province of the medical and health sciences (especially psychiatry, clinical psychology and psychopharmacology). It is here also that Foucault's attention to dominant and subjugated knowledges is of value for informing how to understand how dominant knowledges of schooling's disorders such as ADHD misdirect attention from those practices that enable psychopathology to sit comfortably in contemporary schooling and educational environments.

One of the tasks of this book is to provide an account of how psychopathology has, through extending into the school, reached into the worlds of children and young people. To do this we employ a Foucauldian genealogical approach to foreground practices in the present (Foucault 1997a). This allows us to throw the seeming (and paradoxical) normalcy of psychopathology in schooling into relief. This style provides a historical and contemporary analysis that Foucault's own work exemplified.

Reflecting on analysis of madness, Foucault discusses the 'focal points of experience' (Gros 2008). These 'focal points' comprise 'three elements': 'forms of possible knowledge, normative frameworks of behaviour, and potential modes of existence for possible subjects' (Gros 2008: 3). We suggest that this approach can be used to craft an analysis of the experience of psychopathology. Foucault explained that he sought to 'study madness as experience within our culture' (2008a: 3). To do so he first considered knowledge, 'as a point from which a series of more or less heterogeneous forms of knowledge were formed' (Foucault 2008a: 3). Second, he considered madness as 'a set of norms'. Importantly, this applied as much to the mad as to the non-mad. Notions of madness created norms against which the normal might be demarcated, as well as how the behaviours of those who administer to madness might be regulated. Third, he explained that this required 'studying madness insofar as this experience of madness defined the constitution of a certain mode of being of the normal subject, as opposed to and in relation to the mad subject (Foucault 2008a: 3). This third element involved 'analysing the constitution of the subject's mode of being' (Foucault 2008a: 4). In this regard Foucault posed the problem for his analysis: 'one should try to analyse the different forms by which the individual is led to constitute him or herself as subject' (2008a: 5).

To guide our examination of knowledge and the truths produced about mental disorders we direct our questions as well as our analysis onto how truths about schools and psychopathology are constituted. This allows us to consider psychopathology and truth in certain groups of children and young people, such as children from disadvantaged circumstances. Attention to power enables us to consider the relations of power involved in psychopathology at school. In 'The Subject and Power' Foucault (1983) describes power as 'action':

> The exercise of power is not simply a relationship between partners, individual or collective; it is a way in which certain actions modify others . . . Power

exists only when it is put into action, even if, of course, it is integrated into a disparate field of possibilities brought to bear upon permanent structures.

(Foucault 1983: 219)

We deploy this focus on actions and the relationships of power to consider how, for example, the actions linked to practices of psychopathology have effects that 'modify others'. This enables us to argue that the effects of psychopathologizing are not limited to the simple transaction of the diagnosis, but do indeed reach much further and occur in numerous ways.

Foucault's work on the subject allows us to sketch out how children and young people are constituted as psychopathologized subjects across different age groups and according to differing individual characteristics. This enables us to delve into the way that contemporary schooling can have subjects in which psychopathology inheres. In the example of schooling, holidays and medication discussed earlier, the children were not spoken of; it was paediatric patients. These paediatric patients remained paediatric patients when at home or at school, when on holidays or during term time, and irrespective of whether medication was required (and even not exhibiting medication-requiring behaviours). These children were paediatric patient subjects, and by using Foucault we are able to decipher how these subjects are constituted and how this influences a contemporary schooling landscape where psychopathology is an ever present (and ever looked for) possibility.

We use Foucault's work on knowledge, power, truth and the subject together to inform six key arguments:

1   Within schooling we are passing from an exclusionary technology to an inclusive one and from disciplinary power to biopower and this has led to more children and young people being 'captured' and represented as mentally ill.
2   The diagnosis of mental disorders is an assemblage of desire, vagueness and flexibility.
3   While schools have been a key site for the psychopathologization of children's behaviour, historically, they have also been viewed as a principal *cause* of children's problems.
4   Disadvantage and poverty, as well as other markers of identity such as 'race', disability and gender, are established as 'risk factors', which become intertwined in interpretations of children's behaviours – to the extent that diagnosis becomes inevitable.
5   An optimism, levelled at young children of nursery and primary age, that their mental illness can be resolved through intervention, recedes by the time the young person reaches secondary school and is replaced by concern at the dangerous potential of the young person in higher education.
6   Resistance (from professionals) to psychopathologization generates new forms of recognition of children and young people.

In each of these arguments we draw on key theoretical resources in connection with our considerations from Foucault. In argument two, for example, we draw closely on Schram's (2000) work on medicalization and disadvantage to explore how psychopathology at school has profoundly material dimensions. These dimensions are impossible to ignore given the disproportionate numbers of children from disadvantaged circumstances who are diagnosed with behavioural problems (Allan and Harwood 2013).

In working with these arguments our standpoint is informed by the view that critique is vital to education as a political activity (Harwood and Rasmussen 2013). In this respect we engage with Arendt's (1968b) emphasis on the importance of critique and 'thinking' to confront the problematic, 'to what degree is thinking being brought to bear on psychopathology?' In this respect, Foucault's (1997b) work on critique provides a rationale for our argument that psychopathology needs to be questioned and Arendt's (1968b, 2003) work on thinking, judgement and politics connects critique with political action. We take an Arendtian emphasis on political action and its relationship to thinking and judging in our examination of psychopathology at school and raise the question, 'to what extent is it politicized?' Are there silences, for instance, in the take-up of the knowledges and practices of psychopathology used in the crèche or college years? Silences or gaps are important to our analyses as these can, from a Foucauldian perspective, alert us to actions of power. From an Arendtian viewpoint, silence from critique may signal dangerous depoliticized ground, where psychopathology becomes entrenched in schooling with limited reflection. As we will outline, these silences pose considerable problems for schooling. This is because such silences allow significant changes in the knowledge and practices of education to occur with very little acknowledgement or debate.

Extending on this engagement with critique, we also utilize the idea of territorialization and deterritorialization developed by Deleuze and Guattari (1987) in order to understand challenges by professionals to psychopathology. Here we are conscious of taking up Appadurai's (2009) challenge of being forward-looking in our analyses and seek to mark out both the problems we envisage occurring and also ways of responding to these.

Our discussion of psychopathology and schooling is guided by a grid of analysis that draws on Nealon's (2008) discussion of Foucault's use of intensity. Here we are drawn to Nealon's emphasis on the lateralization of intensity. For instance referring to *Discipline and Punish* (Foucault 1979) he writes,

> As *D & P*'s analysis progresses, the process of 'intensification' comes to refer less to a centripetal force acting on an individual body ('intense pain'), and more to name a 'lateral' or 'centrifugal' smearing or saturation of efforts over a wide field (intensity as a state that strives to be complete and exhaustive, as seamless as possible – as in 'intensive care').
>
> (Nealon 2008: 34)

This depiction of intensity as a 'saturation of efforts over a wide field' aptly depicts the movement of psychopathologization, smearing across and through the numerous and diverse aspects of schooling. Importantly, this reading of intensity is not restricted to experience, 'rather intensity and its modulations are everywhere' (Nealon 2008: 66). Nealon's discussion of intensification in 'mundane financial transactions' provides a cogent example of how this reading of intensification can be applied to an analysis of psychopathologization in schooling,

> Because we don't know what money or value is, such categories are under constant construction, and such modulation moves through intensification – speeding up or slowing down of flows.
>
> (Nealon 2008: 34)

We use this concept of intensification and modulation in our analysis of the 'periods' of schooling covered in this book: from the cradle to the crèche; the primary years; the high school years; and higher education. We use an analytic grid that poses the following questions for each of these periods: 'Who is aroused to concern?' 'What are the relations or networks of power?' 'What are the disorders of interest?' 'What are the modes of practice?' and lastly, 'What are the desired consequences/outcomes in respect of the people who are the focus of concern?'

## The studies discussed in this book

In our discussion of psychopathologization in schools in this book we draw upon three interconnected studies. The first, The New Outsiders, was focused on sites in four Australian states (Western Australia, South Australia, New South Wales and Victoria) where there were both high rates of prescription medications for attention deficit hyperactivity disorder and significant social and economic disadvantage. In these sites, key youth services were targeted and semi-structured interviews were held with youth service professionals. Troubled by the findings that suggested the extent of psychopathologization evident in these young people's lives, we decided to broaden this study to include interviews from two locations outside of Australia: in Cambridgeshire, England, and in the Greater Bay Area of San Francisco.[2] The youth professionals interviewed in these locations (two in England and three in the United States) were working in areas of socio-economic disadvantage that had comparatively high rates of child and youth behavioural problems. Findings from the research conducted in the United States have pointed to the development of 'mobile asylums' (Harwood 2010a) and our research from Australia has examined the issue of disadvantage and psychopathologization (Harwood 2010b). In this book we draw on the interviews with two key youth professionals working in Cambridgeshire, England and discuss diagnosis in the secondary school age group.

The Imagining University Education project is the second study that we draw on in this book. This national Australian study has focused on perspectives of university for young people who live in communities in comparable low socio-economic status (SES) regions of Australia (in Victoria, Tasmania, New South Wales, South Australia and Queensland),[3] all with low rates of university participation. Two hundred and fifty young people have been interviewed in this national project, and a number of these young people were affected by psychopathologization in schools. Across these sites young people were interviewed over a period using semi-structured interviews in youth settings such as youth centres. Participants were recruited through youth sector and related agencies with youth professionals often joining interviews.

The third study discussed in this book, the Medicalization of Child Behaviour, was conducted in Scotland, where the pace at which child behaviour has been medicalized appears to be slower than in other parts of the United Kingdom and in Australia and North and South America. For this study we carried out semi-structured interviews within one health board and two education authorities in one geographically defined region of Scotland, which had lower than expected rates of ADHD diagnosis (not disclosed to maintain confidentiality). This series of interviews was carried out with professionals working with young people who had been referred for behavioural problems, including child mental health professionals, specialist education support staff and youth service workers. In this location we purposively selected a sample of representative services that were working with children with behavioural difficulties. We interviewed ten professionals who worked with children with behavioural problems across several settings including child mental health, specialist education and youth services. Each of the participants was asked about the community that they worked in and the extent to which it was affected by poverty. We asked about the prevalence and patterns of behavioural problems and how these were described in communities experiencing poverty. We were also interested to learn about the commonly used diagnostic terms for child behavioural problems. Using thematic data analysis, our findings were cross-checked between the two authors and themes were defined: processes that medicalized behaviour and processes that interrupted medicalization. We identified three types of interruptions: visual, linguistic and affective. In the discussion of this data, to preserve confidentiality participants are identified only by number and by area of expertise. We cite findings from these studies throughout the book, including quotes from our interviews with young people and professionals. To identify these different studies, the following annotations are used: The New Outsiders project – TNO; Imagining University Education – IUE; and Medicalization of Child Behaviour – MCB.

## The structure of the book

The following chapters are organized to chart the ways mental disorders have become commonplace in childhood and youth, from birth through to college and university. This structure highlights the interface between these educational periods, the educational institutions and how regularization of learning is closely tied with conceptions of mental normality, and, by consequence, to mental disorder. For example, an anticipated prognosis of problems in a toddler, child or youth is frequently linked to expectations of negative outcomes as an adult (future mental disorders, health and social problems).

Prior to discussing psychopathology at school across different age groupings, we consider two important contexts: its history in schooling and the social and cultural characteristics of psychopathology and schools. Chapter 2 takes a Foucauldian, genealogical approach to examine the historical background of the application of mental disorders in education. Using this approach we provide commentary of the distinctive uses of mental disorder in twenty-first-century education settings. We use contemporary examples to illustrate how mental disorders have been referred to, and to demonstrate the changes in the incorporation of mental disorders into and across education settings.

In Chapter 3 we examine the gendered, racialized and classed issues associated with diagnostic practice. Minority groups and children from disadvantaged circumstances are over-represented in educational remediation and disciplinary programmes, an issue that is a problem in the United States, the UK, Australia and elsewhere. Drawing together contributions from the critical literature on ADHD and childhood mental disorders, the chapter details how diagnosis and medicalization in education is heavily affected by social and cultural factors.

Chapters 4 through to 7 focus specifically on a life period of a child or young person, reflecting educational development groupings used internationally. Each of these chapters investigates the presence of the culture of mental disorders at different educational groupings (preschool; primary/elementary school; secondary/high school; college and university). In these chapters we also consider the relationship between schools and health, welfare and related services (for example, public health and child and youth focused health programmes).

Chapter 4 charts the influences of psychopathologization from birth through to the crèche (or preschool years). This period corresponds to what is popularly referred to as 'early childhood', and is a teacher specialization internationally. 'Early childhood' has now been accorded great significance in education and educational research, yet it is a largely neglected area of critical scholarship in relation to the application of psychiatric and psychological knowledge of mental disorders. This chapter begins with a discussion of the influence of mental disorder 'at the cradle' and specialist areas such as 'infant mental health' and moves to toddlers and the rate of diagnosis and medication in this age group.

The primary school is the focus of Chapter 5, covering the ages of five through to eleven or twelve (these ages depend on the country and/or local jurisdictions). We begin by discussing the entry to formal schooling (elementary school or primary school), a moment when considerable scrutiny is made of young children and whether they will 'fit' or 'non-fit' into the school regimen. For many children this period is when medicalization begins in earnest. Starting from these early school-based identificatory practices, the discussion will move to examine the range of services and resources that bring psychopathology into the school.

In Chapter 6 we move to the middle and senior years of schooling (secondary/high school) and outline how psychopathology is present in the schooling contexts that educate young people aged 12 to 17. Here we consider the range of instances where behaviour is pathologized. We also discuss early school-leaving and youth that have become disengaged with schooling.

In Chapter 7 we move from secondary schooling to colleges and universities. Here in addition to discussing psychopathology and medicalization we examine the current wave of concern regarding the dangers and threats posed by young people with mental disorders in tertiary institutions.

Chapter 8 reports on our research into how child and youth professionals interrupted practices that threatened to psychopathologize. These professionals, while recognizing the space in which diagnosis was initiated as particularly forceful and restricted, revealed strategies for interrupting the lines of referral through which a medicalized diagnosis of behaviour was inevitable. Deleuze and Guattari's concept of deterritorialization is used in this chapter to make sense of these interruptions.

The final chapter considers the consequences of psychopathologization in schooling and draws together an argument for the need to put pedagogy ahead of the diagnostic reflex. We contend that the presence of cultures of mental disorder across the life worlds of childhood establishes a pattern that encourages reliance on narratives of mental disorder to account for childhood normality or non-normality. The book will close with a discussion of how the employment of such methods, together with a healthy position of critique, can be deployed.

## Notes

1 Interview excerpt from *Imagining University Education: Perspectives of young people impacted by low socio-economic status and disengagement from school* (IUE), a research project funded by the Australian Research Council (Harwood, DP 110104704). This involved semi-structured interviews with 250 young people from Australian sites representative of disadvantage and a range of geospatial differences (remote, metropolitan, regional and rural).

2 Details of the locations have been altered to maintain confidentially. Due to budget constraints the international site selection was made to reflect the original aims of the project (to investigate the occurrence of the high diagnostic rates of behavioural disorders in areas of disadvantage) and to coincide with the locations where the author took sabbatical leave in 2008 (University of California, Berkeley and University of Cambridge).

3 Site selection based on: (i) proportionately low rates of undergraduate participation by persons aged 18 to 20 (Birrell et al. 2008); (ii) low SES (ABS 2001; Vinson 2007); (iii) rating highly on indicators of disadvantage health, community safety, economic factors and education (Vinson 2007); (iv) high rates of behavioural problems; and (v) school engagement problems as indicated by a) school nonattendance rates, b) rates of school non-completion to year 12, and c) attendance and absenteeism intervention programs (DECS 2010; NSW DET 2009; Stehlik 2006).

# Chapter 2

# A brief history of mental disorders in school

## Introduction

> One simple truth about madness should never be overlooked. The consciousness of madness, in European culture at least, has never formed an obvious and monolithic fact, undergoing a metamorphosis as a homogenous ensemble. For the Western consciousness, madness has always welled up simultaneously at multiple points, forming a constellation that slowly shifts from one form to another, its face perhaps hiding an enigmatic truth. Meaning here is always fractured.
>
> (Foucault 2006: 163)

Anticipation of psychopathology occurs because psychopathology is an integrated thread in the contemporary education landscape. This integration could mistakenly be explained, to bring to mind the above from Foucault (2006), as a metamorphosis from earlier forms. Such a story might dwell upon advancements in explanations of children's difficulties or of the precision of an expanding psychiatric knowledge that naturally lends improvement to pedagogy. It might also tell of new generation pharmaceuticals that magically gather children's concentration and place it on the task at hand. The problem, however, is that, according to the metamorphosis principle, contemporary forms of psychopathology in schools are depicted as not only evidence of improved knowledge, but significantly as homogenous phenomena.

Nothing, however, could be further from the case. The stirrings of modern schooling (which we are taking as building momentum in the nineteenth century with the advent of publically funded schooling) can be seen, to paraphrase Foucault (2006: 163), as the 'welling up simultaneously at multiple points . . . of a constellation that slowly shifts from one form to another'. In reviewing literature of a century ago, we see eerily familiar concerns in the descriptions of children's problems. What differs, though, are the varied emphases on both the nature of the problem and what constitutes it. We can conclude, therefore, that what is consistent is thus: where there is schooling there are problems of children and schooling. We maintain that, following Foucault (2006), this is best viewed as a constellation of problems varying in ways that reveal the significant influences schooling itself has on how children and problems are understood.

The appearance of psychopathology in contemporary educational domains, whether it be crèches or colleges, primary or secondary schools, while not always commonplace is certainly not unusual. This distinction between the commonplace and the unusual is significant. As we outline in Chapter 3, there are patterns in the distribution of psychopathologies, such as more young people from disadvantaged communities described as having behavioural disorders (Allan and Harwood 2013). Concentrations of psychopathology in areas of disadvantage and poverty do not make psychopathology at school an unusual phenomenon more generally. Indeed, psychopathology is quite the contrary to unusual; it is usual, acceptable and anticipated.

## A familiar problem

In the twenty-first century familiar tones of psychopathology can be heard in school meetings, called across playgrounds, discussed in university halls or considered in childcare settings. Sharing an emphasis on psycho-scientific terminology for child problems, these tones appear at times uncannily similar to what might have been heard a century ago; at others the differences could not be more stark.

Take for example a late-nineteenth-century approach to assessing problems in children's mental faculty, and the 'classification of children' in schools (Warner 1890). In *A Course of Lectures on the Growth and Means of Training the Mental Faculty*, Warner proposes that the 'study of mental action thus becomes a study of physical facts, as is the study of any other subject in physiology, or the study of the phenomena of light, electricity or sound.' (1890: 37). This practice of observation is taken to be of importance due to the necessity of teacher skills in the observation of children. For instance, in relation to 'children of defective development' the question is posed, 'how can the teacher know from his observations, who in his school are the children below standard?' (Warner 1890: 100). At end of the book a sizeable chapter provides a 'catalogue of a museum of natural history' and advocates the use of these examples to train teacher education students 'to observe and think about living things' (Warner 1890: 167). This technique of observations included (as shown in Figure 2.1) the close study of hand postures in order to reveal activity in the brain.

By following instructions on how to observe hand postures such as the 'feeble hand', the teacher will be equipped to assess the child and detect conditions such as nervousness.

This concept of assessment (or determining who is and isn't a problem) would appear to be a practice that one can trace with continuity though education from the nineteenth century to the current day. Contemporary assessments of child mental problems are, as we outlined in Chapter 1, informed

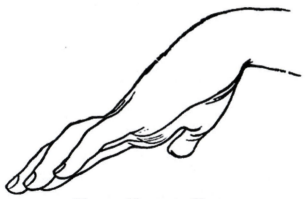

Fig. 7.—NERVOUS HAND.

Wrist flexed; palm somewhat contracted; fingers extended backwards at knuckles, or meta-carpophalangeal joints; thumb
extended.

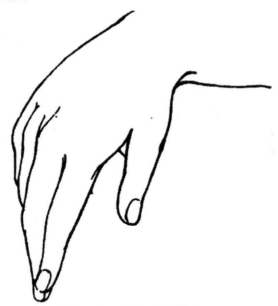

Fig. 8.—FEEBLE HAND.

Wrist and all joints more flexed or bent than in C.; palm or
metacarpus much contracted.

Figure 2.1 Observation and description of facts: hand postures indicative of brain function

Warner 1890: 56–9

by psychiatric categories from the *Diagnostic and Statistical Manual of Mental* (*DSM*), with this system increasingly used in schools, and especially in the determination of the identification of problems that require financial supports (House 2002). The perceptible difference, however, is in the shifts toward an increasing emphasis on this diagnostic terminology. In Australia for example, new standards for teacher training mandate covering knowledge of mental disorders such as ADHD. Uses of mental disorder in education settings in the twenty-first century are distinctive because earlier discussions of education and its problems did not always (or not at all) adhere to this pattern of understanding. There were shifts and movements in what was considered a problem in education as well as what was thought to be the cause (and, correspondingly, how it might be solved). What is undeniably most extraordinary in the contemporary moment is the lack of vacillation; the current climate in education is one of acceptance and promotion of psychopathology as the default explanation of problems. This way of framing problems, has, as we will discuss, not always been the case.

## The problems schooling causes

While contemporary views might pejoratively focus on *students'* problems and how these interact in education, a quite different stance can be found in nineteenth-century discussions concerned with education. Concerns were raised about the problems caused by schools – as opposed to the problems within the student. For instance, in 1822 when the Reverend R.W. Bamford wrote about the issues of corporal punishment in his book *Essays on the Discipline of Children, Particularly as Regards Their Education*, he drew attention to the problems *caused* by the school:

> See even a boy of mild and diligent temper, who naturally desires to please, and study, how he trembles in his run to school! With what palpitation of heart, yet unconscious of wrong he hastens! Sleepless at night, restless in the morning, harassed during the day; his youth is spent in anxiety and fear.
>
> (Bamford 1822: 16)

As is evident in the above description, schooling was seen to be capable of eliciting significant physiological effects on the child, and this may extend to other feelings such as 'disgust': '[t]he disgust, with which many children generally regard the school, induces them often, on very trivial occasions, to prevail on their parents to allow them to remain at home' (Bamford 1822: 131). These effects occurred when corporal punishment was employed, with Bamford's book amounting to an argument against corporal punishment in both public and private schools (Anon 1822).

Attention to corporal punishment would seem to set this book quite apart from present-day considerations of education. On closer inspection, though, it is the emphasis on interpreting the effects of the teacher (and the school) on the child that is paramount:

> Take not then from children the power of discrimination; and be assured that when a boy is obstinate it is for some reason. Examine your conduct towards him, and his previous behaviour. . . . An obstinate boy is generally either very clever, or very ignorant; either wilfully impudent, or stupidly perverse. Both may be managed without beating.
>
> (Bamford 1822: 96)

These concerns were not limited to the teacher but extended to the parents, and especially to those belonging to certain classes: 'How few, particularly among the middle and lower classes of people, enquire what their children have learnt – examine; approve, incite; condemn, lament, and seek cause?' (Bamford 1822: 126). Of course, questions about enquiries about learning depend on whether children have been able to attend school. This lack of access provides a different perspective on the problems caused by schooling, where, on the one hand, there are arguments about the lost opportunities for those children not in education (principally the poorer classes) and, on the other, the 'unnaturalness of schooling'.

Present-day concern that engages with individual pathology as a matter of course varies significantly from interpretations from the nineteenth century where alarm was expressed about the effects of schooling on a child's health. This framing of health is evident in a lecture given to the Royal College of Preceptors; at the time an early professional body formed to 'raise the character of middle-class education, by educating and raising the attainments, ability and fitness of teachers in private schools' (R. Willis 2005: 17). In this lecture, which also emphasized the importance of charity schools, the issue was one of the seats and tables and the effects that these had on the student.

> Comfortable seats enable the pupil to keep up his mental activity, and to work well; whilst the present seats hurt the back, and produce an uncomfortable stretching and straining of the legs and foot joints, thereby making the *pupil fidgety*, withdrawing his attention from school duties, and originating a thousand disciplinary difficulties which comfortable seats would completely avoid.
>
> (Heinemann 1870: 6–7, emphasis added)

The observation of children moving, of the 'fidgety pupil' or of 'withdrawal of attention' and the accompanying 'thousand disciplinary difficulties' are not the pathology of the child but rather the feasible reactions of the child to the seats and tables in the school environment. Likewise, Heinemann warns against interpretations of some postures as meaning laziness on the part of the child:

> You can frequently see boys or girls, spending their play time in the school-
> rooms, lying at full length on the forms. It is a mistake to think them lazy,
> and compel them to go out.
>
> (Heinemann 1870: 7)

Rather than interpret this as laziness and remove the child, what is considered
is the capacity of children's muscles in relation to the physical demands of
classroom settings.

> The fact is, that their bodies are not possessed of sufficient strength to make
> up for the fatigue of long sitting by violent exercise of the muscles. Going
> to their next lesson, they are weary from the beginning, and it is cruel in
> the extreme to keep them in continued bodily torture, and at the same time
> require them to attend to mental work from which their feeling of physical
> uneasiness is constantly withdrawing them. But still more cruel is it to pun-
> ish them for what is called idleness; for it is a natural impossibility for their
> tender frames to fight long and successfully against the force of gravity.
>
> (Heinemann 1870: 7)

At issue is the incorrect interpretation of 'idleness' and the need to correctly
comprehend the physical weariness wrought by engaging in the processes of
schooling. As with the question of corporal punishment, emphasis is placed not
on the *child-problem*, but upon objects or actions that affect the student, thereby
creating problems.

The effect of health on schooling is the topic of *Health at School: Considered
in its Mental, Moral and Physical Aspects*, which claimed to be the first textbook
on school health. Written by Clement Dukes a medical doctor, the book was
published in 1887, was aimed at public schools and included a separate chapter on girls. The focus was on providing schooling suitable for the health of
the child, a focus that differed from ideas from the early twentieth century.
For instance, some sixteen years after the publication of this first textbook
on school health, a rather different one was published. Titled *The Mental and
Physical Life of School Children* (Sandiford 1913), this textbook provided extensive descriptions of different 'types of children'. Unlike this later book, the text
by Dukes places emphasis on overcoming the problems caused by school (as
opposed to problems within the child). *Health at School* (Dukes 1887) covered a
range of topics, from the 'selection of a suitable school, before entering school'
and, arrangements for the 'Master's boarding house' to arrangements of the
'school, work, play' and a chapter on' illness.[1] Again, the emphasis on health
picked up the theme of the possible effects of schooling on the student's health.
Duke connected the physical and the mental, and in doing so put forward a
case connecting the mental and moral training of students with physical health
in order to avoid 'a well-crammed head on a stunted body' (Dukes 1887: 6–7).
The textbook also describes a specific category of students as needing extra

time before entry into schooling. These students, called 'delicate boys', require a dedicated 'school-home':

> There are a certain number of boys in all schools who, though not ill, are not strong enough, for the time being, to bear the usual strain and exposure of school life, but need more home comforts and attention than can be well provided where the number of boys is large.
>
> (Dukes 1887: 236)

Delicate boys who 'are not naturally strong but weakly' might require 'a year or two at the commencement of their school life before they are able to 'rough' it amongst the large number' (Dukes 1887: 236). Delicate boys include:

> Boys from a hot climate . . . boys who *have* a constitutional ailment that needs great care; boys who require extra care during school life in order to *prevent* the development, owing to an unfavourable family history, of a constitutional complaint; boys who have had a recent severe illness, from which they have recovered, but who need the care of home life still for a term or two, the parents not wishing them to lose ground at school by being kept away until they can dispense with this additional attention.
>
> (Dukes 1887: 236, emphasis added)

Interestingly, to counter causing any problems for the parent, decisions on entry into the proposed delicate boys' school-home would be the sole responsibility of the headmaster. This would ensure that 'every parent would not be under the impression that his own boy was delicate and needed extra care' (Dukes 1887: 237). While delicate boys might be a source of concern for parents, the issue is the boys not being ready for school, a place readily acknowledged as a 'strain'.

It is not clear whether the idea of the school-home for delicate boys was ever put into practice. Dukes wrote that in 'no great school is special provision made for these delicate boys' (1887: 236). Whether or not school-homes for delicate boys were put into practice at the time, the very idea of these separate spaces to cocoon boys from schooling reveals much about how schools were viewed as places that *caused* problems. It was not the case that delicate boys were deficient (as they might be viewed by contemporary standards). Rather, it was the case that they were not ready for the school environment. Unlike how it might be viewed today, being not ready did not simply mean they were abnormal.

The school figuring as a place of challenge devoid of home comforts and where strain is expected meant the effects on children were understood as a logical consequence of the nature of schooling. The difficulty was then one of addressing schooling and its structures (its seats and tables, the modes of training, practices of discipline or to provide a school-home to ready boys for the strain of school).

This focus on the school *as the locus of the problem* (as opposed to the child as the locus of the problem) is apparent in discussions of mental concerns of insanity and issues such as the suicide of children. In 1877 William Ireland reported that '[i]nsanity in children is a rare affection' (Ireland 1877: 241) and noted that, for suicide, 'the most frequent motive was being punished or harshly treated by their parents or teachers' (Ireland 1877: 246). In a second book on this topic by Ireland, published some twenty years later, there is an increase in discussion on education. Likely to be influenced by an increased provision of education to the masses (the commencement of free public schooling began with the 1870 Education Act), Ireland's 1898 book *The Mental Affections of Children, Idiocy, Imbecility and Insanity* provided commentary on the issues with education that included discussion of the pressures of the education system. Ireland states suicide is 'now increasing in frequency 1865–74, 81 from 10 to 14 years of age – 45 male and 36 female. The ratio between shows female precocity. Child suicide is increasing in England and in almost all the Continental states' (Ireland 1898: 287).[2]

> In England and Wales for some years past the suicides of children under fifteen years have averaged over 10, while those of persons under twenty have averaged between 90 and 100 annually. It is significant of the increase of this most pitiful form of self-destruction that the Registrar General had latterly found it convenient to add an extra column for the reception of self-destroyers whose ages are between five and ten years.
>
> (Strahan 1893, cited in Ireland 1898: 287)

Notably, schooling is assessed to be a key contributor to increased suicide rates amongst the young.

> No one denies that child suicide is on the increase, and the high-pressure system of education is generally set down as the cause of the greater part of it. In support of this it is pointed out, that in those countries in which education is forced on most strongly, child suicide is found at its highest.
>
> (Strahan 1893, cited in Ireland 1898: 287)

Countries where education is 'forced most strongly' include those that began providing mass public education. In these places Ireland (1898) concludes the cause to be the consequences of 'over-pressure' in education.

> But what undoubtedly causes many cases now is over-pressure in education, while the education itself produces precocious development of the reflective faculties, of vanity, and of the desires. During the last few years

there have been several English cases of children killing themselves because unable to perform school tasks.

(Ireland 1898: 287)

'Over-pressure' relates to the demands of school tasks, and connects with the demands of achieving suitable progress. This requirement for progress was directly connected as a cause of suicide in an example cited by Ireland of a suicide reported by Dr Durand-Fardel (1885). This report found that a 'boy of twelve hanged himself because he was no higher than twelfth in his class' (Durand-Fardel 1885, cited in Ireland 1898: 288), thereby making a strong case for the over-pressures that education has on children. Concern with school as the locus of the problem fluctuates and in the United Kingdom is most visible in documents from the nineteenth century in the years prior to and shortly after the commencement of mass public education.

Discussions of the school as a problem, or at least, reflections on schools as problems are not without comment in sources from the early twentieth century. For example, significant changes were found in the survey of schools and clinics and mental hygiene in the United States, published in *Mental Health through Education* (C.W. Ryan 1938). Remarked upon were the changes from the 'tension' of the past fifteen to twenty years (post World War I) to the 'friendliness' of the schools of the present.

> In many schools of today one finds an atmosphere of friendliness and happy activity. Much of the traditional formality, the forced silence, the tension, the marching, is gone. Children's voices are heard in the halls and 'classrooms'. The younger children come gaily down the stairways (if stairways are there), natural and relatively unrestrained; the older boys and girls throng the corridors or outside walks, making their way to school-rooms, shops, studios, libraries, laboratories, and playing fields – to tasks that mean something to them, that make demands upon their energies and their imagination, that often involve hard, difficult work, but work that they recognize as creative.
>
> (C.W. Ryan 1938: v)

Schools described as 'friendly' were those schools that drew on principles of mental hygiene. Contrasting with these were the opposite, the unfriendly and, not surprisingly, unscientific, a point Ryan (1938) makes clear: 'A very large proportion of the schools have been little touched as yet by recent scientific knowledge of human behavior' (1938: vi). Schools touched by scientific knowledge are the very same schools where changes away from 'traditional formality' have occurred. In these schools we see forms of problem-naming familiar to contemporary education: categories of difference dominated by terms that in a multitude of different ways produce descriptors that demark aberration of the mind.

These descriptors of aberration include the 'subnormal' or 'difficult' and a range of services defined by aberration (whether it be dealing with aberration or avoiding it). Services include:

> Child guidance clinics, visiting teacher staff, or similar services . . . school psychiatric staff, child guidance clinics, visiting teacher service, institutes for child development – and various agencies outside the schools that typify the community concern for the 'happiness and well-being' of children and youth.
>
> (C.W. Ryan 1938: vi–vii)

The picture painted by this report is not all rosy, and it notes that '[s]ome schools are "depressing"' (C.W. Ryan 1938: vi). The importance of the teacher comes to the fore in this book, where a chapter is devoted to the topic of the 'teacher's personality'. Citing psychiatrists and mental hygienists as authorities, Ryan (1938) states that these experts 'consider the teacher second only to the parent in influencing for good or ill the mental health of the child' (C.W. Ryan 1938: 11). Here the teacher's personality is explicitly discussed as integral, having the potentiality for very good or very bad effects. Here the bad effects unflinchingly mark out the teacher as problem. For example, the argument is made that, 'with due allowance for the fallibility of psychiatric prognosis and the unpredictable values inherent in "just growing up," the evidence seems to point unmistakably to the influence of teachers and the educational approach generally' (C.W. Ryan 1938: 20). Ryan's discussion moves to consideration of how teachers are selected and the grave error that teacher personality is not assessed. Underscoring this crisis, we are told that there are high numbers of problem teachers, and that 'most school systems have some teachers who are notoriously difficult in their relations with other human beings' (C.W. Ryan 1938: 21).

With the advent of schooling as a widespread institution available to all social classes different problems arise and prompt different questions. The issue of the school as a place of difficulty appears and reappears, but amongst discussions of schools as problems other problems appear and variously gain attention. Principal of these, as we discuss below, is the student, who increasingly is the identified object that holds the problem. Indeed, as the school as problem was effaced, the child as problem emerged.

## Utilization of schooling and the prompts for psycho-educational concerns

The receding of the school as a key problem co-occurred with an increasing accessibility of education, with the rise of publically accessible education placing different attention onto the school. This attention differed from concerns with the problems that school causes, with the focus shifting to concerns about the utilization of the school. One approach to explaining these changes is to be beguiled by the most obvious denominator: the sheer size of increasing numbers of children attending school. Explanations for the growth in psycho-educational concerns then logically cite the rise in numbers and the attendant challenges caused by the range of students now flooding into schools. With such increases in numbers, so the line of explanation goes, schools are more likely to encounter far greater and more diverse students, and, consequently, child problems. Therefore new forms of interpreting and managing these problems are required. There is much more at work than the issues caused by the mere increase in numbers. How is it, then, that questions about the problems schooling caused could so quietly disappear from the surface of concerns about problems and education? One possibility is that these do not disappear as such, but remain in variously subdued forms. Given the dominance of psychopathology as an explanatory medium in education, such concerns about the school itself have all but been expunged.

Discussion about 'adjustment' and schooling in the 1920s and 1930s, for instance, foregrounds the rise in numbers and attendant changes in schools. Closer inspection, however, suggests that at the same time as changes in enrolments were an issue, so too was the way the schools worked with their new constituents. With the population of young people doubling between 1890 and the 1920s, changes in the education system were the greatest in secondary schools, resulting in a 'shift in the character and social composition of the student population in the secondary field' (Reavis 1926: 4). Thus,

> In the place of the small academically selected body of pupils of three or four decades ago headed toward college, there is now in our secondary schools a cosmopolitan group, the majority of whom are in the school either for purposes of general education or for the sake of limited special study.
>
> (Reavis 1926: 4)

Significantly, pressure was not on accounting for the problem in situ in the student, but rather in figuring how to respond to the issue of adjustment between students and the schools. In his report for the Commonwealth Fund, Reavis states that '[l]arge numbers of pupils 14 to 18 years of age withdraw from the secondary school every year for no other reason than inability to become adjusted to its procedures and purposes' (1926: v). This issue, seen as a misalignment, is taken to be the responsibility of the school. Therefore, '[w]hen the school evades or misuses its obligation to provide what the individual pupil needs, it fails in its fundamental purposes and to that extent forfeits its claim to public support' (Reavis 1926: vi). While this could be interpreted as an early example of contemporary neo-liberal narratives of responsibilization (Lemke 2001), there are significant differences. The sense here is that schools can and are problems, and these need to be addressed to educate students. There is also the view that schools need to change from traditional practices.

A generation ago, a high rate of failure and elimination was universally regarded as *prima facie* evidence of the satisfactory operation of the selective function of the school, but today it should be regarded as positive proof of the failure of the guidance function. The school can no longer place the responsibility for adjustment solely on the pupil. It must share the responsibility, and it must not allow pedagogical stereotypes or tradition to interfere with the rights of the child to be understood and to develop his potential possibilities.

(Reavis 1926: 8, original emphasis)

The call for changes from the traditions of 'a generation ago' points to the perceived need for shifts to be made in education. But these shifts did not herald the positioning of the child as uniquely the problem, at least not in the same manner that child as problem occurs in contemporary manifestations in the late twentieth and early twenty-first centuries. Phenomena such as 'delicate boys' existed in the nineteenth century alongside emphasis and acknowledgement of the 'strain' of school life, and so too did pupil adjustment and the problems of the school in understanding how to develop a child's 'potential possibilities'.

In the early twentieth century, then, key issues were whether children were attending school, if they stayed at school, and who was or was not progressing in school. Such issues are difficult to locate in reports on schooling for the poorer classes in the eighteenth and up to the latter part of the nineteenth century. Matters reported for this group of children were in relation to the amount of schooling available, whether schooling interfered with other activities (such as employment or church attendance) and commentary on movement from school to other training or paid employment (such as servants). Charity schools, for example, aimed to provide education to the poorer classes. Workhouses were notoriously oppressive and permitted little chance of education. Children had some opportunity to attend 'school' for two hours. For example, the Work-House in Bishopsgate Street, London, in the early eighteenth century, allowed '20 or 30 Boys' to attend 'Reading and Writing Schools, about two Hours every Day, Sundays excepted' and 'ten by Turns kept a Reading and Sewing School, for making up and mending the Linnen for the Boys and themselves' (Anon 1732: 4). Another report noted the

Children applying themselves to learn all that is taught in the School with utmost Chearfulnefs [*sic*]; and the Employments aforesaid not at all interfering with their learning to read, and say the Church-Catchism, and attending the publick Prayers of the Church, every Day in the Year.

(Anon 1732: 30)

Reports such as these did not discuss things such as 'adjustment' between child and the school.

Examples of poor children in Victorian England attending charity schools are depicted in literary fiction such as Dickens' Noah Claypole in *Oliver Twist* and Uriah Heep in *David Copperfield* (Brantlinger 2011). In the quote below Uriah Heep describes his (and his family's) schooling.

> Father and me was both brought up at a foundation school for boys; and mother, she was likewise brought up at a public, sort of charitable, establishment. They taught us all a deal of umbleness – not much else that I know of, from morning to night. We was to be umble to this person, and umble to that; and to pull off our caps here, and to make bows there; and always to know our place, and abase ourselves before our betters. And we had such a lot of betters!
>
> (Dickens 1850: Chapter 39)

Uriah's education taught him a lot about 'umbleness', a lesson reflective of the Victorian view that education for the poorer classes was not to achieve 'social mobility', but rather to equip these classes with what is necessary to do their work well (Brantlinger 2011). Another argument for education was to improve morality, a point clearly made by Joseph Lancaster (who instigated the Lancasterian System of Education for the Poor): 'Many thousands of youth have been deprived of the benefit of education thereby, their morals ruined, and talents irretrievably lost to society, for want of cultivation . . . ' (Lancaster 1806: 186). This proposal was underpinned by views about the 'subordinate brethren':

> We present to their consideration a plan for extending to the poor the knowledge of reading, writing, and common arithmetic, more efficacious, and more economical in respect to both time and money, than has hitherto been conceived to be within the sphere of possibility. It is a plan which, while it calls upon the superior and middling classes for nothing that admits the name of a sacrifice, promises to bestow upon them more able and more trust-worthy associates in all the circumstances of life, in which we are dependent upon the cooperation and fidelity of our subordinate brethren.
>
> (Committee for promoting the Royal Lancasterian
> System for the Education of the Poor 1810: 1)

The problem of 'extending reading and writing' to 'our subordinate brethren' gives way to a different set of concerns about physical and mental health in the late nineteenth and early twentieth century. Changes made education available for two hours per day in the Workhouses (Brantlinger 2011) and compulsory education 'for all children from 5 to 10 years of age became law in 1880' (Brantlinger 2011: 221).

The presence of medical expertise in the school environment is one of the key indicators of this new form of concern about schooling. In several European countries 'school physicians' were appointed, including 'Sweden 1868; France 1879; Germany 1889 . . . in England and Wales [the] Education Act of 1907 makes school medical inspection compulsory and universal (even in the most remote rural districts)' (Wallin 1914: 10). In the United States the medical inspection of schools began in Boston in 1894, with the appointment of 'fifty school physicians in the fall of 1894; Chicago followed in 1895, NY 1897 and Philadelphia 1898' (Wallin 1914: 10). Wallin notes that by 1903 'only eight cities had established medical departments in the schools (but without the school nurse)' but that this number increased at a great pace in the first decade of the new century. By 1911 in the United States, '443 cities (or 42 per cent) of 1,038 cities reporting were supporting departments of school medical inspection or school hygiene' (Wallin 1914: 9–10).

The information about US school physicians and medical inspection was provided in a significant US educational publication of the time, *The Mental Health of the School Child. The Psycho-educational Clinic in Relation to Child Welfare. Contributions to a New Science of Orthophrenics and Orthosomatics* (Wallin 1914). Wallin was a professor of clinical psychology and director of the psycho-educational clinic. His book emphasizes not only the importance of medical inspection and the school physician, but also the value of the psycho-educational role in the school. Wallin scorned, however, any, 'crude or amateurish psycho-educational diagnoses', instead emphasizing the importance of qualified 'psychological or psycho-educational clinics in the schools' (1914: 397). This specialized area conducted the 'psychological inspection of our large army of mentally exceptional children'.

> We do not know the complete status of the child when we have merely examined his bodily aspect by the available instruments of precision. The child possesses a mental aspect which needs to be just as thoroughly explored by instruments of precision. For the mental examination the instruments and methods of medical inspection do not suffice; this work requires a technique of its own.
>
> (Wallin 1914: 387)

Inspecting this 'large army' demanded specialized techniques with 'instruments of precision'. Also referred to as 'mentally unusual children', these children included the 'feebleminded' and 'seriously backward', identified by techniques such as 'orthophrenics'.

Wallin refers to 'orthophrenics', a technique attributed to the French Psychiatrist Félix Voisin who in the early nineteenth century described 'four categories of children'. Interestingly (and not surprisingly given that this was developed in the early nineteenth century), among these are included children who are affected by the problem of school. Levy explains that Voisin's four categories are:

> Feebleminded children, children with difficulties attributable to faulty education, children with character difficulties since early childhood, and children born of insane parents and hence considered to be pre-disposed to nervous maladies.
>
> (Levy 2006: 225)

In Wallin's adaptation of 'orthophrenics', the category of faulty education is absent. What is stressed here is the problem of the 'grave social and educational problems which spring from the presence in every populous community of large numbers of mentally abnormal children' (Wallin 1914: vii). The locus of the problem is with the child, and the issue concerns how this problem presents to schools, as well as to the community more generally (as opposed to the problem that schooling presents to the child).

One year earlier than Wallin, a book published by Sandiford (who was a lecturer in education at the University of Manchester) provided a breakdown of categories of exceptional children. This book, described earlier, stated that the '[b]ulk of children [were] normal or mediocre' (Sandiford 1913: 297), with exceptional children consigned to three categories:

1
- a) Those who are supernormal in intellect – prodigies, precocious individuals, geniuses and brilliant children of every description
- b) Those who are subnormal in intellect – the backward children, mental defectives, imbeciles and idiots.

2
- a) Those who are supernormal in morals – the saints of society
- b) Those who are subnormal in morals – the excessively cruel, deceitful, egotistical, passionate, and destructive; the moral imbeciles, thieves, rascals and knaves of all kinds.

3
- a) Those who are supernormal in physique – the excessively tall or heavy, and the very healthy.
- b) Those who are subnormal physically – the undersized, the blind, deaf, crippled and diseased.

(Sandiford 1913: 296–7)

These categories omit (as with Wallin's in the United States) descriptions of children who have been affected by 'faulty education'. In this new generation of concern with children, the terms that can be linked to the part (b) of the first category, the subnormal in intellect, were to become the most topical, and possibly the most commonly used term was 'feeblemindedness'.

## Worrying about mental problems: feeblemindedness, mental defectives and backwardness

So far we have mounted the argument that where once there were express concerns about schooling as a problem that affected students these seem to have faded, with discussion emerging about the various student problems that occurred in the school. Terms such as feeblemindedness, mental deficiency and backwardness were widely used to refer to such problems, along with the diagnostic expertise from psychological, psychiatric and medical specializations.

Yet it would be hasty to presume the turn of the twentieth century heralded a purely scientific vigour for understanding problems in schools. A more nuanced explanation would need to take account of the social circumstances that supported the emergence of this knowledge. Clarke *et al.*, for example, argue that mental deficiency 'is a social-administrative rather than a scientific concept, varying in different countries and within a given country at different times' (1985: xv–xvi). One logical way of explaining the proliferation of concern with the child problem is that increases in the numbers of children in schools brought 'social-administrative' issues to the foreground. Dealing with the problem of children 'who do not easily fit in' created the space for new worries to emerge, as well as those ideas formed to describe and/or ameliorate them. As Unwin outlines,

> [I]t was, of course, in the context of the problem of identifying and possibly treating the child who does not fit that the educational psychology promulgated particularly by Cyril Burt over the first decades of the [twentieth] century found a foothold, giving rise to the concepts of educational subnormality, delinquency and maladjustment.
>
> (Unwin 1988: 6)

These concepts included terms such as feeblemindedness, a term that was difficult to uniformly define and presented challenges to diagnose, since 'there is much overlapping and distortion' (Sandiford 1913: 297).

'Overlapping' of terms had deleterious effects for the administration of students, prompting calls for change from generic names such as 'defective classes' to specific categories (Wallin 1914). Common terms at this time included 'feebleminded' as well as the categories 'backwardness', 'imbecile' and 'idiot'. The definitions below are from Sandiford (1913), who cited the Royal College of Physicians of London for categories 2, 3 and 4:

> Definition of Feeblemindedness. With respect to intellect, feebleminded children come between backward children on the one hand and imbeciles on the other. Since the lines of demarcation are artificial it will perhaps be advisable to define each of the grades of subnormal intellect.

1   *Backwardness* is a 'condition in which mental development is retarded through disease, sense-deprivation or some other adverse condition; if suitable treatment can be adopted the child improves and becomes mentally normal' [cited from Lapage 1911: 323].
2   A *feebleminded* person is one who is capable of earning a living under favourable circumstances, but is incapable, from mental defect existing from birth, or from an early age (a) of competing on equal terms with his or normal fellows; or (b) of managing himself or his affairs with ordinary prudence.

3    The *imbecile* is one who, by reason of mental defect existing from birth or from an early age, is incapable of guarding himself against common physical dangers.

4    An *idiot* is one so deeply defective in mind from birth or from an early age, that he is unable to guard himself against common physical dangers.

(Sandiford 1913: 297, original emphasis)[3]

Sandiford's 'definition of feeblemindedness' distinguished it from other 'subnormal intellects'. These definitions were made 'in terms of economic status and of the ability to take care of the person' and it was advised that they be adjusted for application in education. Thus,

[f]rom the standpoint of the educator the difference is one of educability. Backwardness is eradicable by education; feeblemindedness, imbecility and idiocy persist throughout life.

(Sandiford 1913: 298)

In this sense, a clear demarcation was made between what education could and could not change. 'Backwardness' was the category that had 'educability' and could thus be changed.

The terminology was influenced by either the sense of permanence or the possibility of effecting change. For instance, Coldstream (1856) in *The Education of the Imbecile, and the Improvement of Invalid Youth: Home School for Invalid and Imbecile Children* described two types of idiot, the 'idiot proper' and the 'congenital idiot'. The latter is the result of being 'badly managed' and thus considered idiotic. This group is a

large class of persons . . . who are born with a certain capacity, and who, under proper treatment would have manifested a moderate share of intellect, but who have been badly managed and become idiotic, or have been misunderstood and considered idiotic.

(Coldstream 1856: 9)

As with the description of backwardness sixty years later, there is the belief in the capacity for education to change some individuals but not others. This conviction highlighted those that could be changed, as well as those that could not, creating space for specialization in the education for these children. A second point is what might now seem unrecognizable: the very idea that this thing called education could positively change child problems (despite what might be taken as 'fixed problems' such as idiocy). Such positive change is largely absent in present-day education, underpinned as it is by the knowledge and practices of psychopathology.

Use of these terms changed during the mid-twentieth century. For example in the United Kingdom and the United States in the early to first half of the nineteenth century terms such as feeblemindedness were common, but from the 1950s different terminology was employed. As Clarke *et al.* outline,

> in Britain, the terms 'mental deficiency', 'feeble-mindedness, 'imbecility' and 'idiocy' were dropped in favour of 'subnormality' and 'severe subnormality', in the 1959 Mental Health Act, as being less pejorative. Similarly in the United States the words 'mental retardation' are seen as less offensive than 'mental deficiency'. And now 'mental handicap' has become a more favoured label.
>
> (Clarke *et al.* 1985: 28)

In his analysis of special education, Egan suggests that special education, underwritten by psycho-medical expertise, caused decreased tolerance amongst teachers for 'special' students. Teachers consequently 'became more willing to notify struggling children to school doctors, who certified them as mentally defective' (Egan 2006: 150).

Egan is critical of the histories of 'mental defectives', arguing that these have largely omitted analysis of the role of special education.

> The fact that most mental defectives were children, diagnosed primarily on scholastic criteria and segregated by the education system, illustrates that the historiography of mental deficiency suffers from its frequent omission or marginalization of special education. By concentrating on colonies and institutions, historians such as Jackson and Thomson not only fail to tell the whole story but may not even cover half of it.
>
> (Egan 2006: 147)

The sheer amount of early–twentieth-century literature that concentrates on the problems with children, the school and the issue of scholastic criteria is striking. While it is the case that nineteenth-century literature focused on the school more as the source of problems, scholastic criteria were also used to demarcate certain children from the school environment. For instance, in the Home School for Invalid and Imbecile Children in Edinburgh, 'a general feature attaches to all pupils admitted . . . they are all *unfitted* for the training and guidance of the ordinary home and school influences' (Smith and Coldstream 1857: 5, original emphasis). What comes to the fore here is a shared perspective that children aren't naturally suited for school.

Scholastic criteria, then, can easily be viewed as one of Foucault's (1983) dividing practices (separating children into categories and so forth). Use of scholastic criteria could also occur in non-dividing ways that posited the problem as intertwined between issues of education and issues of school. For instance, when asking 'how far is it possible or desirable for the child's problems to be dissociated from the educational system in which it has arisen' a 1937 publication from the Child Guidance Council of Great Britain makes the case that

The difficult child might be difficult because the educational system is at fault, or because of his own inner conflicts. This raises the whole question of influencing the schools as well as of treating the children. It is also a question as to whether the unadapted child ever occurs without the educational system being involved.

(Child Guidance Council 1937: 6)

Two points are notable in the statement above. First, there is a tension between the source of the problem; is it 'inner conflicts' or is it the 'educational system'? Second, we see the dual issues raised of 'treating the children' and 'influencing the schools'. These are out of place in contemporary discussions of education and psychopathology, which rarely focus on influencing schools because of perceived faults in the education system. Undeniably in the contemporary rubric the focus is placed squarely on the psychopathology of the child and, consequently, the school's management of the psychopathological child.

## Mental health and mental hygiene in schools

Children also should be taught to live one day at a time, to settle their moral accounts every night, never to hold a grudge, never to let the sun go down on their wrath, to look upon each morning as a new day in which to improve, but not to carry over their troubles from yesterday.

(Burnham 1924: 647)

Contemporary emphasis on school management of psychopathology circles around concepts of psychopathological problems. This focus, which differs from ideas about influencing schools to address 'education faults', also differs from earlier movements, as rich and profuse as they once were, to manage mental health in schools. Dealing with mental health and promoting mental hygiene were seen to be a natural fit in schools, where there were so many opportunities for prevention (and intervention). For instance, in the United States in the 1930s, C.F. Ryan observes 'the possibilities for mental health in the everyday work of the schools – in program method, attitude of teachers, administration' (1938: vii). Reflecting this interest, works such as *Mental Hygiene and Education* (Mandel 1934) provided detailed instruction to help teachers understand 'the emotional and personality problems of their pupils and to institute classroom treatment . . . [and] the kinds of problems which cannot be dealt with adequately in the classroom, and should be referred to a psychiatrist for treatment' (Mandel 1934: vii). This type of introduction was necessary as the field of child psychiatry was developing as a 'new endeavor'. Contrary to commentaries that attribute problems to the school, Mandel proposes that while child psychiatric illnesses seen at psychiatric clinics are first reported by teachers, '[t]his does not mean that the school itself produces his problems.

On the contrary, the basis of many, if not most, of the child's difficulties is his home training' (Mandel 1934: 266–7).

Other views at the time contended that the purposes of education and mental hygiene are the same, making the case that 'mental hygiene is quite as important as somatic hygiene' (Burnham 1924: 3) and that this had a place in school:

> [i]n connection with every school subject, even every lesson in child hygiene, and every form of motor training, the dictates of common sense and the plain teachings of scientific mental hygiene are to be considered as well as those of physical hygiene.
>
> (Burnham 1924: 3)

On this basis there was a need to examine children as 'beginners' at the start of school life and to identify the 'normal' and the 'defectives' (Burnham 1924: 7). Not identifying children 'at the chronological age of six' (the beginning of school) was noted as a cause of the issues of problems with school as well as with child problems. By recognizing who was – and who wasn't – ready for school, children would not be placed into the situation of failure. From this standpoint mental hygiene was viewed as a preventative practice for 'the prevention of mental disorder, and the development of habits of healthful mental activity' (Burnham 1924: 8). Such views on prevention of problems were similarly shared by writers in the United States who maintained that:

> The psychopath, the neuropath . . . the criminal, and the delinquent might in many if not most cases have been saved from playing their sad roles by early wise observance of a few simple but fundamental principles of mental hygiene.
>
> (Averill 1928: ix–x)

Significantly, though, mental hygiene did not restrict itself to the 'extremes' but rather defined itself by turning to the larger masses of normal people, ensuring the mental health of all (in this sense we might argue there is some pause to consider how this 'globalized' concern with mental hygiene is echoed in the twenty-first-century 'physical hygiene' of preventing obesity).

> For these throngs of tempest-tossed human beings the calm ministry of mental hygiene in those early days when the tares were being sown would have been a solace and a benediction.
>
> (Averill 1928: ix–x)

Tempest-tossed human beings included college students, with books such as *The Psychology of Personal Adjustment* (McKinney 1947) written expressly to introduce mental hygiene for this cohort. This particular US book included detailed photographic illustrations of examples of good and bad mental hygiene and details of personality analysis (see Figure 2.2).

*In which study environment do you think you could work better? Do these study situations throw light on the personalities of the two students?*

*Figure 2.2* Photographs of college students, depicting bad (top) and good (bottom) practices of mental hygiene

McKinney 1947: 25

The photographs are among several used to depict mental hygiene for college students. The caption below the photos asks, 'Which study environment offers less distraction? Which seems more efficient? Which suggests system and order?' (McKinney 1947: 25).

It is clear that in terms of mental hygiene, education institutions are not absolved from responsibility. Indeed, Burnham indicts schools for the failures to take care of the mental hygiene of their charges, pointing out that '[i]t is a grave reflection upon the schools that so many of their graduates have to be re-educated in the sanitarium or the hospital' (Burnham 1924: 13). Schools are seen as a problem, and in some ways this view echoes earlier contentions about the issues with schooling. Again concern is expressed about the unnatural things that school does, since '[w]hen the school attempts to transfer their attention from their spontaneous interests to the more artificial scholastic interests, care should be taken not to weaken the natural habit of concentrated attention' (Burnham 1924: 646). This concern with concentration is based on the view that 'concentration is vital for integration of the personality' (Burnham 1924: 646). Burnham's (1924) book, *The Normal Mind: An Introduction to Mental Hygiene and the Hygiene of School Instruction*, published in the United States, concentrates on how mental hygiene is important for ensuring that the development of the mind is normal.[4]

Accent on prevention is echoed in the literature of mental hygiene for this period in the UK, and is included, for instance, in discussion of the 'mental hygiene of the pre-school child' (Kimmins 1927). This book includes a report by Pritchard, a medical inspector, who found that 'physical defects' existed in children prior to the commencement of school (Pritchard, cited in Kimmins 1927). Pritchard goes on to discuss how public school and upper class parents should be able to organize physical checks for children prior to their starting school. While this points to the prevention of problems occurring prior to engagement with school, problems are of a physical nature and not the mental or adjustment difficulties that so readily appear to occur with the commencement of schooling.

Concerns with health and mental hygiene also saw an intricate set of analyses of schooling not only concerned with identifying how this could be applied within schooling. Questions were again raised about the effects of school. In a chapter dedicated to the 'School Handicaps to Mental Health', it was noted that it is 'evident that many established school procedures work heavily against some of the fundamental principles of mental health' (C.W. Ryan 1938: 69). In a book on mental hygiene published a decade earlier, topics included 'the mental hygiene of the school day' and 'mental hygiene and school subjects' (Averill 1928). This and other similar works are representative of the application of medical and increasingly psychological and psychiatric knowledge to education. When nineteenth-century education literature engaged with medical discourse this was more concerned with health effects wrought by schools. Early-twentieth-century literature, by comparison, increasingly turned to descriptions of the mental domain and how education interacted with it.

Not surprisingly, commentaries are made on the distinctions between the psychiatrist's and the teacher's points of view in relation to gauging the problems of children and schools, with concern for the variation between teachers' attitudes to children's behaviour and that of psychiatrists (C.W. Ryan 1938). Citing studies by Wickman (1928) and Watson (1933), Rivlin describes the particular attention given by psychiatrists.

> The psychiatrists tended to stress acts of omission more than the teachers did and relegated 'transgressions against authority' and 'violations of orderliness in class' to a position of minor importance . . . Psychiatrists rated 'withdrawing, recessive personality and behaviour traits' as more serious than dishonesties, cruelty, temper tantrums, truancy, immorality, violations of school-work requirements, and extravagant behavior traits.
>
> (Rivlin 1936: 258)

These differences are also extended to an entire chapter about the 'methods of teaching that retard adjustment' (Rivlin 1936: 337). Here psychiatric concerns with teaching include 'the exaggerated importance of marks' and the attendant focus of the teacher on 'the direct results of her lessons' (Rivlin 1936: 338).

Divergence in what was and was not viewed as problematic by psychiatrists and teachers is telling of the different issues brought to their respective attention. It is also of interest to note the potentially different ways that contemporary descriptions of children's problems, couched as these are in psychiatric constructs, now include what eighty years ago was the issue identified by the teacher. 'Violations of orderliness in class' and 'transgressions against authority' are now associated with psychiatrically defined behaviour disorders such as ADHD and conduct disorder (American Psychiatric Association 2013a).

In situating the importance of mental hygiene and its application in schools, the problem arises in the literature of the 1920s and 1930s of how to achieve its application in schools. The Child Guidance Clinic was a key means via which tenets of mental hygiene could be delivered and monitored in schools. While there was considerable growth in these clinics in countries including the United States, the United Kingdom and Australia (Harwood 2006), there were limitations, with Rivlin concluding that 'they do not touch the great majority of the school population' (Rivlin 1936: 337). *Child Guidance Clinics, a quarter century of development* (Stevenson and Smith 1934) credits these clinics as beginning in the United States in 1909, although it wasn't until 1922 that the name 'Child Guidance Clinics' was applied. Stevenson and Smith note Lightner Witmer's Psychological Clinic at the University of Pennsylvania as an earlier psychological clinic operating in 1896.

The function of child guidance clinics was (1) to 'study and treat patients'; (2) 'they seek to interest other community agencies in the prevention of behaviour and personality disorders in children and in promising methods of dealing with them when they occur'; and (3) 'they attempt to reveal to the community, through the first-hand study of individual children, the unmet needs of groups of children' (Stevenson and Smith 1934: 2). In line with the emerging influence of medical knowledge and education, the clinics were overseen by 'a physician specially trained for the practice of psychiatry – that is acquainted with the known range of mental deviations, their origins and therapy, and with the mechanisms of behaviour generally' (Stevenson and Smith 1934: 2). Early examples include Healey's Chicago Juvenile Psychopathic Institute, which had specializations in psychiatry, psychology and social work (Stevenson and Smith 1934) and is also noted for making connections between psychiatric interpretations of delinquency (Alexander and Selesnick 1967).

Efforts to increase the use of child guidance clinics in education are evident in the *Proceedings of the Child Guidance Inter-Clinic Conference of Great Britain* London (Child Guidance Council 1937). Discussions in these proceedings from the late 1930s include reports on contact with schools and reactions by teachers as well as reports of teacher training in Scotland being linked with child guidance clinics. These connections made it

> [p]ossible to bring teachers in training into close contact with the [Child Guidance] work. The ordinary teachers' training course included lectures on objective testing, vocational guidance, the treatment of behaviour difficulties in school children, and child guidance method. Students were enabled to visit the clinic and to observe the work in the playroom.
> (McClutsky, cited in Child Guidance Council 1937: 10)

As well as these approaches, connections between education and child guidance clinics included direct financial support (for example, in Leicester the Child Guidance Clinic was financed by the City's Education Committee). Discussions reported in these conference proceedings made clear the importance attached to distinguishing the Child Guidance Clinic from the school and, accordingly, differentiating between problems that belonged with the school (such as remedial teaching) and those which were within the purview of the clinic.

There were, however, doubts as to the appropriateness of Child Guidance methods being taught to teachers in training, with one discussant at the Child Guidance Inter-Clinic Conference in London, a Mr Hardie, the Deputy Education Officer for Edinburgh, said to have 'doubted the wisdom of giving the psychological outlook to the immature teaching mind' (Child Guidance Council 1937: 13). This strong view about the capacity of teachers to grasp the psychological is confounded by works such as that by school teacher Caroline Zachary (1929), *Personality Adjustments of School Children*. Described as being written to 'know more about the factors which contribute to the development of personality' (Zachary 1929: v), Zachary's book covers topics including the 'troublesome child' and 'polyglandular difficulty'. In another book written to include teachers, Wallin's (1927) *Clinical and Abnormal Psychology. A Textbook*

*Figure 2.3* Apparatus used in psychological and psychoeducational clinics

Wallin 1927: ii

*for Educators, Psychologists and Mental Hygiene Workers* provides detail of the various apparatus used in a Child Guidance Clinic (see Figure 2.3).

The focus on mental health, mental hygiene and child guidance at times refer to taking the child to specialist services, noting the difference between the teacher and the psychiatrist. At times the child guidance literature records the problems caused by the schools, and at others this same literature seeks to absolve the teacher of blame (and describes anticipating teacher reactions to alleged criticism from psychiatric or psychological workers). Such opportunity for debate was to substantially change with the advent of *Diagnostic and Statistical Manual of Mental Disorders* (*DSM*), published by the American Psychiatric Association. This system of classifying mental disorders was to grow into worldwide dominance, and to infiltrate the school to such an extent that mental disorder is now ubiquitous in schooling.

## The *DSM*

The *DSM* came into use as a widely (and arguably, globally) accepted classification system for mental disorders relatively recently with the release of the third and fourth editions (*DSM-III* and *DSM-IIIR* in 1980 and 1987 respectively and *DSM-IV* in 1994). *DSM-5* was published in May 2013, and contains changes to mental disorders that include both removal of disorders and also revised and new categories.

The first edition of *Diagnostic and Statistical Manual of Mental Disorders* was published in 1952, and was reprinted fourteen times (American Psychiatric Association Committee on Nomenclature and Statistics 1952). Since this, three more editions, a revised edition and a text revision have appeared. In 1968 the second edition, the *Diagnostic and Statistical Manual of Mental Disorders* (*DSM-II*) was published. Twelve years later the third edition of the *Diagnostic and Statistical Manual of Mental* (*DSM-III*) was published. Citing Cooksey and Brown (1998), Miller and Leger argue that 'the shift from *DSM-II* to *DSM-III* marked an important moment in the history of psychiatry, as the biopsychiatric model came to dominate over the psychoanalytic model' (Miller and Leger 2003: 15). The *DSM-III* was followed seven years later by a revised edition, known as the *Diagnostic and Statistical Manual of Mental Disorders Third Edition, Revised* (*DSM-III-R*). The next edition, the *Diagnostic and Statistical Manual of Mental Disorders – Fourth Edition* (*DSM-IV*), was published in 1994. It had a 'text revision' published in 2000, the *Diagnostic and Statistical Manual of Mental Disorders-Fourth Edition, Text Revision* (*DSM-IV-TR*). As its authors explain, the purpose of this revision was to correct any 'factual errors', check 'information was up-to-date' and make changes to the text to 'reflect new information available since the DSM-IV literature reviews completed in 1992', make 'improvements that will enhance the educational value of DSM-IV' and 'update ICD-CM codes' (American Psychiatric Association 2000: xxix). It also states that 'no substantive changes in the criteria sets were considered, nor were any proposals entertained for new disorders, new subtypes, or changes in the status of the DSM-IV appendix categories' (American Psychiatric Association 2000: xxix).

The *DSM-IV-TR* contains 943 pages. The first edition of the *Diagnostic and Statistical Manual of Mental Disorders* was published in 1952 and is considerably smaller, containing 132 pages. This is a difference of 811 pages in 48 years. The question to be put is whether the recent edition with its sevenfold increase in size represents advancement in psychiatric science. Or, is it rather that this latter edition represents a more organized practice of knowing and speaking its objects into existence?

The making of this first edition of the *Diagnostic and Statistical Manual of Mental Disorders* appears uncomplicated compared to the procedures used to create *DSM-IV*. Unlike the seven-member committee of the first *DSM*, the creation of *DSM-IV* required a 37-member DSM-IV Task Force, 13 separate disorder workgroups (comprising a total of 98 members) and two separate committees (comprising a total of sixteen members). This information is presented in the opening pages of *DSM-IV*, conveying in detail the credentials (and therefore authority) of those involved in the construction of this classification system. It would seem that this extensive reference to authoritative contributors is particularly necessary given what Caplan describes as the limited numbers of individuals who *actually* make *the* decisions about the content of *DSM-IV*. She maintains that, 'in practice, decisions about who is normal begin with at most a few dozen people – mostly male, mostly white, mostly wealthy, mostly American psychiatrists' (Caplan 1995: 31). This need to substantiate the contributors from the outset indicates how vital legitimation is to making mental disorders and their classification truthful and scientific.

Despite the grand influence of the latter versions, the first edition of the *DSM* was considerably humbler. In fact, according to Jenkins, this first edition met with scant regard:

> its categories were recognized by no organization except the American Psychiatric Association. The National Institute of Mental Health had to translate the diagnostic categories into those of the International Classification of Diseases before reporting them to the World Health Organization. Even the American Medical Association utilized the categories of this International Classification rather than those of the American Psychiatric Association.
>
> (Jenkins 1973: 23)

Additionally, this first edition met with criticism for its 'negligence' of child mental disorders (Clarizio and McCoy 1970). By contrast, *DSM-IV-TR* devotes approximately 100 pages to the mental disorders of 'infancy, childhood and adolescence'. The construction of the second edition, *DSM-II*, appears to have had just such an agenda, since 'there was an organized effort to bridge this gap and build an acceptable compromise' (Jenkins 1973: 23). This attention to the mental disorders of children again occurred in the third edition, *DSM-III*, which had the 'largest increase in diagnostic categories' (Kirk and Kutchins 1992: 101).

In their critique of the *DSM*, Kirk and Kutchins note that '[t]he development of the *DSM-III* by the APA was a major public effort to defend psychiatry by making diagnosis appear to conform more closely with the image of technical rationality' (1992: 222–3). The most recent DSM, *DSM-5* has numerous changes and is arguably the largest version of the manual to be produced (see for example the dedicated website, www.dsm5.org). Considerable debate has occurred over the changes in mental disorders such as autism, with Asperger's syndrome now absent as a distinct category and collapsed into autism spectrum disorder. These are changes that will have repercussions in education, not only in terms of what is and isn't diagnosed but also in relation to how the problems that occur in schools, that are now resolutely child problems, are 'treated'.

Alongside the plethora of diagnosis yielded by the *DSM* there is an array of psychopharmaceuticals, drugs that are ubiquitous in education settings. In an institutional context, the increasing use of these in hospitals was commented upon by Foucault, who tellingly wrote: 'in hospitals pharmacology has already transformed the rooms of the restless into great tepid aquariums' (Foucault 2006: 549). Psychopharmaceuticals in education have altered learning spaces; is it unreasonable to overlay Foucault's description of the changes to hospital onto the educational system, with infant settings, schools and colleges purified of restlessness and instilled with a profound kind of pharmaceutical antiseptic scholasticism?

Accounts of the period in the 1920s and 1930s unabashedly describe scenarios that would be understood quite differently today. The quotation below is a case in point, reminding us of the unwieldy constellation that is the psychopathology of children in today's schools.

> [T]o describe an unsatisfactory pupil as inattentive is one of the most naïve habits a teacher can develop. It is naïve because we usually do not realize that we have thrown a sort of verbal boomerang. There is of course, no such thing as 'inattention'. As long as the human organism is alive it is attending – to something. What we really mean when we say that a pupil is inattentive is that he is not paying attention to us, that we have failed to arouse and hold his attention, that we are simply less interesting to him than something else in which he is absorbed.
>
> (Mandel 1934: 79-80)

How far removed is this view of inattention from contemporary practices, where discussion of the medication of children's inattention is acceptable practice within school (and other educational) environments? The level of discussion might be characterized as far more than a murmur; one of loud conversations. We might characterize the contemporary moment as one that is far removed from the 'silence' of 'classical madness' noted by Foucault (2006):

> In itself it was a silent thing: there was no place in the classical age for a literature of madness, in that there was no autonomous language for madness and no possibility that it might express itself in a language that spoke its truth.
>
> (Foucault 2006: 516)

Madness in education is very far from such silence. Discussion of children and problems of the mind over the course of the early to mid-twentieth century is audible, variously concentrating on problems with schools and problems with children. Although at times discussions in earlier periods of the twentieth century verge towards a singular focus on the student as problem, this is muted in its concentration. For it is at its strongest and most complete when the language of psychopathology, breathed into life by the later *DSMs*, is embraced and furthered in the apparatus of education.

## Notes

1  Topics on illness included: feigned illness; infectious illness; the cause and prevention of infectious illness arising while at school; the prevention of epidemic; disinfection; convalescents

after infectious illness; breaking up a school on account of the advent of malignant infectious illness; the prevention of infectious illness being carried home from school; the prevention of infectious illness being carried from school from home; incubation period of infectious illnesses; duration of ineffectiveness (Dukes 1887).

2  These are much lower compared to other age groups: the 'commonest period is from forty to fifty years' (Ireland 1898: 286).

3  Definitions from the Royal College of Physicians of London were accepted by the Royal Commission on the Care and Control of the Feebleminded, Report, 1908, Vol. VIII, *Report of the Royal Commission on the Care and Control of the Feebleminded*, 8 vols, 1908 (Thorndike 1910, Chapter XI. Cited in Sandiford 1913: 297).

4  For Burnham, 'Normality, as we have seen, is that functional condition where a general integration can be maintained and right adjustment made in spite of certain distracting and disintegrating factors' (1924: 599).

# Chapter 3

# The risk factors? 'Race', social class and gender

## Introduction

> We pass from a technology of power that drives out, excludes, banishes, marginalizes, and represses, to a fundamentally positive power that fashions, observes, knows, and multiplies itself on the basis of its own effects.
>
> (Foucault 2003a: xxi)

> [The medicalization of poverty is] potentially even more dangerous than medicalising welfare dependency. It creates the prospect of subordinating all low-income people to the terms of expert discourses designed to diagnose conditions as primarily or exclusively allopathically treatable.
>
> (Schram 2000: 99)

Much of the scientific and educational literature on childhood and youth behavioural disorders ignores, or at best gives limited attention to, the racialized, classed and gendered issues associated with diagnostic practice. Minority groups and children from disadvantaged circumstances are over-represented in educational remediation and disciplinary programmes and boys are far more likely to receive a diagnosis relating to their behaviour than girls. In this chapter we examine the 'risks' associated with 'race', class and gender and detail how diagnosis and medicalization in education is heavily affected by social and cultural factors. We draw together contributions from the critical literature on ADHD and childhood mental disorders, statistics from the United Kingdom, United States, Australia and Brazil, and upon the findings from our own small-scale research with professionals undertaken in Scotland. These combine to offer critical perspectives on patterns and trends, comparisons of particular contexts and a detailed insight into the professional responses in one specific location. We begin by examining the language used to capture mental disorder within involuntary commitment law and, in so doing, illustrate how the construction of risk provides the cause, the justification and the tone for capturing the mental disorders of children and young people. We also show how this notion of risk is conveyed in the formal discourses and documentation about people identified as experiencing mental illness through a simultaneous vagueness and demand for flexibility. We then examine the risk factors of 'race', class and gender and, taking each of these 'oppressions' in turn, we examine the psychopathologizing that goes on within these arenas through, and as a consequence of, risk. We explore the specific patterns of naming – of disorder – within each of the risk factors and the subsequent practices of spatialization that arise. At one level, following Soja (1996), spatialization concerns all social relations, but here it has very specific – and often segregated – outcomes for the individuals concerned. We are all too aware that in focusing on these three areas we are missing out such key dimensions as sexuality (Harwood 2004), but we have chosen to focus on what appears to be associated with the greatest risk of psychopathologizing the behaviour of children and young people. We acknowledge the powerful added value of intersectionality (Erevelles 2010) and while we take account of cumulative risk effects, we also think it is important to examine 'race', class and gender in their individual intersections with psychopathologization. We draw upon our own work as well as on theoretical perspectives from Disability Studies, Critical Race Theory and sociological analyses of social class to analyse these practices. We argue that belonging to certain minority groups puts children at risk of receiving a medical diagnosis of their behaviour and that this risk is produced through a series of complex naming and spatializing practices. This contention is further explored in each of the following chapters.

## Vaguely flexible

Mental disorder [is] . . . mental illness, arrested or incomplete development of mind, psychopathic disorder and any other disorder or disability of mind.
(England Mental Health Act 1983, §1(2), in Brooks 2000: 15)

[Mental illness is] an affliction with a mental disease . . . to such an extent that the person afflicted requires care, treatment and rehabilitation.
(New York Mental Hygiene Law, §1.03(20), in Brooks 2000: 15)

[O]rdinary words of the English language should be construed in the way that ordinary sensible people would construe them. [Therefore] I ask myself what would the ordinary sensible person have said about [the respondent's condition and behaviour]? In my judgement such a person would have said: 'Well that fellow is obviously mentally ill.'
(*W v L*, 1 QB 711 1974, cited in Errington 1987: 184)

The use of tautology within the law pertaining to mental illness appears to serve a greater purpose than simply indicating the difficulty in defining either mental illness or mental disorder. As Brooks (2000) observes, it provides vagueness combined with flexibility that defers the power to define mental illness to administrative agencies, courts or psychiatrists. These 'experts' are given a certain scientific status and their pronouncements, according to Foucault (2003a), are privileged and accorded the 'presumption of truth' (p. 11). They are also assumed to be benevolent and concerned, not with making judgements, but with understanding what is going on within a child's head, or as Rose (1996: 4) notes, with 'the production and maintenance of social normality and competence'. However, according to Laurence and McCallum, their expertise produces not better understanding but 'discontinuity and fragmentation' (2006: 198) because of their need to assert confidence that their vantage point is the only true and correct one.

In both England and Australia, recognition of the problematic nature of expert opinion has led to the engagement of a 'lay definition' of mental illness (Errington 1987; Hogget 1990). The Queensland Minister for Health defended the need for flexibility in defining mental illness and the importance of deferral to his Parliament:

> The question of mental illness is not decided on whether a person can be given a certain diagnostic label. Mental illness can refer to any degree of mental or emotional defect or aberration, whether from physical or psychological causes. Whether the provisions of the Act should apply depends on a medical assessment of the nature and degree of the disorder, and its effects on the person and on other people.
>
> (Errington 1987: 185)

The former USSR apparently had the most precise definitions of mental illness but has been also credited with using these definitions to incarcerate political dissidents and people who were otherwise healthy (Bonnie 1990; Heginbotham 1987).

The function of definitions and expert diagnosis of mental illness and disorder within involuntary commitment law is to enable measures to be taken, usually incarceration, in order to protect society from any risk that might be posed by the patient, look after the patient's own good and meet basic needs (Stromberg and Stone 1983). However, Foucault notes that in legal cases involving criminality, expert psychiatric opinion confirming mental disorder creates a 'psychologico-ethico double' (2003a: 16) of the offence whereby the offence is set alongside a series of other 'forms of conduct' (1996: 15), which often imply a deficit in relation to development, personality or self-control. This reasserts the offence tautologically, conveys a sense that these forms of conduct are in fact the offence and suggests that these forms of conduct do not breach the law and are therefore of a lesser nature than had the offence been considered on its own terms.

Siegler and Osmond (1966) remind us that a medical explanation is one of several possible axes of mental illness and it is only since the 1960s and 1970s that 'sociogenic' factors took over from 'egocentric' aspects and paved the way for 'bio–psycho–social' understandings of mental illness (Murthy and Wig 1993: 395). These new ways of understanding have shifted the naming and spatialization of mental disorder into more complex forms, involving greater differentiation of responsibility among professionals. They have also intensified the risk associated with being from a particular ethnicity, being poor or being a boy, establishing each as a risk that brings with it further (moral) obligations for those with professional responsibility for them.

## 'Race': The risk of colour

Symonds (1998: 951) suggests that certain groups, for example young black men in England, may have, 'elevated perceptions of dangerousness' attributed to them while Bean *et al.* (1991) note higher rates of emergency detention of Afro-Caribbeans than for whites and higher proportions of the former group at each point within the mental health system. 'Race' appears to be associated with a high risk of diagnosis of special educational needs, with particular racial groups at a particularly high risk (Artiles *et al.* 2010). It is precisely the attention to the dangerousness associated with being black and failing that both encourages a diagnostic gaze and diverts attention from the role of schools and society in producing inequality (Brantlinger 2006). This attention involves, first, processes of naming trouble at the intersection of 'race' and behaviour, and second a series of spatializing practices that protect both the individual and others and, in so doing, separate them. We will explore these naming and spatializing practices but before doing so, will examine some of the available figures on prevalence relating to the diagnosis of special needs and behaviour disorder among minority ethnic groups.

Government figures for England (Department for Education 2011a) indicate that in 2011, 25 per cent of black children of compulsory school age were diagnosed with special educational needs (although only 2 per cent of these had statements of special educational needs). Black Caribbean children were apparently at greatest risk with 29.8 per cent diagnosed as having special educational needs, compared with 20.6 per cent of white children. The overall percentage of Asian children with a special educational needs diagnosis was lower than the average for white children (18.4 per cent) although 23.5 per cent of Pakistani children had received a diagnosis. Only 11.1 per cent of Chinese children had been identified as having special educational needs. The government figures for emotional and behavioural difficulties in England show a similar racialized pattern. The greatest 'at risk' group here appear to be children of mixed 'race', of whom 34.3 per cent were deemed to have emotional and behavioural difficulties even though this group did not figure prominently as having a high proportion of SEN diagnoses: 32.2 per cent of black children were diagnosed, with an eye-watering 39.9 per cent of Black Caribbean children with this label, yet 26.6 per cent of Black African children had been diagnosed, lower than the

27.2 per cent of white children within this population. Asian children again numbered fewer among the population diagnosed with emotional and behavioural difficulties (15.7 per cent), as did Chinese at 13 per cent.

Diagnosis of ADHD among minority ethnic groups is a mixed and indeed changing picture. In the United States, ADHD prevalence increased from 1998–2000 to 2007–9 for non-Hispanic white children (from 8.2 per cent to 10.6 per cent) and for non-Hispanic black children (from 5.1 per cent to 9.5 per cent). In 2007–9, ADHD prevalence was similar among non-Hispanic white, non-Hispanic black and Puerto Rican children. Among Mexican children, ADHD was lower compared with children in the three other racial and ethnic groups (Akinbami et al. 2011). Children of mixed 'race' were considered to be at high risk of an ADHD diagnosis with between 8.9 and 14.1 per cent being accorded this status (Centers for Disease Control and Prevention 2011).

In Australia, national draft guidelines (Royal Australasian College of Physicians 2009) on ADHD admit to not having accurate data on ADHD among Australian Indigenous peoples but indicate that people with ADHD are over-represented in the criminal justice system and that rates of incarceration for Aboriginal and Torres Strait Islander peoples are high. The draft guidelines, advising on cultural sensitivity in the diagnosis of ADHD, point out that it is common for Indigenous children to move around the classroom, checking on one another, and advise that this should not be viewed as an indicator of impulsivity. It should be noted, however, that these guidelines have never been formally endorsed following the identification of a conflict of interest violation by one of the US authors whose work was heavily cited. The individual, a psychiatrist, failed to disclose the huge sums of money he had received from drug companies. Rates of diagnosis of Indigenous children from the Brazilian Amazon are cited as 24.5 per cent (Azevedo et al. 2010) although the difficulty in accessing remote populations to estimate prevalence was acknowledged, as was the case in Australia.

The National Collaborating Centre for Mental Health (2009) suggests that the differential rates among different ethnic groups may reflect different levels of tolerance within cultures for the symptoms of ADHD. This is a conclusion also reached by Timimi and Taylor (2004), Bussing et al. (1998) and Hackett and Hackett (1993), who found vastly different levels of diagnosis of ADHD across different cultures and regarded these as reflecting parental perceptions of what constituted 'normal' behaviour. This cultural distinction was underlined by Rohde (2002) in a study of ADHD in Brazil in which he pointed out that children and adolescents from Latin America are more likely to exhibit emotional distress and to be more talkative and active than their counterparts from Anglo-Saxon cultures and that such tendencies must be taken into account by physicians making assessments. Dwivedi and Banhatti (2005) also point to inconsistency in the way in which assessment criteria are applied and, reviewing several studies, all of which used the Connors rating scale, found diagnosis rates ranging from 16.6 per cent in the UK; 16 per cent in Spain; 15 per cent in New Zealand; and 12 per cent in Australia to 3 per cent in China; 4.5 per cent in Scotland; and 5.8 per cent in both Brazil and Canada.

## Racialized naming practices

The naming of behaviour disorder among minority ethnic groups has some origins in early eugenics research, most notably that of Thomas Russell Garth, whose book *Race Psychology* (Garth 1931) advanced claims about the 'primitive', but superior, intellectual status of American Indian children. Garth (1919) reported Indians as performing better in continuous mental performance tests than their white and black peers. A later version of the test, the Continuous Performance Test, became an accepted means of naming ADHD, but far from demonstrating superiority in reaction time among American Indians, functioned to endorse their negative and inferior status (Barkley *et al.* 1990; Walker 2006). Racialized patterns of naming are so entrenched that, according to Walker (2006), who spent four years in the Yakama Indian Health Clinic, there was a 75 per cent probability of children presenting with behavioural problems emerging with an ADHD diagnosis and prescribed stimulants. This pattern is particularly difficult because the deficit ADHD trajectory is at odds with the strength-based perspective of American Indian cultures and fails to acknowledge the importance of intergenerational and family contexts and to recognize that difficult behaviours may be part of 'an individual's and family's life path' (Simmons *et al.* 2004: 61). This is a point also made by Rohde (2002), who, in his study of Brazilian diagnosis of ADHD, is critical of the lack of regard for culturally specific behaviours as part of what constitutes normal. Walker (2006) is not overstating things in claiming that the indiscriminate translation of ADHD across culture without regard for that culture amounts to a form of colonization of the mind, 'with concepts about themselves and their children quite foreign to their culture' (2006: 78).

Within the school spaces occupied by special education there are distinctive sites of the psychopathologization of ethnicity. The overrepresentation of ethnic minorities within special education has been well documented (Artiles *et al.* 1997; Ferri 2004; Graham 2012) and suspicion has turned on special education and its role in preserving education in the face of ever-increasing diversity (Dudley-Marling 2001). In spite of the convincing empirical evidence of the problem of overrepresentation of particular groups of students, Artiles (2004) questions the appropriateness of the focus on 'representation' of any group, the result of which, he argues, is that 'these students are seen as the passive carriers of categorical markers of difference (e.g. 'race', class, gender) and their assumed nefarious consequences (e.g. low achievement, dropout, delinquent behaviour)' (Artiles 2004: 552). This reductive tendency and the obsession with the physical presences and essences of students generates 'myopic understandings of the role of culture and history' (Artiles 2004: 552) and ensures that agency is denied.

## Mind the (achievement) gap: spatializing 'race'

As Dewey (1934: 23) notes, space is 'something more than a void in which to roam about', but rather is 'a comprehensive and enclosed scene within which are ordered the multiplicity of doings and undergoing in which man [*sic*] engages'. Furthermore, space and the practices of spatialization help to construct particular social realities (Soja 1996). Paperson's (2010) notion of the ghetto is a helpful way of understanding the particular spatialization of minority groups. The ghetto, according to Paperson, is not, 'a fixed sociological space . . . [but rather] a dislocating procedure' (2010: 10) that draws on the 'apparatus of empire' (p. 21) to justify the separation, through diagnosis, of children from minority ethnic groups. Pathology, according to Paperson, becomes a valuable legitimizing device:

> Pathology generously rewrote us as anticolonialists. Our colonial complic- ity erased, pathology also erased the violence of this pushout. Thus, the ghettoed subject appears fleetingly as a problem, then vanishes as a person from the official record.
>
> (Paperson 2010: 9)

Cartography, which Paperson describes as a key technology in colonialism, allows for a kind of space-shifting which is 'trickster magic' (2010: 10) and which leads to the eradication of those who do not fit: 'The trickster is shape shifting again, producing new regions of displacement and mapping these car- tographies of nowhere onto bodies' (Paperson 2010: 10). The diagnosis of children and young people from minority ethnic groups with a mental disor- der maps both them and their ethnic identity as distinctive, and subsequently distances, dislocates and differentiates them from their peers. This cartographic practice is promoted as benign and as functioning in the best interests of chil- dren and young people and their peers.

School failure among minority ethnic groups is spatialized as a 'gap', yet Ladson-Billings is critical of the 'achievement gap' (2006: 3) that has become part of our common parlance, 'invoked by people on both ends of the politi- cal spectrum' (p. 3) and with 'few argu[ing] over its meaning or its import' (p. 3). The achievement gap is 'often characterized as a single unyielding gap between white students and . . . minority students' (Ream *et al.* 2012: 37) but is more accurately conceived 'as multiple gaps that fluctuate between racial, social class, and linguistic groups'. Gillborn (2008: 65) argues that 'Gap Talk' serves a particular strategic and political purpose in enabling a sense of incre- mental progress to be conveyed through messages about narrowing or reducing the gap and calls it 'a deception' (p. 68). Gillborn suggests that the achievement gap is more of an 'educational debt' (2008: 44) which is persistent. Ladson- Billings and other scholars, particularly those writing within the United States, have pointed to an impossibility of ever recovering this debt because of the 'locked in' (Roithmayr 2003: 38) nature of racialized inequalities. These are so deep-rooted, historically and culturally, and so institutionalized that they become almost inevitable. Furthermore, as Gillborn (2008) argues, attending to the narrowing of the achievement gap obscures the real systemic problems that need to be tackled.

## Class and socio-economic striations

The class struggle exists; it exists more intensely.

(Foucault 1989: 18)

Children and young people living in poorer circumstances are four times more likely to be diagnosed with borderline to abnormal social, emotional or behavioural difficulties (Barnes *et al.* 2010; Goodman and Gregg 2010; HM Treasury and DFES 2007), have an increased likelihood of school suspension and exclusion (HM Treasury and DFES 2007) and are connected with high rates of behaviour disorders and medication (Harwood 2006). Children are at greater risk of ADHD as a result of deprivation and this is mediated by both social class and ethnicity (Bauermeister *et al.* 2005). Here, we suggest that children and young people of low socio-economic status experience a naming of their chaotic lives and of the lack in their lives, not just of material goods but also of self-control. The naming of these omissions generates a moral obligation and leads to further spatial practices that situate the children and young people and their families as on the end of professional concern, support and control. These practices produce plural disadvantage (Wolff and De-Shalit 2007) while creating a '*positional* flexibility which puts [the professional] in a whole series of possible relationships with [the child and family] without ever losing him the upper hand' (Said 2002: 1009, emphasis added).

Confirmation has been sought from neuroscience that poverty and disadvantage affects children physically. While in opposition, the UK MP Iain Duncan Smith studied the findings of research on the neural development of children from 'neglected and deprived' families compared with 'normal' families (Tomlinson 2012: 282) and the UK Parliamentary Strategy Office produced a paper contrasting a normal brain with an 'emotionally deprived brain' (Cabinet Office 2008: 87). Similarly, in Australia, during a sitting of the federal parliament in March 2001, Dr Louise Newman, then head of the child and adolescent faculty of the Royal Australian and New Zealand College of Psychiatrists, compared projected images of a healthy and a 'neglected' eight-year-old brain. Media coverage of this event records Dr Newman calling for awareness of the 'forgotten epidemic of child maltreatment' and inferring poor parenting as potentially brain-damaging (Ellingsen 2001: 1). As Tomlinson notes, this is not very far away from eugenics theories and from medical textbooks showing the 'warped brains of criminals and the mentally retarded' (Tomlinson 2012: 282). One of the profound consequences of medicalization is that diagnosis obscures other interpretations and this has particular implications for understanding the behaviour of children from poorer backgrounds. This concern echoes Schram's (2000) critique of the medicalization of welfare. In Schram's view, 'poverty can be an important cause of psychological problems, but correcting those psychological conditions will not necessarily correct the poverty that produced those conditions in the first place' (Schram 2000: 92). More broadly, this points to the need for medicalized treatment in poorer communities to be given careful scrutiny.

The UK study *Poorer Children's Educational Attainment: How Important are Attitudes and Behaviour?* (Goodman and Gregg 2010) identifies the markedly lower levels of educational attainment reached by children from poorer families, pointing to behavioural problems as a key element contributing to this. A Scottish study found one in four persistently poor children (aged three-to-four and five-to-six) rated as having social, emotional or behavioural difficulties (Barnes *et al.* 2010). Children in these circumstances experience multiple social, health and behavioural problems, with rates of 22 and 23 per cent for five-to-six-year-olds living in short-term and persistent poverty, and a sharp increase of 28 per cent for three-to-four-year-olds living in persistent poverty (Barnes *et al.* 2010). Research has predicted that young people aged 14 living in poverty have an increased likelihood of school suspension and exclusion as the number of family problems increases (HM Treasury and DFES 2007) and Gorard's analysis (Gorard 2010; Gorard and Smith 2010) highlights the confounding effects of children from poor families, from particular ethnicities and with additional learning needs clustering in specific schools. In the United States, national statistics show that, from 1998 through to 2009, ADHD prevalence increased to 10 per cent for children with family income less than 100 per cent of the poverty level and to 11 per cent for those with family income between 100 per cent and 199 per cent of the poverty level (Akinbami *et al.* 2011). Patterns of higher diagnostic rates in low socio-economic areas are evident in Australia, a country which has rates of diagnosis of 11.2 per cent and which has the third highest use of stimulant medication for ADHD, after the United States and Canada (Harwood 2010b). The rates of medication are highest within disadvantaged communities in Australia, among unemployed families (Sawyer et al. 2002) and among children in care (Graham 2008). Concerns have been raised in Australia about the risk of paediatricians 'medicating for social disadvantage' (Isaacs 2006: 44). The implication of social class and disadvantage as a risk factor has been recognized in urbanized Brazil, where lower class young people were more likely to be identified for behavioural diagnoses by both clinicians and school staff (Béhague 2009), and where distinct socio-economic inequalities have been recorded between black and white Brazilians (Gradín 2007).

Several researchers have discerned classed and racialized parental strategies that determine particular outcomes for their children, revealed through different discursive representations. Gillies (2005), for example, comparing Scotland and England, distinguished between middle-class parents who emphasize the individuality and competences of their children and working-class parents who stress characteristics such as social skills, working hard and staying out of trouble. Similar differences were observed in the United States by Lareau (2003), who also distinguished between the intensive cultivation by middle-class parents of their children and the concern to provide adequately for the physical needs of children by working-class parents. A UK study by Vincent et al. (2012) found subtle differences among a group of middle-class Afro-Caribbean parents in terms of their strategies for involvement and support and identified a continuum with parents doing whatever it took, including employing tutors, to get the best for their children at one end; parents merely hoping for the best at the other end; and those in between who were described as, 'watchful and circumspect' (Vincent et al. 2012: 347) and being guided by what was deemed to be appropriate parental involvement. Whilst these studies appear to show the value of an intersectional analysis, Strand (2010) warns that social class has limitations in accounting for ethnic-based differences. His UK research found that Pakistani, Bangladeshi, Black Caribbean and Black African children achieve, at the age of 14, three points behind their white peers and he suggests that these differences are better explained by pre-existing effects of ethnicity at age 11 than by factors relating to socio-economic status.

As Deleuze and Guattari (1987) have noted, many of the spaces in which we work are heavily striated or lined and the rigid nature of these spaces may give rise to particular practices and patterns of behaviour. Social life, they argue, is 'machinic', leading to a distribution and differentiation of people's existence, production and consumption (Deleuze and Guattari 1983; Patton 2000). This is no accident, argue Deleuze and Guattari (1987), since the striation of space is one of the main tasks of the state and this functions to include some people and exclude others.

> The *relative global*: it is limited in its parts, which are assigned constant directions, are oriented in relation to one another, divisible by boundaries, and can interlink; what is limiting (*lines* or wall, and no longer boundary) is this aggregate in relation to the smooth spaces it 'contains', whose growth it slows or prevents, and which it restricts or places outside.
>
> (Deleuze and Guattari 1987: 382, original emphasis)

Striated spaces dominated by medicalizing processes were an ongoing presence in the work of the professionals we interviewed in the Scottish study. These occurred along directional flows, especially for children and families who were perceived as poor and working class. This was explained to us using the metaphor 'wedded': 'By the time somebody comes to us and they have a referral accepted to us, by then they're getting, you know, quite wedded into a mental health service' (Professional 5, Child Mental Health, MCB Scotland). Financial ability to choose medical care distinguished the flow of medicalization, with middle- and upper-class parents being in a position to pursue diagnosis and treatment strategies that were unavailable for children from poorer families. This was apparent in whom the professionals saw, with our respondents noting higher referrals for disadvantaged families and social class distinctions. Patterns of who receives which diagnosis and what clients used free public services were, for instance, closely associated with class-related treatment choices and diagnostic practices,

> When you're working within the middle-class and the upper-class areas, it's often related to attachment or trauma . . . and there'll be psychotherapists involved; whereas when you're working in areas like that [poorer areas] . . . ADHD's often the one that's given and medicated quickly.
> (Professional 7, Headteacher, MCB Scotland)

Class-based differences in diagnostic practices were also described as occurring for dyslexia where, 'for middle-class parents, if a youngster is struggling a bit with literacy, it's almost more acceptable to go for dyslexia' (Professional 1, Educational Psychology, MCB Scotland). One of the sites that children and parents were directed to was specialist child mental health services. Yet, as another professional noted, parents from disadvantaged areas did not always take up or continue these appointments.

> A number of the kids that we recommend and take forward, the parents for whatever reason don't engage and that's maybe particularly those from your kind of poorer backgrounds . . . A lot of the parents for whatever reason do not engage, and do not look for that level of support. They don't appear for appointments, they don't turn up or they constantly re-arrange and they put no barriers up to stop it happening.
> (Professional 6, Educational Support, MCB Scotland)

While our study did not include data from parents or children, this professional did state that children 'don't want to go' to mental health services. He went on to explain that this could be due to 'a fear thing [as for] a number of kids with behavioural needs with self-esteem issues, going and seeing something like that is pretty scary . . . they'll look for any reason to avoid doing it' (Professional 6, Educational Support, MCB Scotland). The professional described how the service would attempt to alleviate these types of fears, including offering to accompany children and parents to appointments.

As well as distinctions between the types of diagnoses, comments were made about the processes leading to a diagnosis. What stood out in these observations were comments about how diagnoses are made more frequently, at younger ages, and sometimes occurred without 'full consultation':

> I think there's always that question of how the diagnosis came about, because it's not always done in full consultation . . . Certainly in my

previous post you would have looked at home, school, community, or lots of different areas to build up the diagnosis. I don't know if that's always the case, I think it's often just . . . from family or social work for example.
(Professional 6, Educational Support, MCB Scotland)

The importance of a child's context was a shared concern, with several professionals describing how context could become obfuscated, such as when 'the route goes from a parent to a GP to a specialist mental health team, then the assessment can be very much about the young person without looking at a wider context' (Professional 1, Educational Psychology, MCB Scotland). Other professionals described how increases in school-based support services resulted in lower diagnostic rates.

Despite efforts to understand and support, children and families would frequently become subjected to the force of striations that medicalized and territorialized social class. This pattern of subjection was apparent in situations such as when, despite efforts by services, children and families did not attend specialist mental health settings. As outlined above, the children experiencing poverty would be more likely to be directed along a different route to that of their middle-class peers.

### Naming chaos and lack

As discussed above, children and young people living in poor circumstances were especially marked by the manner in which problems were explained, with depictions of the chaos of their lives and of what they lacked, both in material terms and in their capacity for self-control. One of the professionals described this need to recognize the chaos in the child's life and the judiciousness required by services:

That's maybe part of the worry – that if too much store is being put on an ADHD diagnosis, actually if you really saw what that youngster's coping with, day by day, both in terms of traumatic situations and routines that are not routines, then maybe you would see exactly the same behaviour in school and describe it in a different way, or attribute it in a different way.
(Professional 1, Educational Psychology, MCB Scotland)

In emphasizing an understanding of the context of the child's life this professional was critical of an over-emphasis by the school on the medicalization, resulting in the emphasis on diagnosis of behavioural disorders such as ADHD.

Depictions of poverty and 'the poor' as chaotic and lacking organization are recognizable characterizations. The drawing *Après la saisie* ('after the seizure') by Jean Louis Forain (Figure 3.1) conjures this meaning, while at the same time the title itself could be said to prompt an understanding of the family's chaotic or disorganized presence.

*Figure 3.1 Après la saisie* by Jean Louis Forain, c. 1870–1900

This nineteenth-century depiction of a destitute family with its jagged lines is evocative of the chaos of their life as they move from the structure of home to the unknown. While current depictions of poverty with chaos echo the sentiment of this drawing, we want to suggest that the practices that medicalize poverty and child behaviour territorialize social class in new ways. This contemporization of poverty was readily apparent when the medicalizing apparatus focused on matters of attendance at specialist services and on the uptake of medications. In terms of the latter, several of the professionals described the way both the prescription of medication and compliance in consumption were classed. One professional observed that while 'the chaotic use of medication is perhaps more linked to demographics . . . equally there can be some families who simply feel, on a principle, that, that they don't want to use the medication' (Professional 1, Specialist Education, MCB Scotland). Although this professional was acknowledging that parents might not comply 'on principle', often adherence to medication regimens is couched in terms of compliance (Harwood 2006, 2010a). Yet the view that decisions can be related to principle is probably a less common way of understanding the interaction between parents from poorer circumstances and the uptake of medication regimens. In the main it seems that children's not taking medication or adhering to medication regimens is conceptualized as a problem that originates from a lack of organization, structure and consistency in poor and working-class families. This interpretation is evident in the following description:

> Parents from poorer or deprived backgrounds find it much harder or, in some cases, are unable to actually help support their kids because they don't give them the consistency, they don't insist upon the medication, you know, a number of things, and that's where it can become an issue.
> (Professional 5, Child Mental Health, MCB Scotland)

Unpredictability in a child's medication regime was discussed as an issue for primary schools, one that could serve to magnify the depiction of chaotic life.

> We've got some schools that have to guess almost whether a youngster's had their Ritalin before they come into school – or their medication. Part of the work around supporting the young person is actually supporting the whole family.
> (Professional 1, Educational Psychology, MCB Scotland)

Thus, notions of chaos are named and serve as justification for the territorialization of the child, the family and the home as a site for support and control.

With families characterized as lacking order, children are, by implication, unable to exercise control over their own conduct. They are also, however, named as pathologically incapable of self-control and of being often driven by extraneous impulses. One of the professionals we interviewed described an individual as lacking the part of her that could intervene before she spoke:

> I'm just thinking of a young girl that's quite impulsive and she comes out with some very impulsive type things that then upset people . . . her 'stop and think muscle' doesn't work and so things that, you know, all of us would think and just wouldn't say she just blurts and she's not intending necessarily to hurt it's just unfortunately that's come out.
> (Professional 5, Child Mental Health, MCB Scotland)

Although the professionals were firm about seeking to avoid such a pathologizing gaze, which we discuss in more detail in Chapter 8, they acknowledged the difficulties for individual children who lacked self-control, and the professional speaking above attributed lack of control and inattention to more contemporary causes within society:

> Children now are not taught to tolerate boredom . . . We were taught to tolerate boredom . . . Children are not now expected to develop their own strategies for amusing themselves, are they? You know, car journeys, now you can have DVDs and your Xbox and you know, how to learn just to notice what's going on around you or learn to just be still in yourself and learn self-containment. There's always some external stimulation, so I would be amazed if the rates haven't gone up, when you think about what . . . we're doing to [children].
>
> (Professional 5, Child Mental Health, MCB Scotland)

This argument is also made by Ken Robinson (2006), the creative arts guru, who alleges that schools kill creativity while actively producing boredom among children and young people. The professional quoted above went on to offer a contrasting picture of how children who are able to become controlled, through stimulant drugs, experienced this positively:

> They've suddenly found themselves joining in with the class, focusing on their work, paying attention, not getting into trouble and their lives have taken a very different direction.
>
> (Professional 5, Child Mental Health, MCB Scotland)

This lack of control over conduct was first determined by George Still, who presented, in 1902, 43 child cases of 'moral defect' to the Royal College of Physicians.

> I would point out that a notable feature in many of these cases of moral defect without general impairment of intellect is a quite abnormal incapacity for sustained attention.
>
> (Still 1902)

For Still, moral control meant 'the control of action in conformity with the idea of the good of all' and his presentation of the characteristics of a 'morbid passionateness' exhibited by the children is generally accepted as marking the start of the medical record on ADHD (Wallis 1994).

### Territorializing the home

The classed thematic becomes a tell-tale characteristic of the way in which classed-medicalization produces the behaviour assemblages of children from poorer backgrounds and territorializes the family and the home as a site for support. A professional in our study illustrated the intensification of the gaze 'into' both the home and the school with her comment,

> You can get some that can be well managed within school, but you get great stories of very difficult behaviour at home. And sometimes that may depend on how the family chooses to maximize medication, in the course of the day, but there are other times where . . . they can be fine at home but difficult at school – that says to me you need to drill more into the setting, and see what's going on.
>
> (Professional 1, Educational Psychology, MCB Scotland)

Another professional described how the support actively reached into the territorialized space of the home:

> Trying to help with . . . homework strategies . . . finding the optimum level of stimulation that works for [the child], so we can help the families think about strategies that . . . before there would have ended up being rows about.
>
> (Professional 5, Child Mental Health, MCB Scotland)

Following Fox and Ward (2011: 1015), we view behaviour assemblages as 'confluences of relations that *pattern* the psychic landscape of a subject and establish the boundaries of "what a body can do"'. Behaviour assemblages can result in limits that pathologize poverty. The salience of this consideration is made clear in Schram's (2000) analysis of the medicalization of poverty, stated in the introduction to this chapter.

One consequence of the depiction of parents as 'erratic' in the administration of medication is that it can serve as a rationale for services to focus concern onto the amelioration of inconsistent medication regimes and medicalized engagement.

The idea that parents need to be supported to engage productively with medication serves to compound identification of social classes with specific medical problems – and thereby medicalizes their experiences of poverty. Being poor and working class can therefore mean child behavioural issues fit neatly into striations that have the twofold effect of both creating and bolstering classed and medicalized modalities. The danger is that the problem becomes one of engagement with this classed-medicalized striation and in so doing risks missing other ways of conceptualizing the issues involved with child behaviour problems.

## Gender: the danger of being a boy

> Boys' behaviour at school is still more challenging than that of girls, but the behaviour of both is getting worse.
>
> (Association of Teachers and Lecturers 2011)

The trouble with boys

They're kinetic, maddening and failing at school.

(Tyre 2006)

Bad behaviour in schools fuelled by over-indulgent parents.

(Paton 2012)

A salutary reminder is given by Roberts (2012) of the way in which attention to extremes of behaviour and achievements, in particular boys' underachievement, leads to 'ordinariness' (McDowell 2003: 204) being overlooked. Much of this appears to be associated with intense media interest in 'bad boys' and even though, as Ashley points, out gender is a smaller risk factor than 'race' or class, 'it is boys to whom media often turn first for good stories' (2009: 181). At the same time as it can lead to the less dramatic, but nevertheless troubled, behavioural disorders exhibited by girls being missed, it can lead to an over-dramatizing and intensified regard for the behavioural problems that boys may present with.

Boys outnumber girls in diagnoses of ADHD by three to one, and this is the case in most neuropsychiatric conditions, but Cantwell (1996) notes a referral bias, whereby boys are more frequently referred than girls because of their aggressive behaviour, which takes the ratio of boys to girls within mental health clinics or hospitals to between six and nine to one. Girls are considered more likely to exhibit the characteristics of the less prevalent attention deficit disorder, which include sluggishness and anxiety, but because, by its nature, it does not involve hyperactivity, they may not be referred or may be misdiagnosed (Myttas 2001; Quinn 2005; Quinn and Wigal 2004).

Whilst ADHD prevalence is increasing across the board, this prevalence is markedly higher among boys than girls and is noted as a worldwide phenomenon (Skounti et al. 2007). Also consistent across countries are the higher rates of prevalence where there is a clinical referral, going from a ratio of 3:1 to as much as 9:1, for example in New South Wales, Australia (NSW Department of Health 2002). Skounti et al. (2007) suggest that variation between countries may be due to cultural factors, reflecting, as in relation to ethnicities, different levels of tolerance of hyperactive behaviour, but these are not gender specific. Indeed reporting on ADHD in Brazil, Rohde (2002) notes similarities in the male–female ratio, the prevalence of the combined type of ADHD, and the pattern of comorbid disorders with those reported in the United States. As O'Dowd (2012) points out, reflecting on Australian statistics, most of the studies of ADHD are biased towards males.

### Naming the gender danger

The first reported portrayal of a behaviour-disordered boy was Fidgety Phil, who appeared among the poems of the German doctor, Hoffman, in 1864.

**Fidgety Phil**

Let's see if Philip can
Be a little gentleman;
Let me see if he is able
To sit still for once at table
Thus Papa bade Phil behave;
And Mamma looked very grave.
But fidgety Phil,
He won't sit still;
He wriggles,
And giggles, . . .
See the naughty, restless child
Growing still more rude and wild
Till his chair falls over quite . . .
                    (Hoffman 2004)

The majority of the children presented by George Still to the Royal College of Physicians were boys and, as many researchers have suggested, and as we have noted above, the higher rates of prevalence are linked to higher rates of referral of boys, which is associated with the troubling and troublesome behaviour exhibited by them. This in turn appears to be tied to a fear of a risk of further pathology and dangerousness. The guidelines of the Australian National Health and Medical Research Council (NHMRC) make this association explicit:

> [H]yperactivity which persists from early childhood, associated with defiance or aggression, increases the risk of Conduct Disorder, antisocial personality, substance abuse and criminality in adulthood.
> (cited in Van Acker 2007: 5)

Such risks are less commonly associated with girls and, as Donnelly (2007) suggests, it is only when the risk of academic underperformance is identified among girls that any attribution of a behaviour disorder surfaces.

A major UK teachers union (Association of Teachers and Lecturers 2011) named boys' behaviour as still remaining more challenging than that of girls, but girls' behaviour has become increasingly problematic over recent years. A survey conducted with its own teacher members also identified gender differences in the problem behaviour, noting the boys as exhibiting aggressive behaviour, which teachers experienced as more challenging. Girls, according to the teachers, undertook more subtle forms of disruption, but this was nevertheless still challenging and the recent increases in forms of cyber-bullying using social media, which often spilled over into the classroom, had been most prevalent among girls.

### Taking boys out

Department for Education figures, which cover England and which report 3,020 suspensions and 40 expulsions of five-year-olds during 2010, show boys were three times more likely to be suspended than girls and four times more likely to be expelled (Department for Education 2011b). O'Regan (2010) notes that school exclusion impacts disproportionately on children with special educational needs, and although the relationship between ADHD, boys and exclusion has been under-researched, Daniels and Porter (2007) suggest that rates of exclusion are higher among children with ADHD. The Attention Deficit Disorder Information and Support Service (ADDISS) (2006) documented rates of 11 per cent of exclusion among children with ADHD, over ten times higher than the average in 2006. O'Regan suggests that the significantly lower proportion of girls than boys with ADHD being excluded may reflect an under-diagnosis of girls' ADHD rather than anything else. Being excluded from school has clear 'knock on effects' (CALM 2010) on educational attainment, for the obvious reason that children who are not in school will be not participating in lessons (although they may well be learning). Recent UK government exclusion figures provoked concerns among education groups and teachers unions that those with diagnosed behavioural problems and/or special educational needs were not having these diagnoses taken into consideration (Wainwright 2011).

At the same time as there have been concerns that insufficient attention is given to behavioural disorders in the discipline practices within schools, leading to their physical exclusion, there has also been an intensification of regard for troubled boys and of spatialization practices. These practices are *inclusive* and therefore retain boys within the school, but mark them as both troubled and troublesome, either actually or potentially, and territorialize them as objects for special attention by specialist staff and for particular intervention programmes that may be gendered or that at least try to take account of masculinity. They also distinguish them as the future beneficiaries of drives, such as that by the Teacher Development Agency in England, to recruit more male staff teachers as 'role models' (Guardian 2008).

## Taking intersectionality apart

There have been increasing calls for critical analysis that is intersectional, that is, that attends to the interaction between particular arenas of difference. Some of those making the calls appear to be motivated by concerns at a lack of attention to certain aspects such as disability (Davis 2002; Ware 2005), while others see the importance of attending to the interaction itself (Brah and Phoenix 2004; Erevelles 2010).

Those academics concerned with a lack of attention to disability have been critical of how 'the majority of academics do not consider disability as part of their social conscience' (Davis 2002: 35). Davis illustrates his argument with examples of hate crimes in which disability is overlooked by the focus of attention being given to 'race'. This 'eclipse of disability' by 'race' occurs because anti-discrimination legislation revolves around a 'single axis framework' (Crenshaw 1994: 40), but it could be argued that this is also how academics orient themselves in the world, only able to handle one form of oppression at a time. Berubé sees the refusal to acknowledge disability as part of what he calls the 'politics of disavowal' (1997: 5) or a form of ableism, which sits alongside other forms of oppression such as sexism or racism, but expresses a hope that scholars are moving disability studies from being a 'sideshow to midway' (Berubé 2002: xi). Berubé reminds us, however, that, 'the importance of disability as a category of social thought may depend more on the practices and politics of people with disabilities than on the work of academic disability studies' (2002: x).

Arguments for greater attention to the intersections, for example between disability and social class/disadvantage, between disability and 'race' or between 'race' and social class/disadvantage are based on the perceived greater value to be had from intersectionality than on single-issue thinking. Delgado-Bernal, calling for attention to the 'intersectionality of subordination' (2002: 118), argues that 'one's identity is not based on the social construction of "race" bur rather is multidimensional and intersects with various experiences' (p. 118), while for Solórzano and Yosso to neglect intersectionality is to 'omit and distort' (2002: 27) individuals' experiences of oppression. There is, however, a danger that the proclamation of intersectionality provides an excuse to dodge the issue (Gillborn 2008) and this phenomenon was identified by Troyna (1994, cited in Gillborn 2008: 37), who referred to the tendency for 'commatization' ('disability – comma – gender – comma – age – comma – sexuality'). People cited in this way, Troyna suggested, could be ignored. We wonder what it might mean to insert the term psychopathology to the list – or to add a list of commatized descriptors to discussions of psychopathology. One problem is how commatization would obfuscate the complexity of the individual's experiences.

The challenge of intersectionality is paradoxical. On the one hand, researching and writing about generic constructs of 'social reciprocity and redistributive justice' (Brantlinger 2004: 497) or analysing the 'five faces of oppression' (Young 2000: 39) – exploitation, marginalization, powerlessness, cultural imperialism and violence – takes us out of the essentialist trap and reduces concerns about privileging one area over another or about the silencing effects produced in discourses. On the other hand, 'race' and identity may themselves become entangled in discourses (Reid and Valle 2004) and there is the possibility that this may be overlooked. Cognisant of this danger, Ferri calls for more self-conscious research practices:

> LD scholars and researchers must turn the research gaze back on ourselves; a reflexive turn is necessary in order to transform our past and present complicity with racist hierarchies and agendas.

> (Ferri 2004: 512)

A key question is: 'Whose voices are validated, acknowledged and taken into account in defining the future of the field?' (Artiles 2004: 553).

The question of whose voices are validated, acknowledged and taken into account are indeed key to the next four chapters, where we begin to unfold the processes of psychopathology at school. We begin, as one might say, at the beginning, from the cradle to the crèche, and including what precedes this phase of schooling.

# Chapter 4

# From the cradle to the crèche

Yes we have to get our babies young, from the time they are born. Many of the mental health problems that emerge in teenagers and adults have their start in what happened to them when they were little babies, before memory and before language, certainly before they can make sense of what is happening to them.

(Infant Mental Health 2012: 33)

In truth there is a vast gallimauphry of neuroscience research, but little settled knowledge.

(Wastell and White 2012: 402)

The earliest times of life have become vital sites of intervention for future life. This is a time to garner knowledge and devise programmes of intervention. The newborn, as well as the prenatal (or antenatal), are critical sites because they are viewed as the points of life holding the most potential. These are the life-points where there is the greatest possibility for the potential of mental health problems to be avoided, detected or corrected. On a downward slid-ing scale, where potentiality decreases as age increases, the unborn, newborns, infants, toddlers and preschoolers have an 'inherent' potentiality for optimiza-tion; an inherent potentiality that no other age can lay claim to. According to this logic, the longer existence continues the less potential there is for interven-tion and correction. This is a logic necessitating a sense of moral urgency to act and intervene and it is the logic that underwrites much of the contemporary emphasis on the very young. Needing to 'get our babies young' highlights the prominence of 'future proofing' the infant experience; a set of beliefs that Nicholas Rose (2010) has described as the risk discourse of mental health. This experience concerns far more than the infant itself, relying upon what Foucault describes as 'focal points of experience' (2008a: 3).

The focal points of experience, as discussed in Chapter 1, comprise three elements: 'forms of possible knowledge, normative frameworks of behaviour, and potential modes of existence for possible subjects' (Foucault

2008a: 3). In relation to the first 'focal point of experience', knowledge of the very young has relatively recently seen a rapid increase. 'Infant psychiatry' is said to have been first used as a term in 1976 (Sameroff *et al.* 2004), with terminology such as 'infant mental health' (or 'early childhood mental health') increasingly recognized as a specialization (Kope and Lansky 2007). Infant mental health, for instance, is defined as 'the healthy social and emotional development of a child from birth to three years' (Zero to Three 2013) and is distinguished from the mental health of adults, young people and older children. Egger describes the field of infant mental health as having two important tenets, with the first emphasizing the importance of the developmental perspective and the second emphasizing an understanding of mental health, 'within the context of the child's relationships and environment' (Egger 2009b: 561).

The 'set of norms' (the second focal point) encourages awareness of the ways in which babies, infants and toddlers are identified, understood and judged. As Valerie Walkerdine has argued, developmental norms produce criteria against which infants can be assessed as normal or non-normal (Walkerdine 1984). The norms that mark out this early period of life extend in a range of ways. For instance, the time of birth is the subject of normalization, with research suggesting the seasonality of birth (the time of year babies are born) as associated with certain psychiatric disorders. A recent UK study reported that babies born in January had higher rates of adult schizophrenia and bipolar affective disorder (Disanto *et al.* 2012). This interest in seasonality of births and psychiatric disorder has spurred studies in equatorial regions 'without seasonality' (as compared, it would seem, with Europe or North America), where studies have found there is no 'seasonality' of birth date and psychiatric disorders (Parker *et al.* 2000). While those living in equatorial regions might challenge assumptions about the 'lack of seasonality', the very idea of seasonality of psychiatric disorder for those born in January could be of concern. Likewise, families with babies born at this time could also experience a sense of alarm at the 'greater risk' their child has of developing schizophrenia. There are numerous other examples of the sets of norms that are applied in relation to babies and young children to identify the non-normal, and that by consequence carve out the sphere of the normal infant.

Taking up these ideas to consider the infant experience it becomes clear that the first two elements, knowledge and norms, appear more amenable to analysis of the infant than the third. The heterogeneous forms of knowledge of the infant experience can be accessed, as can the set of norms on which the infant experience is established. But to speak of how the infant constitutes him or herself demands the assumption that first the infant is constituting his or her experience, and second, we can, in one way or another, access this or presume to understand its meaning. While the former can be assumed, the latter is arguably impossible, aside from via extensive speculation. The breach created by this necessity of speculation is filled, it would seem, by what has become the orthodoxy of baby brains and neuroscience.

## Points of arousal

Parents of prenatal babies, caregivers of very young children and preschool teachers are the principal points of arousal for this age group, but these individuals also find themselves the focus of concern by professionals. While professional service staff such as preschool teachers are targeted, arguably the primary locus of concern is with the caregivers of young children, and this is whether these are born or unborn. At the same time there is a whole enterprise that expands around the baby, the infant, the preschooler and their parents/ caregivers. Babies born too early, the 'preterm babies', are argued to be at risk of psychiatric illnesses (Allin 2010). Thus while the well-being of young children is pressed as an issue of societal concern, responsibility rests with caregivers, especially mothers (Wall 2004). This in effect translates to a moral imperative. Indeed, as Wastell and White maintain, 'the present argument for early intervention is part of a longer-term project of moral regulation' (2012: 408). Hence caregivers are a key point of arousal that is in need of regulation and intervention.

Emphasis on the very young child and the yet-to-be-born is not in itself a 'new' concern heralded by contemporary technology. For instance, concern with the prenatal is evident in the passage below, taken from the *American Journal of Public Health* in 1933:

> The psychic well being of the preschool age child is bound up in such problems as are concerned with the prenatal care, maternal mortality, rational spacing of pregnancies, adequate obstetric attention, and a lessened use of forceps, especially among primipara. The fact of birth itself is a psychophysical factor, in so far as it subjects the child to physical strains and cerebral pressures, and it may occur in a psychological atmosphere which may be disadvantageous from many angles.
>
> (Wile 1932: 192)

There are some unusual comments about the child's psychic well-being in this quote, such as the reference to 'primipara' (first time pregnancy), the spacing of pregnancies, and the reference to maternal morbidity, which has significantly decreased in the western world and global north. Amongst the quoted list, however, is the consideration of prenatal care and the preschool child. This is an emphasis linking the actions occurring pre-birth to a period in the future, and in this case, two to four years later. Striking in this quote from 1932 is the way the prenatal is defined against preschool age, and in this instance the prenatal does not hold its own status. Some eighty years later the prenatal does not disappear from view in this manner: it is now a site that demands intervention. The reason that this is possible is because things can happen at this site of life that are of consequence to this site of life.

Given the focus on intervening as early as possible, it is unsurprising that the parents of the yet-to-be-born are a point of arousal. Thus while concerned with the foetus, the target is women who are pregnant with unborn children. In this regard, prenatal mental health of the baby is implicitly coupled to the mother–baby dyad and this is done in a fashion that intensifies the emphasis on the behaviours of the woman. The extent of this prominence can be grasped when it is understood that the contemporary emphasis on the gene and genetics loses out: 'there is evidence that fetal adversity on postnatal mental health is not due to genetic factors. Taken together, the findings suggest programming effects of a prenatal adverse environment on postnatal mental health and behaviour' (Schlotz and Phillips 2009: 912). Maternal behaviour is thus critical as an instigator of problems and this now competes against the traditionally held problem behaviours such as smoking and drug use (for example cocaine) seen to cause foetal mental health problems. Maternal behaviours such as responses to psychosocial stress are considered causes of foetal development problems that are linked to later mental health issues such as ADHD (Schlotz and Phillips 2009).

The foetus focus draws on the familiar gendered emphases made on the mother–baby and mother–infant couplet. Maternal physiological factors such as high cortisol levels are reportedly connected with behavioural and emotional problems in children at the age of four (Glover and O'Connor 2002). Assumptions about neural pathway connections and developments post-birth enable the application of neural connection logic (and thus, the influences on these connections) occurring pre-birth and caused by the woman.

The metaphor of 'programming' describes a process termed 'foetal programming', which has been employed to depict the effects of the mother on the foetus in utero. In this schema it is the mother's physiological activities such as 'stress hormones' that programme the foetal brain in ways that may be adaptive or in a manner that is in conflict (Del Giudice 2012). The adaptive view holds that foetal programming occurs via the mother transmitting hormones about the 'state of the external world' that 'forecasts the environmental conditions it will eventually face after birth' (Del Giudice 2012: 1615). At the cellular level this has been argued to affect telomere biology. 'Telomeres . . . cap the ends of linear chromosomes . . . The telomere structure facilitates full replication of the chromosome, and prevents chromosome ends from engaging in fusions' (Nature 2013). In this view the mother's reactions to the world create hormonal responses that reach to the telomeres and thereby affect cellular structures of the unborn.

The opposite of the adaptive view is the conflict view. In this scenario a 'conflict of interest [occurs] between mother and fetus about the outcomes of fetal programming' (Del Giudice 2012: 1614). Foetal programming is not only about the foetus, but also about the mother's needs. Thus this 'is the crucial dilemma in prenatal stress: the fetus is going to receive a mixture of useful information and manipulative signals' (Del Giudice 2012: 1617). This would have effects beyond the uterus, where

[m]aternal stress hormones do not only carry information about the features of the external environment, but also make the fetus more open to later behavioural influences from the mother (and other caregivers).

(Del Giudice 2012: 1624)

Del Giudice (2012) cites research by Kaiser and Sachser (2009) that reports on outcomes of maternal stress including 'female masculinization' and 'male infantalization' in the offspring of guinea pigs exposed to maternal stress. Effects on humans apparently include a range of mental health problems such as 'higher anxiety and fearfulness, temperamental difficulty, impulsivity, reduced executive functions, impaired attention, higher aggression and risk taking' (Del Giudice 2012: 1616). In sum, the argument is mounted that there is a clear and definite link between foetal development and mental health status later in life (Schlotz and Phillips 2009).

Concern is also aroused by a range of parental behaviours and attitudes towards their children (and, as described above, by parents, principally mothers, towards the unborn). The 'emotional availability' of parents is cited as a difficulty (McGrath et al. 2012) and described as affecting things such as children's behavioural problems at school (Yurduşen et al. 2013). The gendered focus on women is consistently emphasized in the literature on young children and mental health, with studies reporting the importance of 'maternal sensitivity' for 'social-behavioral adjustment' (Jacob 2009). 'Poor maternal caregiving' is, for instance, linked to behavioural and emotional problems (McCartney et al. 2010; Stein et al. 2012). While the extensive research and health practices emphasizing the prenatal care of the mother may well have benefits, intensification in concern with the mental health of the unborn as well as the newborn infant places a specific responsibility onto the mother for the mental health of her foetus.

The extraordinary absence of research on fathers and early childhood is noted by Jacob (2009). In addition to this lack, there is a dearth of research on the diversity of families, with little available on lesbian, gay or intersex headed families. The majority of work in this area has focused on how such families (mainly lesbian headed families) produce 'healthy children' (Andre 2009).

Other researchers point to the impact of parental personality, highlighting problems such as neuroticism, inability to control anger (Wahl and Metzner 2012) and depression (Goodman et al. 2011). Allin et al. (2006) describe the concern about the impact of preterm birth on future adult psychiatric problems as 'complex and multigenic', involving a range of factors. This includes reference to the effect of 'increased parental monitoring . . . of children born prematurely (Hack et al. 2002) as well as the influence of "higher parental behavioural restrictiveness"' (Reti et al. 2002, cited in Allin et al. 2006: 315).

The attention on prenatal life and on young children is not evenly distributed, with some parents and caregivers arousing more concern than others. This includes people where 'risk factors' are identified such as living in poverty and disadvantage, mental health problems, substance use, single mothers and young parents, as well as certain cultural groups. The effects of racism on parents has been investigated as an issue, but the focus has been on how parents respond to racism, with certain responses said to negatively affect the mental health of young children. Parents who 'denied experiencing racism [had] the highest behavioural problems among their children' (O'Brien Caughy et al. 2004: 2122). Consequently although this important issue has been raised, the shortcoming is the potential for some parents affected by racism to be held as causative of (and responsible for) mental health effects on their young children. This diverts attention away from the substantive causes of racism and racialization (and responsibility), placing the onus onto the individual who has been subjected to this abhorrent action.

Childcare and preschool are also key points of arousal and a locus for both scrutiny and intervention. It is also a site that is reported to be causative of mental health problems, although, unsurprisingly, this can be linked to a discourse of maternal absence. Early exposure to childcare (before the age of two) is associated with more difficult behaviour at older ages (Eryigit-Madzwamuse and Barnes 2013). A review of fifteen US studies into effects of childcare on children's social and emotional well-being found that 'more hours per week in non-maternal childcare and entry into non-maternal care in the first year of life are the most consistent and significant childcare predictors of negative social-behavioural adjustment' (Jacob 2009: 564). A similar conclusion was reached in another study, which reported that:

> having only a few months of center-based care experience before age two was not detrimental to child behavioral outcomes but that prolonged experience of dominant center-based care before two years old is likely to be a risk factor for anger prone and unmanageable behaviour at later ages.
> (Eryigit-Madzwamuse and Barnes 2013: 113)

Children in preschool are more likely to be expelled due to behavioural problems than older children in primary schools, with a US national study reporting it was three times higher (Gilliam 2005). According to one UK study, nursery care has also been reported to be linked to children developing behavioural problems, with those receiving childcare again more likely to have behavioural problems (Stein et al. 2012).

The relationship between the early childhood/preschool/kindergarten teacher and the child is held to be of significance (Amini Virmani et al. 2013). Attention on preschool teachers places emphasis on factors such as their relationships with children to prevent mental health problems such as anxiety (Anticich et al. 2013). Problems with behaviour include issues for teachers that were so severe they resulted in expulsion of children (including three-year-olds) from their preschool (Gilliam and Shahar 2006). Teacher concern with behavioural problems is reflected in the outcomes of a review of the literature between 1991 and 2002, which ranged between 14 and 52 per cent of children aged three to five rated as having behavioural problems (Upshur *et al.* 2009). Interpretation of behavioural problems by preschool teachers has been shown to be affected by gender bias, with boys considered to more typically have disruptive behaviour disorders (Maniadaki *et al.* 2003).

Preschool/kindergarten is viewed as a site for early detection, remediation and prevention of future mental health problems in the adult population. Correspondingly, childcare teachers are assumed to have a role as a link to mental health services (Alkon *et al.* 2003). Efforts are thus made to foster and improve connections between childcare centres and mental health services, especially for children with behavioural problems (Upshur *et al.* 2009). One angle taken in this regard is how future problems (such as mental health or criminality) can be predicted in very young children.

> [T]his study has shown that an early designation of high risk status can effectively predict service use (and thus predict emotional and behavioural problems serious enough to require services) . . . early conduct problems represent an obvious risk factor among most populations of children.
>
> (Jones *et al.* 2002: 255)

Proposed interventions include physical exercise, which in addition to being emphasized as a health measure is also described as contributing to the prevention of mental health issues (Tubic 2013).

As preschool is deemed a valuable intervention site, concern has been raised about populations that do not access preschool and consequently may miss out on interventions. Not surprisingly, then, the lack of access and engagement in preschool by families considered to be 'at risk' is a matter for alarm (Reid *et al.* 2002). This is because it is typically those on low incomes that do not attend, and these are among the demographic group of young children considered to be especially 'vulnerable' or 'at risk'. Childcare and preschool as points of arousal are thus complex spaces: they are places where non-involvement by risk groups is problematic and where too much participation, especially at a young age, can cause future behavioural problems.

## Relations (networks of power)

The infant experience (as well as the prenatal and the toddler) is less a network of power and more a web of relations in which the young child is caught in any number of threads. These threads are drawn for a similar reason: the sense of urgency of the need to act to intervene. As outlined by Foucault, power can be understood as an 'action' and 'is a way in which certain actions modify others . . . ' (Foucault 1983: 219). Two points are important to this conceptualization of power. First, that 'power exists only when it is put into action', and second, that one instance of an effect or an action such as a young child considered at risk of mental disorder is not a single instance of power. Rather, the presence of such an action implies multitudinous relations, or as Foucault (1983: 219) states, relations of power are 'integrated into a disparate field of possibilities'. Foucault further clarifies this concept of action as follows:

> In effect, what defines a relationship of power is that it is a mode of action, which does not act directly and immediately on others. Instead it acts on their actions: an action upon an action, on existing actions or on those which may arise in the present or the future . . . It is a total structure of actions brought to bear on possible actions; it incites, it induces, it seduces, it makes easier or more difficult; in the extreme it constrains or forbids absolutely; it is nevertheless always a way of acting upon an acting subject or acting subjects by virtue of their acting or being capable of action. A set of actions upon other actions.
>
> (Foucault 1983: 220)

As an action that acts on another action, power is an entity that can exist only through a relationship. Foucault emphasizes that power relations 'is a field of analysis and not at all a reference to any unique instance' (1998: 451) and that

> if power is in reality an open, more-or-less coordinated (in the event, no doubt ill-coordinated) cluster of relations, then the only problem is to provide oneself with a grid of analysis which makes possible an analytic of relations of power.
>
> (Foucault 1980b: 199)

A useful way to devise such a grid is via Foucault's (1983) five-point analysis of power, which entails

> the analysis of power relations demands that a certain number of points be established: 1. The system of differentiations which permits one to act upon the actions of others . . . 2. The types of objectives pursued by those who act upon the actions of others . . . 3. The means of bringing power relations into being . . . 4. Forms of institutionalisation . . . 5. The degrees of rationalization.
>
> (Foucault 1983: 223)

The first point of Foucault's (1983) analysis of power draws attention to the mechanisms that define knowledge about the mental health of young children and how this creates a 'system of differentiations'. The second point prompts the questioning of the types of objectives pursued in this relation of power. This style of question seeks to disturb the legitimacy of the relations of power and questions the objectivity of the expert. The third point draws attention to the means through which the actions producing knowledge of mental disorders of young children are brought into being. The fourth point raises awareness of the multiple levels at which the relations of power function. This includes the way action can be inflicted onto prenatal life, onto a newborn, or to an infant or toddler via health practices, childcare settings or via the regulatory effects enacted through health and welfare systems. The last point highlights the rationality of power relations that substantiate the actions made on the actions of the very young.

The third point of Foucault's (1983) analysis, 'the means of bringing power relations into being', can be used to focus on the indirect actions on the actions of others. These are the power relations implicit in constructing knowledge about childhood mental disorders. This can include the power relations that facilitate 'psychiatric expertise' as well as the numerous professionals who use this expertise to identify and act upon young children (for instance nurses or midwives who cite psychiatric expertise in order to substantiate the rationale for how a mother should act in order to prevent mental health problems in her unborn child). This third point includes the power relations that enable this expertise to permeate preschool settings.

This 'five-point analysis' is useful for comprehending the web of relations that are implicated in the production of truths about the mental problems of young children. Certainly it assists us to understand how truths about *potential* have such force and impact, operating through a complex of power relations. For instance, this notion of potential relies upon systems of differentiation, it is tied to the objectives of those who act on the actions of young children (as well as their caregivers), it requires a means to bring power into being, and it is connected to forms of institutionalization. Would it be possible, for example, to have such potentials without the institutions of psychiatry or education? Lastly, it must have a form of rationalization that makes it acceptable to act upon the very young and to do so with certainty about their future.

Concentrating upon the potential of the child and the prenatal paradoxically creates constraints about the potential for mental disorder. This occurs because, as Foucault points out, truth is 'produced only by virtue of multiple forms of constraint. And it induces regular effects of power' (1980c: 131). In this sense, the focus upon these young ages produces greater and greater constraint, and in so doing is a remarkably productive site for infantile mental health 'truth making'. The period once left predominantly to mothers (or for the wealthy to wet nurses) is now the period of life that must be acted upon as early as is possible.

This effect is most obvious in the moments when the truth of potential mental disorder persuades parents/caregivers to construct the potentiality of mentally disordered subjectivity within their young child (born or yet-to-be-born). This relationship is not restricted to the individuals who appear directly involved in the subjugation (the childcare worker, the mental health consultant). Relations of power reach to the depths of truth making (at once producing truths and the effects of truth) that affect the everyday lives of those who live with, care for and work with very young children. To consider power relations as operating only in the moments of diagnosis is to adopt a superficial view, one ignorant of the cacophony of competing actions to exert power over others.

## Disorders of interest

Mental disorders are an issue of concern for the very young and include problems pertaining to sleeping, eating and behaviour. Prevalence rates for preschool children are cited as being up to 20 per cent of children having 'behavioural or emotional problems' (Alkon *et al.* 2003). This figure is higher in special groups. For example, in the United Kingdom a study of 43 pre-school children in care identified that 69.8 per cent had mental health issues (Hillen *et al.* 2012). Yet an alarmingly low number of these children were receiving support.

Defining mental disorders of childhood (let alone those of babies or in infancy) is not a straightforward matter, especially in clinical practice. For instance, a comment by Achenbach (a leading child psychologist) expresses the problems:

> Mental health workers devote a great deal of time to diagnostic issues during their clinical training. Yet there is little agreement about the proper nature and role of diagnosis with respect to child psychopathology.
>
> (Achenbach 1998: 64)

Despite Achenbach's observation, specification remains as persuasive as the scientific rhetoric legitimating the disorders that are considered to affect young children and their futures.

Questions concerning mental disorders in very young children have been a topic of debate (Carter *et al.* 2004; Emde *et al.* 1993), with unease as to whether it is possible to diagnose the very young. Despite such questions, attention to mental health in the period from birth to school age has only increased (Egger 2009b). This has seen intensification in the specialization of infant mental health, an intensification that has seen the creation of psychiatric classifications tailored to the 'developmental needs' of infants and young children. This has included growth in the use of the modalities of treatment that are commonly used by adults and older children. Very young children, for example, are being prescribed more psychopharmaceuticals, such as stimulants, antipsychotics and antidepressants, than ever before (Zito *et al.* 2007).

Egger (2009a) describes 'three approaches to defining mental health problems': descriptive, dimensional and diagnostic. Descriptive approaches involve case reports and place emphasis on the parent–child interaction (and on attachment theories). Dimensional approaches are based on the notion of a normative point, and consequently use dimensional scales to determine the presence or absence of mental health problems. Examples of dimensional scales include the Child Behavioral Checklist (Achenbach and Rescorla 2000) and the Infant–Toddler Social Emotional Assessment (Carter *et al.* 2003). The *DSM-5* (the most recent *Diagnostic and Statistical Manual of Mental Disorders*) is a diagnostic approach that uses categories of disorders (accompanied by definitions/descriptors). This system is by far the most influential, with for instance the categories used to define disorders that receive financial support through government health initiatives (such as for pharmaceutical prescriptions, reduced or free access to psychological services, or educational support). Popular disorders defined by this system include the ubiquitous ADHD (which is applied to young children).

> [In infants at 12 months] . . . lower levels of adult activity and lower levels of adult speech significantly predicted caseness and the diagnostic groups of: any ADHD, inattentive ADHD, any emotional disorder, any anxiety disorder, DBDs, oppositional defiant and/or DBD-NOS, and CD at seven years of age.
>
> (Marwick *et al.* 2012: 564)

Here again we see how diagnoses are explicitly linked to the actions of parents/caregivers.

The *DSM-5* (American Psychiatric Association 2013a) does not include a specific section on children. The previous edition (*DSM-IV*) included a chapter entitled 'disorders usually first diagnosed in infancy, childhood or adolescence'. Disorders affecting infants and toddlers in the *DSM-5* are the feeding and sleeping disorders: insomnia disorder and avoidant/restrictive food intake disorder (Bolten 2013).

The first edition of the *Diagnostic and Statistical Manual of Mental Disorders* met with scathing criticism for its 'negligence' of child mental disorders. Clarizio and McCoy (1970) draw attention to this omission of 'childhood disorder' in the first edition, explaining:

> Clinicians have long decried the inadequacy of the American Psychiatric Association's *Diagnostic and Statistical Manual of Mental Disorders* (1952, 1968), the nosology[1] which has been applied to children's disorders since the initiation in 1954 of reporting by psychiatric clinics nationwide . . . In short, the most commonly used classification system today fails to take into consideration the differences between child and adult disorders.
>
> (Clarizio and McCoy 1970: 58)

Disorders related to child behaviour are prominent in the *DSM-5*. While the *DSM* is the dominant form of psychiatric classification, there are criticisms of its application to young children. For instance, as Egger points out,

There have been real questions within and without of the infant/early childhood mental health field about whether is it possible to define a developmentally appropriate classification of psychiatric symptoms and disorders in early childhood that stays true to the central tenets of the infant/early childhood mental health approach. The foundation of the infant/early childhood mental health field is the understanding that mental health in young children is defined by healthy social and emotional development: development of capacities to experience and regulate emotions, to form close and secure relationships, and to learn. From this definition of mental health the field focused as much on fostering healthy development and preventing mental health problems as on identifying and treating young children's mental health problems.

(Egger 2009a: 560)

The focus on developmentally appropriate classification places a significant emphasis on interpreting 'where the child is at'; for instance language issues may give rise to frustration and need to be taken into account.

Although mental disorders in the unborn are as yet, to our knowledge, to be clinically diagnosed, it may be reasonable to argue that this is almost accomplished with the raft of predictions that are made and 'risk factors' that are identified. For instance, maternal stress is linked to the breadth of childhood disorders that includes ADHD as well as autism and schizophrenia (Del Giudice 2012). Stress in mothers is also viewed to lead to 'heightened anxiety' and 'greater negative emotional behaviors' in offspring (Lee and Goto 2013). Responses to maternal stress that result in behaviours such as ADHD have been viewed by evolutionary biologists as possible adaptations, where the pressures of 'modern society' mean that 'hyperactivity enables greater exploration of surrounding environments for threats and opportunities' (Lee and Goto 2013: 5).

Birth weight is another variable linked to mental health disorders. Disorders associated with low birth weight include behavioural problems (Lee and Goto 2013: 5) and mood disorders such as depression (Indredavik *et al.* 2005). Links are also made between obstetric problems and schizophrenia (Costello *et al.* 2007). Preterm birth is associated with a number of mental disorders including depressive disorder, ADHD and anorexia nervosa (Cannon *et al.* 2002). It is also considered to affect personality, where 'reduced extraversion and increased neuroticism . . . may be at risk of developing personality traits that could predispose them to later mental illness' (Saigal and Doyle 2008: n.p.).

## Modes of practice

Foucault's (1983) 'grid of analysis' provides a way to consider the modes of practice involved in the psychopathologization of young children. Point one of this grid, the system of differentiations, can bring the focus upon diagnostic repertoires, and point two alerts us to the objectives of power (which we have argued are tied to the notion of potential). Points three and four, however, offer a way of conceiving the modes of practice. Point three emphasizes the 'means of bringing power relations into being' and point four emphasizes the 'forms of institutionalisation'.

Practices premised on the concepts of the 'developing brain' of very young children are a major site of activity and weave throughout a plethora of activities. In this sense 'attention on the brain' can be argued to be a key mode of practice in the prevention of mental problems in young children. Recent social policy in the United Kingdom, for instance, now draws heavily on the infant brain and on the imperative to act early in order to ward off future mental health problems (Allin *et al.* 2006). Such policy imperatives are based on the popular discourses on the trajectory of the developing brain and the problems that may result. Ideas drawn from neuroscience are fundamental to contemporary knowledge of the very young. This affects even the yet-to-be-born, with projects now under way to conduct perinatal scans (Infant Mental Health 2012: 11). This form of knowledge has attained a level of fame with the functional MRI (fMRI) an instrument that enables the hidden inner spaces of the brain to be seemingly opened out (Ramani 2009). Indeed as one researcher, Steven Peterson (of Washington University) explained, 'The problem right now with imaging is that doing experiments right is really, really hard, but getting pictures out is really easy' (Centre for the Developing Brain 2013). In addition to the ease with which images can be produced, they are also visually appealing and attention-grabbing.

> [F]unctional MRI scans . . . display a topography set out in colour schemes like real-world maps, thereby greatly adding to their verisimilitude. That such images are the result of very complex processing and dependent on a technology that is unimaginably sophisticated, and yet crude in terms of what it tells us about the brain, is quite invisible to the enchanted viewer.
>
> (Wastell and White 2012: 406)

These images help to promote ideas such as the developing synaptic connections in the brains of babies (as well as prenatal brains). Yet in addition to the difficulties in accomplishing experimentation, there are also questions concerning the use of this instrumentation in children (G. Miller 2008).

Despite such questions being raised, the discourse of brain development, with its synaptic narratives, has become a popular conversational point in everyday conversations about babies and young children (for instance, just recently at a local library a bystander commented on Valerie's seven-month–old, stating: 'all those synapses so hard at work it is like he is completing hundreds of PhDs'). Synapses of babies are especially evocative, given the popularism of neuroscientific ideas about baby brains (Bruer 1999).

Sources of such information stem from the popularization of scientific ideas about the infant brain, and these are cemented in the popular imagination via images (such as from fMRI). In the book the *Myth of the First Three Years* by

John Bruer, a psychologist turned critic of the wide-reaching claims made based on neuroscience, he claims 'three strands' of key influence are held responsible for the focus on infant brains. These strands are: the idea of synaptic growth; the critical periods of brain development; and third, the idea of 'enriched or complex environments'.

> This interpretation of critical periods assumes that the brain learns best and is unusually plastic only during the early, superdense years. It also assumes that the experiences we have during those years are particularly powerful and have long-term, irreversible consequences.
>
> (Bruer 1999: 1962)

The crucial importance of intervening as early as possible is evident in UK national news media discussion (Mundasad 2013) of a research report into 'Developing Brains'. The report is based on new research into understanding the neural connections in the brains of unborn babies undertaken by the Centre for the Developing Brain, King's College London. The article contained the statement: 'by the time a baby takes its first breath many of the key pathways between nerves have already been made'; which was followed by immediate comment about how such research 'may have a role to play in the development of conditions such as autism' (Mundasad 2013). In this way getting in early to understand the brain and via its wiring is fundamentally linked with the goal of intervening in the development of mental health. 'First Years Last Forever' is another campaign that is an exemplar of this ideology (Bruer 1999) . These campaigns or public health messages buy into the 'now or never imperative' (Wastell and White 2012).

The centrality of neuroscience and the wiring metaphor is evident in material distributed to parents, which uses metaphors of wiring and neural connections. This conveys to parents not only how the child, via the child's brain, is made, but how this is irreversible (Wall 2004). Imagery of wiring and computers permeates this space of the imagination of children's brains,

> Castenda (Reiner Foundation 1997) notes that the computer metaphor that pervades current child development discourse, with its emphasis on 'electronic circuitry' and 'hard wiring' conveys both the exciting potential of appropriate stimulation and the irreversible consequences of inappropriate or absent stimulation.
>
> (Wall 2004: 78)

The metaphor of 'hard wiring' is suggestive and powerful, exhorting the belief that wiring is unchangeable and that, consequently, we must act before it is too late. Ideas of acting before it is 'too late' also connect to 'neuro discourses' such those using neuroscience to tackle crime (Wall 2004: 43).

The concept of wiring in baby brains is used commercially to market products such as The Baby Brain Box (Rose 2010). This commercial product marketed to parents and caregivers contains a box of materials that is 'a unique patented educational product for caregivers to use with children from birth to 5.5 years old' (Baby Brain Box 2013a). The website for the product contains a page titled 'Brain Wiring Facts' that includes the two statements 'The brain is the least developed organ at birth' and 'At three years old, a child's brain is about 90 per cent of its adult size' (Baby Brain Box 2013b).

John Bowlby's (McGrath *et al.* 2012) ideas on attachment contribute foundational knowledge in the neuroscientific-wiring space, linking notions of attachment with the materiality of brain physiology. For instance, Bowlby's description of the 'gnawing uncertainty about the accessibility of responsive attachment figures [which] is a principal condition for the development of unstable and anxious personality' (Bowlby 1969, 1998) can be explicitly connected with the third strand of neuroscience that champions 'enriched and complex environments'. This means such phenomena as the movements and actions of caregivers can be understood to directly link with the neural connections/ non-connections in the infant's brain.

The examination is another key mode of practice with very young children. This mode of practice brings into play the diagnostic repertoire as well as drawing in those with expertise in mental health (such as child and mental health specialists) and the corresponding institutions. What gets assessed in the mental health examinations can be quite extensive, including not only the child but his/her caregivers and environment. Table 4.1 is an example of an inventory of the points used for psychiatric examination of young children.

This list contains 23 separate items to be noted in a psychiatric examination, clearly indicating the intricacies of the examination and how this encompasses the individual child, its caregivers, the childcare environment and the demographic setting.

In relation to the use of mental health services, there is a strong impetus to bring mental health practices into childcare settings and these can take the form of mental health consultations in preschools (Egger 2009a). Joining the sense of urgency that action for babies and the very young requires, such consultations are viewed as being of vital importance. Along these lines it can be claimed that 'it is imperative that early childhood educators receive the support necessary to engage children in sensitive, responsive, and developmentally appropriate ways to support children's healthy development' (Perry *et al.* 2008). Systems described as 'Early Childhood Mental Health Consultation' work from the perspective that:

> Mental health consultation in early childhood settings is a problem-solving and capacity-building intervention implemented within a collaborative relationship between a professional consultant with mental health expertise and one or more individuals, primarily child care center staff, with other areas of expertise. Early childhood mental health consultation aims to build the capacity (improve the ability) of staff, families, programs, and systems to prevent, identify, treat, and reduce the impact of mental health problems among children from birth to age 6 and their families.
>
> (Amini Virmani *et al.* 2013: 156)

*Table 4.1* Domains to be assessed in the comprehensive psychiatric assessment of a young child

---

- Current and past history of emotional and behavioral symptoms, including frequency, duration, content, onset, relationship context, and triggers for positive symptoms
- Developmental history including history of pregnancy, maternal prenatal care (e.g. use of alcohol, tobacco, or drugs during pregnancy), neonatal history, and developmental milestones and delays (e.g. motor, language)
- Sleep, feeding and eating, and toileting history
- Child's play (e.g. content, enjoyment of, variety)
- Parent–child relationship (e.g. affect of parent and child during interaction, child's reactions to separation and reunion, level of conflict/coercion/intrusiveness)
- Current cognitive and developmental assessment of expressive/receptive language ability, gross and fine motor capacities, and adaptive functioning
- Medical history . . .
- Recent physical examination results, including height, weight, BMI, and blood pressure
- Medication history . . .
- Laboratory tests, including genetic testing, if indicated
- History of potentially stressful life events, including major traumas (e.g. death in the family, abuse, witness to violence), 'minor' stressors (e.g. birth of sibling, changing daycare/school), and ongoing stressors (e.g. economic hardship, parental illness)
- Family structure and functioning, including discipline practices, such as use of corporal punishment
- Relationships with siblings, peers, and other-age children
- Child's and family's culture as well as appreciation of the impact of cultural differences/conflicts between this culture and the culture of the wider community
- Daycare/school experiences, including type of setting, teacher/child ratios, length of time in setting, relationship with teachers/childcare provider, and relationship with peers
- Three-generation family psychiatric/substance abuse/criminal history (ideally collected as a genogram) with a record of symptoms/diagnoses/events, age at onset, treatments, including in-patient and out-patient interventions, psychotherapy, and medications (name, dosage, any adverse side effects), including details about anxiety disorders and depression
- Current history of parental psychiatric symptoms, including symptoms of depression, anxiety, and substance use/abuse
- Current and past history of domestic violence between adults and between adult and child in the child's home
- Assessment of the child's impairment in activities and relationships from symptoms
- Assessment of the child's strengths and competencies
- Impact of the child's symptoms on the family's functioning (e.g. unable to leave the child with a babysitter due to the child's anxious distress)
- Degree of parental stress, both overall and in relationship to the child being evaluated
- Demographic and environmental information, including living conditions, parental employment, number of people living in the home, socioeconomic status and stress, neighborhood resources and violence, community participations, religious participation, and faith practices

(Egger 2009: 571)

---

Emphasis on the childcare setting, as indicated above, does not only concentrate on the childcare professionals but also connects to the young child's family. Interest in the family can incorporate very specific modes of practice, such as parent-based therapies for preschool ADHD (Cohen and Kaufman 2005: 4). This concern with child behaviour is also integrated more broadly into practices with children. For example, 'tutoring, social skills training, and parent training might enhance positive outcomes even among children with subclinical levels of conduct problems' (Sonuga-Barke *et al.* 2001). Despite this type of specialist attention being instigated and, in some cases, woven into practices within the childcare setting, it has been pointed out the childcare is not necessarily going to 'fix' problems with young children. This viewpoint reorients the focus from the childcare environment to the child, and in so doing serves to reinscribe the locus of the fault to the child. Indeed it is arguably a logical explanation, given the attention paid to notions such as the wiring of the infant brain or the problems caused by the child's early environment.

Issues such as behaviour problems (and possible disorders) are common reasons for childcare workers to refer children to child mental health workers. These actions, which can be described as a caregiving practice, 'have two modes: program centered and child-and-family centered' (Cohen and Kaufman 2005: 33). In this way early childhood mental health consultation has two foci: (i) the child and its family and (ii) the child centre programme (Amini Virmani *et al.* 2013).

Dispensing medication can be applied to very young children. Medications that are dispensed to very young children include drugs such as methylphenidate (commonly known as Ritalin and used for ADHD). This, however, is not the only medication used. Indeed, there is a range of psychopharmaceuticals that are increasingly dispensed for a number of disorders.

> Preschool psychotherapeutic medication use increased across ages 2 to 4 for stimulants, antipsychotics, and antidepressants, reflecting use for psychiatric/behavioral disorders. However, the use of anxiolytic/sedative/ hypnotics and anticonvulsants was more stable across these years, suggesting medical usage. Additional research to assess the benefits and risks of psychotherapeutic drugs is needed, particularly when such usage is off-label for both psychiatric and nonpsychiatric conditions.
>
> (Zito *et al.* 2007: 195)

Worry over medicating children has prompted reactions that are not always in favour of mental health practices that diagnose and medicalize. The drive for childcare workers to refer to or seek the help of mental health professionals is not always done as obligingly as it might appear in the published literature championing such actions. In the United Kingdom there are reports of some reticence, with teachers preferring to use education-based services rather than mental health services such as CAMHS (Child and Adolescent Mental Health Service) (Kurtz *et al.* 1995). Similar findings were found in our research in Scotland, with education professionals describing how they would at times avoid mental health services as a means to avoid the medicalization of children (Allan and Harwood 2013).

## Desired consequences/outcomes

Strategic timing and interception are prominent features in the attention given to the mental health of very young children. For this age group (from the prenatal to the preschool) the 'focal points of experience' (Foucault 2008a) are dominated by a fragility of time whose purpose is to assuage the threat of the mental health problems. Forms of knowledge are accordingly bounded by the urgency to 'get in early'. This prompts normative frameworks of behaviour that support extraordinary activities, such as the quest to investigate the brains of the unborn or to create charts of children's 'wiring' based on assumptions that are argued to be flawed. The third of Foucault's (2008a) three elements of experience, 'the constitution of the subject's mode of being', remains illusive and yet is able to become the malleable subject of infant determinism (Kagan 1998).

A question that needs to be asked, amongst these early interventions and 'future proofing' of the individual/society, is why other viewpoints are far less frequently heard. Why is it, for instance, that views that question the turn to neuroscience and the gospel of hard wiring are seldom heard? These include views such as that put forward by Bruer, who wrote over ten years ago:

> [W]e should be wary of claims that parents have only a single, biologically delimited, once-in-a-lifetime opportunity to help their children build better brains.
>
> (Bruer 1999: 73)

Likewise, it would be useful to be less acquiescent to the beliefs about synapses.

> The argument that there is a simple, proven connection between brain power and synaptic profusion is not sustainable. It is abundantly clear that more synapses does not mean greater intellectual prowess in any simple way.
>
> (Wastell and White 2012: 403)

Returning to Foucault's (2008a) three elements of experience, the problem posed in attempting to analyse this third element, the 'infant experience', brings to the fore one of the vexing issues in the domain of knowledge of the mental health of the baby and the infant. In recognizing the impossibility of accessing the prenatal, baby's or infant subject's experience we can at last throw light on the enormous extent to which this experience is projected onto the tiniest of human subjects. Nevertheless, this field of knowledge speaks convincingly of the subject's experience by relying exclusively on processes of speculation. In this regard it is vital to be mindful that when we consider the baby and the discourses on their mental health, problems pertaining to the subjective are greatly magnified. Issues of accessing experience that occur for adults and older children (for instance, understanding the experience of an adult who is hearing voices) become greater and much more complex when we contemplate the youngest amongst us. From this perspective it should be continually difficult to accept claims to knowledge of the infant subject's experience; yet, as we well know, this is far from the case when synapses and brain images are brought into play.

## Note

1  Nosology is 'the branch of medicine concerned with the classification of diseases' (Hanks 1981: 1005).

# Chapter 5

# Primary school

> [Consider] whether it is worth your while to pay less than a shilling to have your boys and girls measured . . . either to learn their powers or to obtain timely warning of remediable faults.
>
> (Galton, cited in Ministry of Education 1955: 7)

For the child entering the primary school, scrutiny is intensified, directed at whether he or she will 'fit' into the school regimen and be accommodated in its expectations and practices. For those children who arouse concern, psychopathologization begins in earnest and they become subject to a whole regime of practices that amount to 'officially sanctioned developmental truths of the child' (MacNaughton 2005: 30).

Ball (2013) takes up Rose's (1999) notion of 'abjection' (which he takes from Judith Butler) to denote educational practices which target children as abnormal and which amount to a 'casting off or a casting down . . . into a zone of shame, disgrace or debasement' (Rose 1999: 252). Here, where children with mental abnormality are concerned, we see the opposite. Children singled out for psychopathologization are given a kind of exaltation and become privileged, protected and readied for special treatment. At the same time, however, this process enables a certain security – for mainstream education and for society in general – assured by teachers and schools using techniques that 'are at once enlightened, reflected, analytical, calculated and calculating' (Foucault 2009: 71). Foucault describes the power being exercised here as 'biopower', which is markedly different from discipline, but which does not exclude it:

> But it does dovetail into it, integrate it, modify it to some extent and, above all, use it by sort of infiltrating it, embedding itself in existing disciplinary techniques . . . Unlike discipline, which is addressed to bodies, the new nondisciplinary power is applied not to man–as–body but to the living man, to man–as–living–being.
>
> (Foucault 2003b: 242)

Biopower is directed towards life itself, rather than at the body or mind (Nealon 2008), working on individuals 'really and directly' (Nealon 2008: 46), and seeking to understand, rather than resolve, individuals' behavioural problems: 'Biopower's norms are efficient and continuous calculations of alterity, not the binary banishment or exclusion of it' (Nealon 2008: 51). The understanding that is sought is no longer of mental abnormality but of the mentally abnormal 'life and lifestyle' (Nealon 2008: 48) of the child and his or her parents and, as Foucault notes about sexuality, the effect of this new form of power is that psychopathologizing discourses become 'multiplied rather than rarefied' (Foucault 1976: 53). Both the professionals and those with whom they interact (the child and his or her parents) acquire 'surplus-power' (Foucault 2008a 269) and consequently confidence and authority is invested in professionals while the child and parents are exalted for their capabilities in exhibiting abnormality. These surpluses circulate and maintain each other as psychiatry is now able to

> plug into a whole series of disciplinary regimes existing around it, on the grounds of the principle that it alone is both the science and power of the abnormal. Psychiatry will be able to claim for itself everything abnormal, all these deviations and abnormalities in relation to school, military, family and other forms of discipline. The generalization, diffusion, and dissemination of psychiatric power took place in our society by way of this carving out of the abnormal child.
>
> (Foucault 2008a: 222)

At the same time the abnormal child, the patient, is able to say to the professional:

> It is thanks to me, but thanks only to me, that what you do to me – confine me, prescribe me drugs, and so on – really is a medical act, and I crown you doctor to the extent that I provide you with symptoms. Underneath the doctor's surplus-power is the patient's surplus-power.
>
> (Foucault 2008a: 269)

## Point of arousal

Teachers are central figures in determining whether children entering primary school are 'ready' and able to 'fit in' and in triggering reactions where their suspicions are aroused about particular individuals. Their attention is, to an extent, guided by their knowledge, acquired through training and which may be vague or partial, of expected stages of development, and a sense of the *normal*. Depending on the teachers' education, their knowledge of what is normal may have been influenced by a series, and perhaps a contradictory mixture, of child development theories. These are likely to include some or all of Freud's notion of children developing through a series of stages (albeit developed with adult psychiatric patients); Piaget's stages of cognition; Erikson's theory of psychological development through the resolution of psychosocial conflicts; Maslow's hierarchy of needs; and Bronfenbrenner's ecological theory of development through family functioning (Atkinson and Hornby 2002). The experience of acquiring knowledge of these theories as 'theory junk sculpture . . . a cacophony of incompatible explanations' (Thomas 2007: 1) may leave teachers uncertain about what to make of individual children, but nevertheless resolute in raising suspicions where something – or someone – appears extraordinary.

The 'maladjusted child', a term abandoned in the United Kingdom with the publication of the report of the Warnock Committee in 1978, is nevertheless of interest because of the explicit intention, enshrined in legislation, to 'discover' it (Ministry of Education 1955). Concern was expressed at the uneven 'rate of discovery' (Ministry of Education 1955: 13) across the UK. It is at school where the 'first signs of maladjustment in a child may appear . . . and show in his reactions to his contemporaries, his teachers and his work' (Ministry of Education 1955: 4). And it is here that attention to particular individuals consolidates their identities as 'peripheral subjects' (Foucault 1980d: 98), even though the process of identification amounts to a 'bewildering spectre of incoherence' (Erevelles 2005: 48). There is a continuing concern about the variable rates of discovery, or diagnosis, of mental health conditions (Hyman 2010; Wakefield *et al.* 2002) and while this may be down to variations in practice among professionals, it has legitimated calls for strengthening teachers' capacity for *noticing* abnormality in their classrooms. Even the UK Government's declaration that '[c]urrent practice harms children who do not have SEN but who are identified as having SEN' (Department for Education 2011b) assumes that things would be so much better if diagnostic procedures were more reliable (Thomas 2013). Researchers have also noted different perceptions between parents and teachers about what counts as abnormal behaviour, with a low to moderate overlap reported in the UK (Tizard *et al.*1988), New Zealand (McGee *et al.* 1983) and the Netherlands (Verhulst and Akkerhuis 1989), and with parents tending to raise more concerns than teachers.

Hyman (2010) observes that the increasing pressure to produce inter-rater reliability in the *DSM* came at time when understanding of mental illness was still relatively underdeveloped and the diagnostic criteria which dominated *DSM-IV* also produced some 'epistemic blinders' (Hyman 2010: 121). As Hyman notes, this occurred because although there was an understanding that *DSM-IV* diagnosis was an heuristic, in practice, and in research, it functioned as a kind of reifying 'prison' (Hyman 2010: 123) that controlled the kinds of questions that could be asked. The revised edition of *DSM-IV* contained a warning about its fallibility and refused to guarantee the inclusion of new categories such as pathological gambling as bona fide disorders:

It is to be understood that inclusion here, for clinical and research purposes, of a diagnostic category such as Pathological Gambling or Pedophilia does not imply that the condition meets legal or other non medical criteria for what constitutes mental disease, mental disorder, or mental disability.

(American Psychiatric Association 2000: xxxvii)

Nevertheless, the *DSM* continues to function as a formal witness to pathological disorder, providing its own warrants for truth telling:

> In crude terms, psychiatric power says: The question of truth will never be posed between madness and me for the very simple reason that I, psychiatry, am already a science. And if, as science, I have the right to question what I say, if it is true that I may make mistakes, it is in any case up to me, and to me alone, as science, to decide if what I say is true or to correct the mistake. I am the possessor, if not of truth in its content, at least of all the criteria of truth . . . I can attach myself to reality and its power and impose on these demented and disturbed bodies the surplus-power that I give to reality.
>
> (Foucault 2006: 134)

The *DSM-5*, published in May 2013, sees a whole new wave of pathologies, including adult ADHD, temper tantrums, captured as 'disruptive mood dysregulation disorder' and 'generalized anxiety disorder', previously understood as everyday worries. These new inclusions, according to Frances (2012), will 'medicalize normality and result in a glut of unnecessary and harmful drug prescription', and a *Lancet* editorial (2010: 390) echoes the concern that 'inclusion of more mental disorders in *DSM-5* might be of greater benefit to drug companies than to the patients and their families'. Frances, arguing for a reduced hold by the American Psychiatric Association on mental illness through *DSM*, suggests that things have gone out of control:

> Indeed, the D.S.M. is the victim of its own success and is accorded the authority of a bible in areas well beyond its competence. It has become the arbiter of who is ill and who is not – and often the primary determinant of treatment decisions, insurance eligibility, disability payments and who gets special school services. D.S.M. drives the direction of research and the approval of new drugs. It is widely used (and misused) in the courts.
>
> (Frances 2012)

## Relations (networks of power)

The submission of the child to the scrutiny of experts – doctors, child psychologists and child psychiatrists – allows for the examination, not of an illness, but, as Foucault (2003a) suggests, of a *condition*. At the same time, such a submission grants that a child 'will be ill for a knowledge that will then authorize me to function as medical power' (Foucault 2003a: 309). A condition, that is non-medical or non-pathological, allows for recognition of infinite possibilities of abnormality or deviance, which may be pathological but which could also accommodate physiological, psychological, sociological, moral and legal aberrations. An individual's condition, thus, is their structural whole or their background that may give rise to particular (abnormal) features that merit pathological scrutiny and/or intervention. Those professionals involved in the 'medicine of mental alienation' (Foucault 2003a: 302) have a mandate to exercise medical power over the body and mind of the person suffering from the condition and upon the various social and ecological dimensions in which abnormality may surface. They are also permitted to look away from structural causes of school failure and to seek instead 'explanations for children's failure, disengagement, distraction, anger and defiance in their genetic and medical profiles' (Slee 2011: 151). Psychiatry, in particular, the reference point of which is childhood, functions through infantilism rather than delirium, dispensing with illness in pursuit of the science of the normal and the abnormal. Yet the discipline and its practitioners remain troubled by the recognition of the difficulty in establishing 'the frontier between rationality and madness' and the 'dangerous question of the coexistence of madness and rationality, of partial delusion and lucid interval' (Fontana 1975: 272–3). Foucault clarifies the relations of power in opening up children and childhood to the psychiatric gaze:

> Psychiatry will effectively ask the family to provide it with the material it needs in order to make its profit. Psychiatry says, more or less: 'let your mad little children come to me' or, 'you're never too young to be mad,' or, 'don't wait for the age of majority or adulthood to be mad.' And all of this is translated into the institutions of supervision, detection, training and child therapy.
>
> (Foucault 2008a: 125)

## Disorders of interest

Mental abnormality's 'confiscation' (Foucault 2008a: 211) by psychiatry from medicine was initially based on a demonstration of 'instincts' (p. 210) rather than symptoms, the former being supposedly more natural, 'an indefinite series of small refusals opposed to any will of the other person' (p. 215). Instinct itself is normal but becomes abnormal when it is not controlled (Foucault 2008a: 222) and it is that pinpointing of the failure of mastery that allows for the 'carving out of the abnormal child'. Foucault talks of how the early diagnosis of madness, at the beginning of the nineteenth century, was characterized by an absence of differentiation. The issue for the psychiatrists was a binary matter of simply whether behaviour by particular individuals 'belonged to madness' (Foucault 2008a: 267) or not. Current diagnostic practices do rely on differentiation but this takes place within a sphere of absolutes, whereby the professionals are required to specify whether children's behaviour belongs to a particular diagnosis – or not. Even a condition as specific as attention deficit hyperactivity disorder has a differentiation within it, distinguishing children whose behaviour amounts principally to inattention (ADHD-PI or ADHD-I) from those with predominantly 'hyper-active-impulsive' (ADHD-HI or ADHD-H) and from those exhibiting both types of behaviour (ADHD-C) (Miller *et al.* 2011).

The mental disorder of primary aged children that is captured with particular intensity is attention deficit hyperactivity disorder (ADHD), but the professionals working in child mental health that we interviewed mentioned a whole panoply of 'disorders', including obsessive compulsive disorder, post-traumatic stress, Tourette's (which one professional qualified as 'mini-Tourette's', presumably because it was child-based), self-harm and eating disorders. In the research we carried out in Scotland, one professional indicated that the child mental health service also saw children with developmental disorders such as autism or Asperger's syndrome and children with physical problems but with concomitant psychological problems, such as diabetic children who may be needle phobic. However, another professional child mental health worker suggested that very few of those referred 'actually' fitted the reality of mental illness:

> [We're] getting inundated very, very fast by children who are, you know, varying degrees of difficulty, none of them probably have got mental health – a very small percentage are mental health but the majority of them are to do with dealing with . . . poor circumstances, domestic abuse, unemployment, you know, those kinds of issues.
>
> (Professional 9, Child Mental Health, MCB Scotland)

The professional's dropping of the word 'disorder' from the tag of 'mental health' seems to signal an obligation to verify a child's membership within the field of (mental) abnormality. This professional also, however, acknowledged a lack of agreement over what constituted membership:

> I think it's a useful reflection to say the team is probably quite split, I mean we have psychiatric colleagues who would disagree with that view and see that as a disorder . . . and then there's people like myself who probably kind of . . . tries to take a middle ground but is leaning to the non-disorder group more and more and more given my own training and background . . . but I think that there . . . it's coming from within the service but it's also coming from our customer if you like, I mean, sometimes they . . . you know, we can have referrals or children or parents of very affluent people who are looking for reasons for antisocial behaviour that are a disorder, therefore explains sort of behaviour but we also have parents with children who are very impoverished and come from impoverished backgrounds emotionally and socio-economically and you know sometimes that disorder label can increase – well, it increases their benefits.
>
> (Professional 9, Child Mental Health, MCB Scotland)

## Modes of practice

The practice of diagnosis is, according to Foucault (2008b: 342), a 'psychiatry of zero production' because of its function in ensuring that illness, once diagnosed, 'no longer has to figure in the medical process' (p. 342). Subsequently, pharmaceutical practices, directed enthusiastically at the primary aged mentally abnormal child, have a 'pasteurizing' (Foucault 2008b: 342) aim at their heart, looking to suppress (or ideally make disappear) the symptoms. Finally, segregation, even if it is only virtually, from the power of the family enables the teacher to become 'the absolute master of the child' (Foucault 2008b: 216). Each of these forms of practice that are directed at the child exalt the child through its abnormality and at the same time invest him or her with 'surplus-power' (Foucault 2008b: 216) that circulates through the therapeutic relationships within the school, through 'onto-epistemological strategies called modern pedagogy that rest heavily on selectivity, differentiation, and out-of-jointedness' (Baker 2007: 26), and in the home.

Working alongside these therapeutic practices and focused on the child's parents, teachers and school systems are various forms of educational training. There are also more generalized modes of practice that target low achievement as a phenomenon, usually in areas of low socio-economic status, and these often are accompanied by psychopathologized assumptions about the need for intensive behaviour management of particular groups of children (Allan and Harwood 2013). These modes of practice, and the accompanying assumptions, reproduce the child as a set of attributes: 'Things themselves become so burdened with attributes, signs, allusions that they finally lose their own form. Meaning is no longer read in an immediate perception, the figure no longer speaks for itself' (Foucault 2001: 16). As far as the behaviour-disordered child of primary age is concerned, the key ambition is to 'understand' (Nealon 2008: 47) the nature of the abnormality and this is achieved through the exercise of biopower and by means of the normative gaze. This in turn allows for the child to experience not abjection or exclusion, but an exalted state whereby he or she is cared for and included.

### Diagnostic qualifiers

The problem psychiatry faces becomes precisely that of constituting, of establishing, the kind of test, or series of tests, that will enable it to meet this requirement of absolute diagnosis, that is to say, the kind of test that will accord reality or unreality to what is taken to be madness, to inscribe it within the field of reality or disqualify it as unreal.

(Foucault 2008b: 267)

Foucault suggests that the referral, by the school, of a child for assessment of mental abnormality takes place when the 'power exercised at school ceases to be real power and becomes a both mythical and fragile power, the reality of which must consequently be intensified' (Foucault 2008a: 190). This is a point of exquisite reification whereby the reality of the individual child, and the school's knowledge of this, no longer works and has to be elevated – by the 'expert' – to a higher domain. The psychiatrist's or educational psychologist's function, thus, is paradoxical: 'to intensify reality as power and to intensify power by asserting it as reality' (Foucault 2008a: 190).

> The complexity of many of these [neuroimaging] studies and the methodological variation among them make it difficult to discern whether these inconsistencies are apparent or real.
>
> (Baumeister and Hawkins 2001: 2)

One of the professionals we interviewed, working in child mental health, conveyed a sense of children 'qualifying' for their subsequent referral by meeting particular (abnormal) conditions.

> [Referrals occur where] both of the following conditions are met . . . [the] child or young person has or is suspected to have a mental disorder or other condition that results in persistent symptoms of psychological distress . . . then the existence of at least one of the following . . . there is an associated serious and persistent impairment of their day-to-day social functional or an associated risk that they may cause serious harm to themselves or others, and then there's a kind of caveat that where there's evidence of an associated significant social variable such as maybe a child in care or a sibling or parent with significant mental or physical health problems.
>
> (Professional 5, Child Mental Health, MCB Scotland)

The professional implies a form of diagnostic tautology, whereby the child is suspected of having a mental disorder in order to qualify for a full-blown suspicion of a mental disorder that plays out in the multi-disciplinary assessment.

In spite of the 'elusive' (Visser and Jehan 2009) aetiology of ADHD and uncertainty about treatment (Timimi 2008), diagnosis is pursued enthusiastically, hunting down the child's 'inability to marshal and sustain attention, modulate activity level, and moderate impulsive actions' (Rappley 2005: 165). A diagnosis of ADHD amounts to an assumption, based on neuroimaging studies, of the presence of low levels of activity in the neurotransmitters in the frontal lobes of the brain. These lobes control impulses and thereby the amount of attention a child can marshal (Wheeler 2010). The assumption of the child's brain as a 'circuit' with faults to be pinpointed, enables a diagnosis of 'developmental failure in the brain's circuitry that underlies inhibition and self control' (Barkley 1998: 67). Here again, as described in the previous chapter, the 'scientific-neuro' magic of the fMRI scan is invoked together with the emphasis on metaphors of circuits, networks and neurons. Adding to the mechanical techniques of fMRI, familial investigation through molecular genetic research has strengthened the notion of a genetic association, if not causally, by specifically identifying rogue, dysfunctional dopamine receptors (Daley *et al.* 2008; McCracken *et al.* 2000; Todd and O'Malley 2001). Yet this outstanding reach capability of the neuroimaging research is not deployed for most diagnoses of ADHD; the majority are instead reached through the checklist text and therapeutic talk of the professionals, who nevertheless rely on this surplus-power to generate a new reality. One of the professionals we interviewed mentioned a geographical dimension of surplus-power at play, whereby children in particular areas were more likely to become diagnosed because of the particular professionals in charge:

> I know of [one local municipality] that has a high level [of ADHD diagnosis] because there's an individual there who is very vocal and very pro-ADHD.
>
> (Professional 9, Child Mental Health, MCB Scotland)

This particular professional was described as, through his private work, being sought out by parents for diagnosis and influencing levels of diagnosis in another local municipality. The diagnosis of ADHD (or other disorders) becomes an end in itself (Wheeler 2010; Hjörne and Säljö 2004). But it also opens the patient up to a whole new set of pharmaceutical realities, surpluses and arousals.

### Pharmaceutical arousal

Children diagnosed with a mental abnormality such as ADHD become objects of arousal, the better to ensure they can both control themselves and attend to what is appropriate within the school. This is achieved through psychostimulant drugs – methylphenidate (Ritalin and Concerta) and amphetamines (Li *et al.* 2006; Visser and Jehan 2009) – which work on the brain to alter its structure and function, correct the errant dopamine function and eradicate symptoms of ADHD:

> Methylphenidate increases dopamine by blocking dopamine transporter and amphetamines (like methamphetamines) increases dopamine by releasing dopamine from the terminal.
>
> (Volkow and Swanson 2003: 1909)

Doctors prescribing these drugs have to weigh up the costs and benefits, comparing the fast-release Ritalin with the slower-releasing and therefore longer-lasting Concerto, and with the acknowledgement that the latter, as a cocaine-like substance, gradually becomes less effective, requiring higher doses by its users. These dangerous stimulants provide further excesses for the child and for his or her prescribers:

[S]timulant medication such as methylphenidate (*Ritalin* and *Concerta*) shares many toxic properties with pure amphetamines, including rapid uptake, high addictive qualities and occasionally a proclivity to reaction.

(Baldwin 2000)

While Visser and Jehan (2009) claim that pharmacogenomics research has established justifications for the use of pharmacological interventions to treat ADHD, this is questioned by Wheeler (2010), Baldwin (2000) and others, who have expressed serious reservations about the impact on children. Furthermore, the failure to ask children about how they felt when taking psychostimulant medicine means that key side effects such as depression, worry and loss of spontaneity have not been picked up (Baldwin 2000; Visser and Jehan 2009). Drawing on Illich, Breggin (1999: 303) suggests that we are currently witnessing an 'iatrogenic drug epidemic' whereby undesirable behaviour is controlled and supressed by drug treatment that produces 'mindless obedience that suppresses emotions and ideas, diminishes self esteem, and takes away the sense of self' (Miller and Leger 2003: 46). According to one of the professionals we interviewed, while medication such as Ritalin is advised as a last resort, after all other interventions have been tried, in reality it is used as 'the first line of defence' (Professional 9, Child Mental Health, MCB Scotland).

## Separation

While, as we discussed in Chapter 2, much effort has been given over to mental hygiene in education as a means of preventing mental health problems from arising, the favoured mode of practice for the treatment of discovered mental disorder has been segregated special schooling, but latterly more intensified forms of within-class separation have prevailed. The first school, in the United Kingdom, for 'maladjusted' girls was opened in 1932, following the discovery of a 'nervous, emotional and restless' female (Ministry of Education 1955: 11) by the Tavistock Clinic in 1929. The clinic recommended that she be afforded 'sympathy, knowledge and circumspection' (Ministry of Education 1955: 11) and made the Education Authority's responsibility in this regard clear. By 1939, there were 24 clinical provisions in the UK for 'nervous, difficult and retarded children' (Ministry of Education 1955: 12). The number of establishments catering specifically for mental disorder had risen to 80 by 1954, alongside some 300 child guidance clinics. The importance of their existence was affirmed in both education and health legislation, which placed a clear obligation on education and health authorities to 'secure improvement in people's mental as well as physical health, and the prevention of illness as well as its diagnosis and treatment' (Ministry of Education 1955: 13). At the same time, it was recognized that mentally disordered youngsters are 'not readily capable of improvement by ordinary discipline' (Ministry of Education 1955: 22).

The separation of children with abnormal behaviour for specific and special levels, although continuing on disproportionate levels and often directed at minority populations (Thomas 2013; Artiles 1998), is no longer practised so blatantly. There is, however, an intensive practice of separating the child from his or her family through the process of schooling. This is achieved by granting the teacher a therapeutic power, which is of a higher order than that within the family. Thus, 'the teacher becomes the absolute master of the child' (Foucault 2008b: 216).

## Training parents to be 'good'

Although their children are 'removed' from them under the aegis of special education and schooling, parents of children with identified behavioural abnormalities experience some of the same exaltation and privileging as the children themselves and are marked out for training to become a 'good' parent. They also experience biopower through the scrutiny of their child's mental abnormality 'life and lifestyle' (Nealon 2008: 48). The rendering of parenting into the verb form brings with it an array of normative standards of *good* parenting, which, as Vincent (2000) observes, are neither class nor gender neutral, but also take on deficit and moralistic tones (Power and Gewirtz 1999). The family, that 'huge fantastical body of the family', is required to submit to examination in the expectation that some origin can be identified in a kind of 'meta organic substratum, but one which constitutes the true body of the illness' (Foucault 2008b: 271). Such hereditary attention to the family allows the body of illness to be uncovered and given materiality in the absence of any physical manifestation in the body of the patient under examination. The taking of family history can be seen to be extended in current psychiatric consultations through the taking into account of 'context', with the scrutiny of 'factors', relating to home background, conditions of living and trauma which could be considered to have a bearing on the child's mental health. The family has also become 'an instrument, a point of application, in the monitoring of a larger group (the population) rather than a unit concerned with monitoring itself' (Baker 1998: 131). Armstrong (1995) found that the processes of assessing children's special educational needs, including behavioural problems, involved parents and their children in a bewildering array of interviews and tests which left them 'deprived of information' and 'deliberately misinformed' (Armstrong 1995: 37). Strategies for assisting parents to support their children are bound up with judgements about their capacities – as parents – and often convey a view to the parents that they are part of the problem (Armstrong 1995). As Stoughton (2006) notes, this may drive parents away from professionals and from the help offered. One of the professionals we interviewed highlighted the dangerous effects of drawing parents into the diagnostic gaze:

> We looked at four young people who had very negative outcomes in their lives . . . one was in prison for murder, one . . . in poor accommodation . . . another one was just leaving a residential school . . . one

was . . . looked after outwith the authority. In all four cases . . . the mothers had experienced significant mental health issues, significant trauma, grief and loss, domestic abuse. They'd all been to residential schools. The pattern was there; these children did not stand a chance and what did we do? We treated them like they had the behavioural difficulties and it was their fault and we sent them to residential schools so I think there's learning in that for all of us and I think we need to be very careful . . . to make sure that we are dealing with the root cause and not necessarily with the result, with the result being the behaviour.

(Professional 3, Educational Psychology, MCB Scotland)

Another professional described the kind of support directed at parents:

The ADHD course is developed from [The Positive Parenting Programme] . . . so parents could just come to a group or we would work with them individually, but you know, we're just using social learning theory . . . and helping them to be thinking about different ways of interacting.

(Professional 5, Child Mental Health, MCB Scotland)

The Positive Parenting Programme (or 'Triple P'), in use across some 25 countries, 'takes the guesswork out of parenting' and offers simple and practical measures that promise to help parents to 'confidently manage their children's behaviour, prevent problems developing and build strong, healthy relationships' (www.triplep.net). Parents are assured that this programme has been 'scientifically shown to work', but are also warned that it is not a 'one size fits all'. Thereafter parents can self-select themselves into a range of levels, starting from the generic and general advice (level one), through to a 'light touch', for 'one or two concerns' (level two), then (at level three) specific behavioural problems or issues. Level four is aimed at parents of children with 'severe behavioural difficulties' while level five offers 'intensive support for families with serious problems'. Parents can only qualify for this top-level course by completing a level four course either before or in conjunction with this course, and those who participate in one of these level five programmes may be deemed to be 'at risk of child maltreatment'. At the same time, strenuous efforts are made within the programme to destigmatize parenting support: 'a parenting program becomes a natural thing to do. It's no longer something to be avoided or something that is considered the mark of a "bad parent".' Triple P appears to function as an unashamedly public population approach, aimed at improving the security of the family and society; at the same time, it allows parents to select, or for them to be assisted through professional guidance and support to select, a level of 'risk', including risk of harm to the child from the parents themselves. Those children deemed at greatest 'risk' are exalted and marked for an intensification of care and a power surplus (Foucault 2008a). Triple P has come to be linked, in England and Wales, not just with supporting parents of secondary aged children with various degrees of behavioural problems but with introducing forms of control where children have exhibited antisocial behaviour (Home Office Police and Justice Act 2006). This means of punishing parents for their children's behaviour (Arthur 2005; Muncie 1999) rather than tackling the 'social and familial roots of behaviour disorder' is discussed more fully in Chapter 6.

### Training systems

Programmes aimed at pupils identified as being 'at risk', particularly in relation to behaviour, form part of the analysis of 'case, risk, danger and crisis' (Foucault 2009: 61) that have enabled mentally abnormal children to be placed at the very centre of the discipline of schooling (Foucault 1979; Ball 2013). This allows, in turn, for education to be at the heart of the control of societies. These programmes have been 'delivered' to whole schools and local authorities with the promise of intervention, prevention and mitigation. Such positively couched promises are posited in relation to and are necessitated by what Foucault (2003a: 44) calls 'an entire arsenal of negative concepts', which include 'disqualification, exile, rejection, deprivation, refusal and incomprehension' (p. 43). Yet these educational interventions often benefit those who need them least and can bypass those who would benefit most from them. Other targeted programmes such as the Early Intervention Literacy and Narrowing the Gap programmes have had some success but their exclusionary effects on, or failure to reach, some individuals and groups has been identified (European Commission 2011; Bagley 2006; Demos 2009). These programmes have also been particularly vulnerable to economic pressures with drastic reductions or removal of services in recent years. Structural interventions, involving radical system changes, are currently prevalent in England, but there have been criticisms that these are likely to increase, rather than decrease, inequality and exclusion (Weller 2009).

Advice, in the form of support materials, to beginning or established teachers on how to manage classroom behaviour pathologizes the badly behaved child as not just lacking the capacity to behave but as having some malevolent potential. These materials foster a view of the child with behavioural problems as a present risk and danger in the classroom, and this is a view that has currency within the teaching profession, evident in the teacher's comment quoted by Stoughton (2006: 145): 'I'll tell you what makes me mad: when the "good" kids stop learning because of "those kids".' Slee (2011) is also critical of the emotive nature of these forms of support and takes to task high-earning titles such as *Getting the Buggers to Behave*, for their offensive language, ignorance of politics and the positioning of teachers and students as in confrontation with one another.

The UK Government's expert adviser on behaviour, Charlie Taylor, insists on 'getting the simple things right' (Department for Education 2012a) but his 'behaviour checklist' is impressively simplistic rather than simple:

**Classroom**

Know the names and roles of any adults in class.

Meet and greet pupils when they come into the classroom.

Display rules in the class – and ensure that the pupils and staff know what they are.

Display the tariff of sanctions in class.

Have a system in place to follow through with all sanctions.

Display the tariff of rewards in class.

Have a system in place to follow through with all rewards.

Have a visual timetable on the wall.

Follow the school behaviour policy.

**Pupils**

Know the names of children.

Have a plan for children who are likely to misbehave.

Ensure other adults in the class know the plan.

Understand pupils' special needs.

**Teaching**

Ensure that all resources are prepared in advance.

Praise the behaviour you want to see more of.

Praise children doing the right thing more than criticising those who are doing the wrong thing (parallel praise).

Differentiate.

Stay calm.

Have clear routines for transitions and for stopping the class.

Teach children the class routines.

**Parents**

Give feedback to parents about their child's behaviour – let them know about the good days as well as the bad ones.

(Department for Education 2012a)

Teachers are simultaneously advised to 'differentiate' and 'stay calm' in a list that itself does not differentiate between a pedagogic approach and an emotional state. Surprisingly, the government expert also advises teachers to know the names and roles of adults in their class, as if they might be tempted to disregard these individuals, and to maximize rules, sanctions and rewards, and children's understanding of these. He issues an entreaty to teachers to 'understand pupils' special needs' but does not qualify how this might be done or distinguish those needs that might be related to behaviour. Taylor, who in September 2012 became the Chief Executive of the Teacher Training Agency, an increasingly powerful arm of education governance in England, has also turned his gaze on, and specified a responsibility for, teacher education providers (which is now shared by universities and schools within England) to improve the training of beginning teachers in behaviour management. As a consequence, providers now have to ensure that beginning teachers can

> vary the tone and volume of their voice to teach effectively and manage behaviour;
>
> stand, move, make use of the space and use eye contact in order to be an authoritative presence in the classroom;
>
> use praise effectively to improve behaviour, and understand how to apply rewards and sanctions to improve behaviour;
>
> manage behaviour in a range of different situations such as whole class teaching, group work, the corridors and the playground;
>
> plan and teach lessons that take account of individual children's special needs, so that they are less likely to misbehave;
>
> take appropriate and effective action when they are confronted by more extreme behaviour.
>
> (Department for Education 2012b)

These new requirements upon teacher education providers, which are now incorporated in the standards for qualifying teachers, are part of a framework for inspecting the universities and schools. Michael Gove, the much-criticized education minister, hailed the behavioural component of the new standards, and the standards more generally, as having 'real teeth' and setting 'clear expectations', compared with the 'bland statements and platitudes' (Department for Education 2012b) of the previous set. Yet what they seem to have done is to provide a framework for ensuring that effective behaviour management, and the training of this, is merely *displayed*.

Teachers in New South Wales, Australia are treated to a similar array of simplified checklists and 'ABCs' (New South Wales Department of Education and Communities, undated) that are endorsed by the government, and among the most popular is Dr Mac's 'amazing behaviour management' (BehaviourAdvisor. com, undated), which promises 'safe harbour for captains of the classroom' and is endorsed by the United Federation of Teachers as providing a 'definite mental health destination for teachers at their wits end in managing challenging behaviour' (BehaviourAdvisor.com, undated). Foucault warns against staking such claims for health and takes a certain pride in the danger to health that he may pose:

I'm very proud that some people think that I'm a danger for the intellectual health of students. When people start thinking of health in intellectual activities, I think there is something wrong.

(Foucault 1988: 13)

Dr Mac's multiple-award-winning web-based resource is indeed amazing, not just for its promise to save the minds of teachers, but also for its certainty in its capacity to deliver, 'powerful & positive procedures for helping kids make better behavior choices' (BehaviourAdvisor.com, undated). Furthermore, through its claim of rationality, extending to a 'humorous and informative podcast', 'DSM: An Overview & Semi-Rational Analysis', it provides a new set of regulatory practices that achieve greater intensity and effectiveness through their apparent humanity and warmth (Olssen 1993).

Tips and checklists about managing 'challenging' behaviour abound in the United States, again orienting the teacher to clarify, set ground rules, establish expectations about acceptable conduct and encourage the routinization of schooling. For example, the South Florida *Creating Teaching Tools for Young Children with Challenging Behaviour* (Vaughan *et al.* 2009) again presents such children as dangerous, threatening to 'compromise learning' and 'disrupt classrooms damaging peer and teacher relationships'. This sentiment is echoed by Crone and Horner, who warn, in their Oregon manual, that '[s]tudents who engage in violent, disruptive and dangerous behavior compromise the fundamental ability of our schools to educate children, making violent, defiant, disruptive, and dangerous behaviors an issue for all students and all schools' (2003: xi). The South Florida User's manual, developed with a Government Health Department Grant, lists what can be expected from young children and, like the UK Government adviser, advocates simultaneous application of practical actions alongside achieving a calm disposition. Crone and Horner attempt to steer professionals away from a pathological view of the child's behaviour and to practise, instead, what they call 'functional behavioral assessment' (Crone and Horner 2003: xii). This involves collecting information about the conditions in which problem behaviour arises in order that interventions may be designed that limit or eradicate it. Such an approach posits behavioural problems as a pathogen that can be wiped out, given the correct treatment.

The professionals we interviewed acknowledged the availability of such forms of support for teachers and regarded them as having some utility. However, they were more concerned with interrupting teachers' understandings of behavioural problems as disorders and minimizing their sense of a need for intervention of any kind. We discuss their efforts in this regard in Chapter 8.

## Desired consequences/outcomes

Like power, desire circulates around the primary aged child with mental illness and produces its own surplus. Much of this is directed at the diagnosis itself, with the securing of a diagnosis of ADHD (or other disorder), recognized, by professionals and by parents, as an accomplishment in itself. Beyond that, however, the 'compliance and sustained attention' (MTA 1999: 1077) of a child within the ordinary classroom, albeit achieved through the exercise of biopower which is manifested as a type of exaltation, is desired by the professionals, to an extent by the parents, and even, perhaps, by the child. This desire is invested with hope, perhaps even faith, that the primary aged child can be rescued from the grip of mental abnormality. The abnormal designation is not merely accepted but is coveted, together with a submission to the excesses of biopower, a temporary sacrifice made against the promise of a normal life to come.

# Chapter 6

# Secondary school

Well sir I'm maladjusted.

That's an interesting word. What does it mean?

Well can I put it this way if you don't mind. If I see my pal across the road and he shouts 'you're a bastard', I'll shout back, 'ya bastard' and if I wasn't maladjusted I wouldn't say nothing.

(McKay 2006: 128)

Adolescence, generally accepted as a period of 'instability' (Ministry of Education 1955: 19), is likened more to infancy than to childhood on account of the many adjustments that are required and the conflict with authority that often arises. The secondary school-aged adolescent is no longer considered capable of repair or remedy in respect of his or her mental health problems, and with this loss of potential comes a new set of identifications of individuals as 'troubled' and 'troubling' and who are:

Noticeable for their difficult character, a profound dissimulation, a wild self-esteem, a boundless pride, burning passions and terrible tendencies.

(Voisin, cited in Foucault 2008b: 221)

The secondary aged mentally abnormal child is also seen as presenting danger and risk to the population because he or she is

more or less defective from the intellectual point of view but affected by perversions of the instincts: thieves, liars, masturbators, pederasts, arsonists, destroyers, murderers, poisoners, etcetera.

(Bourneville, cited in Foucault 2008b: 221)

With these new identifications come a set of intensifications which are concerned with control, containment and governance. Biopower takes on a further and more sophisticated dimension and becomes 'lighter, more ubiquitous, less attached to "negative" objects or practices . . . and more saturated within formerly ignored realms of social practice' (Nealon 2008: 71). It also becomes more effective and with fewer apparent options for resistance. Psychiatry has shifted its force and its interest in the diagnosis of mental abnormality and has acquired a heightened capacity and 'power over the abnormal, the power to define, control and correct what is abnormal' (Foucault 2008b: 221).

## Point of arousal

Secondary school teachers are, as at the primary stage, key individuals in raising suspicion of mental disorder but are largely considered incompetent in this domain, lacking awareness, knowledge and skills (Atkinson and Hornby 2002; Daniels *et al.* 1999) and often 'out of their depth' (Atkinson and Hornby 2002: 4). They struggle to place children on the somewhat unhelpful continuum of emotional and behavioural difficulties, contained in official guidance, between 'occasional bouts of naughtiness' at one end and 'mental illness' (Department for Education 1994: 4) at the other.

One of the professionals we interviewed described the big push for an ADHD diagnosis at the secondary stage, precipitated by the pressure on schools to meet targets:

> I think the schools push [ADHD] as a disorder because they think it would explain away children who are not performing quite so well, and I think with . . . expectations on schools to reach certain standards if they get children who're not achieving the standard . . . that then explains away the child's behaviour as being in the child not in the environment that they're in.
>
> (Professional 9, Child Mental Health, MCB Scotland)

However, this was challenged by another professional who thought diagnosis at secondary stage was too little, too late:

> When you hit Year 11, or Year 10, and these things start to happen then there's no point in the schools getting them . . . statemented . . . Basically, in this country, if you've not been statemented by the time you leave primary school . . . it's kind of viewed that it's a bit too late for you. . . . I think it takes a couple of years to get a statement. . . . And to get the extra support. So by the time they're in Year 10 and 11 it's not really, sort of, worth it for the school.
>
> (Professional 11, Youth Work, TNO England)

Yet another professional thought there was an increase in diagnosis in the secondary stage and saw this as having political origins:

> I suppose, political culture has also quite markedly pushed about . . . reforms to the justice system . . . and social behaviour being the, kind of, big political bogeyman really.
>
> (Professional 12, Youth Justice, TNO England)

Parents are, like teachers, seen as suspect in their capacity to recognize their adolescent children's behaviour as normal because of their limited opportunities to compare this with that of other children (Sibley *et al.* 2013). But, as will be discussed later in this chapter, parents are also key targets for intervention and regulation of their parenting practices, often viewed as a contributory factor in children's disordered behaviour as well as part of the means of redress.

## Relations (networks of power)

The secondary aged young person (or 'adolescent') with an ADHD diagnosis that has been previously, or more recently, established experiences a similar intensity of professional interest and concern as the primary aged child. But with these young people, the medical gaze is directed less towards the condition itself and more to protecting the individual, and those around him or her, from its manifestations. Mental disorder among the 'adolescent' does not, thus, need to be explained, since abnormality is, by now, certain, but must instead be contained and managed.

At the same time, however, the diagnosis itself, and its concomitant label, remains powerful and one professional we interviewed talked about how she had been drawn to, and drawn in by, this particular form of biopower:

> I almost think that has changed, but maybe it's just me that's changed about that actually, 'cause certainly in an idealistic view of it, a few years ago, and on my route to this job I'm doing now, and when I was studying for post-graduate modules and things, I was very much writing about . . . the fact that there's a society push to have young people diagnosed, but that's a labelling process which is not positive and it's not positive for someone's long-term good, that if we're talking about true inclusion, we're talking about acceptance of everybody, with everything they bring, regardless of what it's called, you know. But, you know, so that was my view and then as time goes on, you become part of a system where diagnosis and so on is part of it, and in fact is part of the gatekeeper, for making sure we have status for the children when they need it, and that's important as well, and that doesn't mean that I've changed my view completely . . . but you just do what you're doing and it works because of categories.
>
> (Professional 4, Specialist Education, MCB Scotland)

The permanence – and the power – of the diagnosis were also underlined by another professional:

> The core bit for most of these kids and young people is that they believe they're bad and it feeds into that . . . it's still alive and well, you know, children are still identified . . . as bad children and that can impact on the rest of their lives which is a huge concern . . . it suggests there is no potential for change and we're not naive – there is no potential for change in some entrenched positions, but in others there is.
>
> (Professional 2, Educational Psychology, MCB Scotland)

The biopower exercised in relation to the behaviour-disordered young person of secondary age shifts significantly towards a form of governmentality whereby the individual is managed with regard for the wider population to which he or she belongs. According to Foucault, the reach of governmentality or of government, which he often used interchangeably although he did distinguish between the two, is extensive:

> This notion being understood in the broad sense of procedures for directing human conduct. Government of children, government of souls and consciences, government of a household, of a state, or of oneself.
>
> (Foucault, cited in Senellart 2009: 388)

Governmentality, according to Foucault (2009), involves pastoral power, exercised on a population and akin to a shepherd looking after his or her flock.

> It is a power that guides towards an end and functions as an intermediary towards this end. It is therefore a power with a purpose for those on whom it is exercised, and not a purpose for some kind of superior unit like the city, state or sovereign . . . Finally, it is a power directed at all and each in their paradoxical equivalence and not at the higher unity formed by the whole. . . . Is it not exercising power over a flock?
>
> (Foucault 2009: 129)

Foucault draws parallels between the shepherd and the teacher and highlights the function of governmentality in serving the state, suggesting that it is to the state,

> what techniques of segregation were to psychiatry, what techniques of discipline were to the penal institutions and what biopolitics was to medical institutions.
>
> (Foucault 2009: 120)

Governmentality has become a vital element of the relations of power concerning the secondary aged young person with a diagnosis, serving the state and the professionals who will encounter these 'dangerous' individuals. For the individuals themselves (and their families) there is a new dimension of security that comes with both a suspicion that their behaviour could worsen (and hence become more dangerous) and an acceptance that it is unlikely to improve. Thus, the secondary aged young person finds him or herself the object of both fear and disregard.

## Disorders of interest

In respect of the 'adolescent' population, ADHD is of particular interest. The adjustment, in *DSM-5*, of the onset criteria for ADHD from the age of seven to twelve reflects an acknowledgement that the original choice of age seven was not empirically validated (Sibley *et al.* 2013) and that symptoms were more likely to emerge in adolescence (Applegate *et al.* 1997; Barkley and Biederman 1997). In addition, whereas *DSM-IV* requires the presence of 'symptoms that cause impairment', its successor asks only for previous symptoms but not impairment prior to the age of twelve and only requires evidence of current impairment caused by symptoms. Assumptions that children would 'grow out of' ADHD once they became adults have been replaced by an acceptance that it is a chronic lifetime disorder (Barkley *et al.* 2002; Sibley *et al.* 2013). However, Sibley *et al.* note the significant under-diagnosis among secondary aged young people and attribute this to a variety of inaccuracies, many of them stemming from previous versions of *DSM* and its limited capacity for capture. Some of this relates to the limited time spent with young people, even by their parents, in order to produce the necessary cross-verifiable evidence. However, Sibley *et al.* also point to some problems with the criteria itself and note particularly that impulsivity in ADHD is difficult to differentiate from that in other conditions such as bipolar disorder.

In addition to ADHD, conduct disorder, obsessive compulsive disorder, Tourette's, self-harm, depression and eating disorders, the professionals that we interviewed also described developmental disorders such as Asperger's syndrome and autistic spectrum disorder as being discussed and/or diagnosed in the children with whom they worked. These individuals also noted, however, that ADHD referrals by parents of secondary aged young people, which might be motivated by the possibility of financial benefit through disability living allowance, made up a significant part of their case load:

> I think because people can obtain disability living allowance for having that diagnosis as well, then, um . . . sometimes if, if we're diagnosing – if we DON'T diagnose children with it, um, the families, you know, are not happy with that.
>
> (Professional 5, Child Mental Health, MCB Scotland)

One of the professionals working within youth services expressed concern about what he saw as a creeping rise of referrals as well as confusion between criminality and antisocial behaviour in the minds of both professionals and the public. He argued that the criminal justice system 'kicked in' with youngsters who, through no fault of their own, had found themselves in trouble, and this was a particular problem with 'looked-after children':

> They start offending because they're unhappy, they don't like it there . . . they break things and then they get arrested. And what the [care] homes say is 'you've done something wrong and you're responsible, we're making you be responsible, and we're going to take it to court to prove how responsible you should be' . . . Now, my argument with that is that, er, actually, they're not really very responsible for the circumstances they find themselves in. . . . And if they were in a placement that actually, sort of, met their needs then they wouldn't be behaving in that particular way.
>
> (Professional 12, Youth Justice, TNO England)

This individual suggested that the public heat and anxiety within the United Kingdom around disordered behaviour had been created by New Labour and had been further stoked by the media.

## Modes of practice

The modes of practice directed at the secondary aged student reflect an acknowledgement of a reduced potential both in the individual to be rescued and for psychiatry to facilitate this rescue. They also represent a shift away from efforts to understand and address the abnormal behaviour and towards control, containment and governance. This is achieved through a series of measures which involve the specification of danger and risk posed by the 'mentally abnormal' young person; moral treatment of the young person and his or her family which is palliative in its orientation; and mechanisms of security which ensure the population of school and society is protected from the excesses of mental abnormality.

### Specification of danger and risk

Whilst the diagnostic imperative has passed for these young people, there is, nevertheless, an intensification towards specifying the precise nature of the danger and risk they present to school and society. Foucault identifies the discourse that surrounds this process as one of:

> fear and of moralization, a childish discourse, a discourse whose epistemological organization, completely governed by fear and moralization, can only be derisory, even regarding madness.

> (Foucault 2003a: 35)

The process of specifying the danger and risk posed by the secondary aged young person is, however, dominated by the acceptance of a certain 'incorrigibility' (Foucault 2003a: 58), whereby the young person, by his or her very nature, cannot be properly understood or verified as being mentally ill; 'he verges precisely on undecidability' (Foucault 2003a: 58). As a consequence, establishing the danger and risk has to involve some fictional and hyperbolic representations of the individual in order to establish the case for individuals' behaviour being 'monstrous' (Foucault 2003a: 74) and for the individual him or herself to be recognized as 'degenerate . . . someone who, at all events, cannot be cured' (Foucault 2003a: 318).

The risk and danger posed by young people of secondary age with ADHD is associated strongly with their inability to control their impulsiveness and their 'extreme' behaviour.

> Teens with ADHD are inattentive, overactive, impulsive, and disorganized. These behaviors may resemble normal teen behavior. They are, however, persistent, extreme, and truly outside the control of the teen with ADHD . . . And even more impulsive than their non-ADHD peers, these teens seem incapable

of curbing their automatic reactions of thinking before they act. During stress-ful situations, these already exaggerated behaviors become more extreme. Because of these troublesome symptoms, the adolescent may have trouble developing a sense of mastery and positive self esteem.

(Pruitt 2000)

Experts in adolescent mental health have suggested that, in adolescence, individuals become less overactive but more impulsive, inattentive and restless (Harpin 2005), which may become compounded by aggressive and antisocial behaviour (Edwards *et al.* 2001). Furthermore, young people with an ADHD diagnosis are said to be more inclined to lack friends and friendships. These present risks to individuals of significant academic failure, increased detention and expulsion and low rates of high school graduation and post-secondary education (Loe and Feldman 2007). The youngsters' typical behaviours are considered to create problems for their learning.

They demand attention by talking out of turn or moving around the room.

They have trouble following instructions, especially when they're pre-sented in a list.

They often forget to write down homework assignments, do them, or bring completed work to school.

They often lack fine motor control, which makes note-taking difficult and handwriting a trial to read.

They often have trouble with operations that require ordered steps, such as long division or solving equations.

They usually have problems with long-term projects where there is no direct supervision.

They don't pull their weight during group work and may even keep a group from accomplishing its task.

(www.helpguide.org)

Youngsters exhibiting these behaviours are said to 'pay the price for their prob-lems in low grades, scolding and punishment, teasing from peers, and low self-esteem' (www.helpguide.org). The risks of ADHD are also thought to include peer rejection (Barkley 1997) and systemic risks to the individual's person,

In general, youngsters with ADHD are at higher risk for academic failure, social isolation, accidents, low self esteem, demoralization, and disruptive behavior (including antisocial behaviors).

(Pruitt 2000)

These 'adverse risks', particularly of crime, were spelled out by one of the professionals we interviewed who described a pattern of descent into crime, whereby youngsters become disengaged with school, they become disaffected, their life chances are more adverse . . . they can't get . . . a decent job, they fall into . . . low-skill stuff, and then their life outcomes are going to be that much poorer so people start offending to try and improve their situation

(Professional 12, Youth Justice, TNO England)

The risks to 'behaviour-disordered adolescents' are heightened, according to one US doctor, by the increased manifestation of impulsivity in adolescence, a key feature of risk-taking behaviours (Bilkey 2013). According to this expert, young people with ADHD may be 'at risk' of certain risk-taking behaviours, for example drinking, smoking and underage sex, but also such things as verbal impulsivity and impulsive spending, which in turn place him or her at greater risk of harm. These behaviours, to which youngsters without ADHD are also susceptible, seem, according to Bilkey, more likely to be practised, and to more damaging effect, by those who have been diagnosed. The notion of ADHD as a 'gateway disorder', leading young people down a path towards substance abuse later in life, has been suggested by leading US medics (Charach *et al.* 2011; Lee *et al.* 2011), although Lee *et al.* stress that the drug treatment for ADHD does not itself lead to a heightened sensitivity or susceptibility to recreational drugs. One of the professionals we interviewed expressed a concern about the risks faced by young people who were prescribed Ritalin and who might also be engaging in typically adolescent behaviour:

My concern especially about Ritalin for ADHD, especially at the secondary age, there comes a time when kids are into other things; they might be taking other substances, which for me was pretty dangerous with Ritalin, and also a time when kids are kicking against it. At what point do they stop taking Ritalin?

(Professional 3, Educational Psychology, MCB Scotland)

Charach *et al.* and Lee *et al.*, while highlighting the susceptibility of young people with ADHD to recreational drug use, also emphasized the role of medical professionals in interrupting this inevitable trajectory and we report on the interruptions practised by the professionals we interviewed in Chapter 8.

The risk and dangers posed by primary aged children with ADHD to their peers is discussed in Chapter 5; secondary aged young people diagnosed with ADHD are regarded as 'unruly and even abject subjects who are rendered unrecognizable by these designations and the educational discourses that they circulate in' (Youdell 2011: 74). These are dangerous individuals who pose a threat to those with whom they share a classroom and a major challenge.

These students pose extreme challenges to the State, both in meeting their needs and the needs of the students with whom they are to be educated.

(National Council for Special Education 2012: 12)

Miller (undated) suggests that behaviour-disordered young people can create tension in the classroom and encourage disruptive behaviour among other children in the classroom.

Teachers face risk and danger from secondary aged students with ADHD, where their behaviour is aggressive, and find themselves caught in a tension between trying to manage the behaviour-disordered young person and teaching the rest of the class,

> Meanwhile, you, the teacher, wind up taking complaints from parents who feel their kids are being cheated of your instruction and feeling guilty because you can't reach the child with ADD/ADHD.
>
> (www.helpguide.org)

Foucault, elaborating on the pastoral nature of the power exercised within governmentality, notes a similar tension.

> The shepherd owes everything to his flock to the extent of agreeing to sacrifice himself for its salvation. But, on the other hand, since he must save each of the sheep, will he not find himself in a situation in which he has to neglect the whole of the flock in order to save a single sheep?
>
> (Foucault 2009: 128)

One of the professionals we interviewed described how the perceived risks posed by behaviour-disordered children to others in her care led her to decide to refuse to take such individuals in the future.

> And if you'd had asked me four years ago 'Is – how is that boy gonna be in Year 11?' I'd have said, 'He'll probably have been kicked out, he'll be offending and in trouble.' And he's the only child I work with that, like, we wouldn't take him away any more. We have done in the past but if he wanted to come on a residential now I probably wouldn't take him . . . by including him we might actually exclude other kids on the trip . . . But also because you can't have a conversation with him. You can't sit down and say, 'Look, what just happened wasn't really acceptable, you know, it was dangerous, other people could have [been] hurt' . . . He just wouldn't listen. It's just, like, there's no one at home all the time.
>
> (Professional 11, Youth Worker, TNO England)

Concerns about the trouble posed by young people with disordered behaviour have been taken up by teachers' unions.

> The strain imposed by social inclusion in some of our schools is in danger of becoming a time bomb waiting to explode unless properly resourced . . . we all want inclusion for all young people in Scotland, including asylum seeker children, so that they too can look forward

positively to the future. However, that future inclusion which all politicians are happy to sign up to and pay lip service to comes at a price. And in too many schools at the present time that price is the health and well-being of Scottish teachers . . . disruptive pupils may be a minority, but they are a growing minority. Now is the time to say enough is enough. This trend must be reversed. These pupils will not be included in mainstream provision unless their behaviour can be guaranteed. All schools must be given the ability to exclude the disruptive.

(Mackie 2004)

The UK Association of Teachers and Lecturers reported that 62 per cent of its members said there were more children with emotional, behavioural and mental health problems than two years ago and 56 per cent said there were more than five years ago (Sellgren 2013). Members felt they had been inadequately trained to deal with such problems. The UK National Association of Schoolmasters and Union of Women Teachers and the National Union of Teachers (Shakespeare 2005; Macbeath *et al.* 2006) have expressed concerns about the cost of inclusion for other pupils in the school, particularly where there is disruptive or violent behaviour from disabled pupils. The American Federation of Teachers polled its members and found that 24 per cent of urban secondary school teachers thought they lost four or more hours a week through disruptive behaviour, usually relating to a few disordered children, and the misery caused was made clear:

Their aggressive, disruptive, and defiant behavior wastes teaching time, disrupts the learning of all students, threatens safety, overwhelms teachers – and ruins their own chances for successful schooling and a successful life.

(Walker *et al.*, undated)

Teachers in Australia have also expressed concerns at the increasingly problematic nature of the young people in their classrooms. A letter that a member of the Queensland Teachers Union wrote to the Shadow Secretary of State for Education attracted widespread support from within his union, the media and beyond. He invited the minister to defend his position on class sizes with a recognition of a breakdown of his class as including '6 behaviour management students; 5 learning support; 3 English as a second language; [and] 4 gifted and talented', attention to whom meant that in a 70-minute lesson, 'without a teacher aide the needs of these students are so demanding that other children rarely receive any time at all' (Chilcott 2012). These concerns were echoed by Queensland Association of State School Principals and the Queensland Secondary Principals Association, who declared behaviour to be 'the critical and daily issue confronting staff' and saw this as getting worse.

In the United States, an incident in which the police, called to a school following an 'outburst' by a six-year-old, arrested and handcuffed her and removed her from school, led to concerns about the increasing criminalization of child behaviour and the greater reliance on police to manage schools' discipline problems. According to a civil rights lawyer in Albuquerque, hundreds of children have been arrested for minor offences, including having mobile phones in class, burping, refusing to change seats and destroying a textbook. At the same time, however, the Albuquerque teachers' union president has indicated that 'students' bad behaviour is more extreme these days . . . there is more chronic and extreme disrespect, disinterest and kids who basically don't care' (Martin and Clausing 2012).

A further threat posed by young people with a diagnosis of ADHD has been identified as relating to economic factors and the additional costs associated with managing disordered individuals. Pelham *et al.* (2007), reviewing existing research with a cost of illness (COI) framework, estimated an average cost per individual child, in 2005, of $14,576 for ADHD treatment, including special education and health-related costs. A more recent study estimated costs in 2011 of between 21 and 44 billion dollars in health care for children with ADHD and between 15 and 25 billion dollars for education (Doshi *et al.* 2012). This study also estimated spillover costs borne by the family as between 33 and 43 billion dollars. One of the professionals we interviewed, remarking on how much more cost-effective it was to medicate children, commented on the high cost of behaviour interventions:

> We get into a discussion with psychology colleagues, in particular with commissioners, of services, you know, it's not cost-effective to do behavioural interventions.
>
> (Professional 9, Child Mental Health, MCB Scotland)

The threat thought to be posed by behaviour-disordered youngsters may be negligible compared with what the individuals encounter at the hands of their own peers. In the following extract from an interview conducted in Australia, young people describe the risks and dangers to behaviour-disordered youngsters that stem from the irresistible nature of labelling.

I:    Is discrimination an issue here?

C:    Kind of.

I:    Kind of?

C:    Yes, it depends . . . well depends who the person is. Like, if you have a lad, which is like . . . thinks that they're all cool and stuff, they would usually pick on the depression . . . like those depression people . . . or something like that?

N:    They pretty much put labels on people.

I:    And who are they? The lads?

N:    Yes, pretty much everyone puts a label . . . you can't live in pretty much anywhere without getting a label put on you.

C:    For no reason . . .

I:    So they put labels on people did you say with depression?

C:    Yes, like if someone had depression they will like judge them and stuff. They won't ask why or ask why they're allowed to go off; they'll just straight up 'You're an idiot. Go fuck yourself' or 'Go die in a hole.'

I:    You're an idiot, go fuck yourself, go die in a hole?

C:    Pretty much.

(Caine and Nadia, 15 and 17 years old,
IUE Interview, Australia 2013)

### Moral treatment

Adolescent youngsters with behaviour disorders are subjected to regimes of training which constitute moral treatment and which are directed at their souls. These programmes seek to instil some level of discipline and self-control but acknowledge the potential for failure. In this sense, the treatment has a palliative dimension, looking to relieve the adolescents and those around them from suffering associated with the symptoms of disordered behaviour but with no expectation of effecting a cure. Young people are offered training in social skills, given access to cognitive behavioural therapy or involved in programmes with positive behaviour in their titles and their orientation and self-control as their goal. Positive Behaviour Support (PBS) programmes, which are a widespread 'brand name' (Johnston et al. 2006), have been extended to youngsters with learning disabilities as well as those with behaviour disorders. It has also enjoyed widespread adoption in New South Wales, Australia as a framework for school disciplinary policies (O'Neil and Stephenson 2010). The PBS programme has its origins in Applied Behavioural Analysis (ABA) and its proponents accord it a high status as

> an applied science that uses educational methods to expand an individual's behavior repertoire and systems change methods to redesign an individual's living environment to first enhance the individual's quality of life and, second, to minimize his or her problem behavior.
>
> (Carr et al. 2002: 4)

The PBS approach has been lauded as a non-aversive intervention although its complexity has been obscured in the efforts to provide teachers with a non-technical version of PBS. Thus, what were initially constructed as interventions have become converted into 'supports'. In spite of this, claims have been made of the scientific superiority of PBS over ABA (Knoster et al. 1993), which Johnston et al. (2006) refute. The success in the United States, at least in marketing terms, of PBS seems to be as a result of the close ties that PBS leaders have with federal governments, pursuit of federal funding, the creation of a high visibility of PBS, its adaptation to serve market interests and its non-technical presentation to practitioners, minimizing the need for high levels of expertise. Whilst Johnston *et al.* (2006) acknowledge the accomplishments of PBS, they express concern about the negative impact on the status of ABA, and, as has frequently been the case within the field of special education, the weapon of choice against the opposition is ideology (Allan 2010):

> We believe that the PBS movement represents a well-intended attempt to disseminate a more or less behaviorally based treatment model. That effort, however, has been driven more by ideological and marketing interests than by research findings and professional considerations.
>
> (Johnston *et al.* 2006: 74)

An expert advised giving children a mantra to recite: 'Zip my lip and I won't get into trouble' (Taylor, cited in Gentschel and McLaughlin 2000: 343) and also advocated the kind of treatment used with alcoholics, the 'six A's of apology' (Taylor, cited in Gentschel and McLaughlin 2000), whereby the child is forced to confess and acknowledge their misbehaviour and undo their mistakes.

One professional we interviewed expressed a lack of hope that young people with behavioural problems could be rescued and described an alternative treatment track that these youngsters were submitted to:

> There's alternative curriculums for those who are resisting school, for those who are . . . either their behaviour does not allow them to be involved in, sort of, formal education, or they're school phobic, or they're disaffected with school. And it's a way of engaging them in some form of education . . . and keeping them learning and engaged.
>
> (Professional 11, Youth Work, TNO England)

Another professional compared the effectiveness of treatment of the adolescent unfavourably with that of the primary aged schools and attributed this to systemic factors:

> Our primary schools by and large are extremely supportive, but there's always . . . the work to be done to make sure that people are totally on board and totally understanding of . . . what they're getting from the children. . . . secondary schools are bit more complex, obviously they're larger organizations, the support structure isn't the same . . . within the secondary schools clearly we have an old-fashioned traditional structure here where the class teachers might not get that much contact with individuals, the information is not necessarily passed on as it should be and with the best will in the world they sometimes have to respond to what they're getting, not really understanding where it's coming from, so clearly there's more work to be done there.
>
> (Professional 3, Educational Psychology, MCB Scotland)

Voluntary sector organizations were seen as valuable places for teaching adolescents certain values and social interaction skills.

> Where we have identified a child that we think is at is at risk of developing a conduct disorder one of the things that we say to the parents is that if you've only got a limited amount of money . . . get him in Boys' Brigade, get him in Scouts, get him in, in these sorts of . . . places that are going to be teaching him pro-social values.
>
> (Professional 5, Child Mental Health, MCB Scotland)

While these efforts sought to offer assistance through the teaching of 'pro-social values', these measures did not occur outside of the pressures to psychopathologize.

## Supporting parents

Parents of 'behaviour-disordered adolescents' find themselves, like the young people in their care, targeted for intensive support. The professionals in our interviews described some of the moral treatment that was directed towards the whole family and that was aimed at easing them away from using ADHD as an 'excuse' for family dysfunction and for the aggressive behaviour of the young person,

> We do have a self-education pack so we can set them to work through . . . there's a 'full of beans' book and things like that they can go and look at . . . I think sometimes there's a tendency for families to use it as an excuse for aggressive, for planned aggressive behaviour which it is now, and so there's quite a lot of education has to be going on that you know that that doesn't excuse that behaviour . . . what behaviours it could lead to, what behaviours . . . are not to do with ADHD . . . I think that that's quite a good task.
>
> (Professional 5, Child Mental Health, MCB Scotland)

One of the professionals we interviewed talked of nudging the parents into their own community:

> Yeah, it might just be . . . I think you know it might be . . . you need to have . . . more . . . going on in your life socially and it might be that there'd be a task that they're going to go . . . to the library and read what's available . . . we can set little kind of tasks that that they would do out in their community really.
>
> (Professional 5, Child Mental Health, MCB Scotland)

Advice on parenting was similar to that given to teachers, involving high levels of structure and, as Foucault observes of the routines within prison, occupying the child and keeping them busy, since 'idle time may exacerbate their symptoms and create chaos in your home' (www.helpguide.org).

As was mentioned in Chapter 5, the 'Triple P' approach to parenting, the scientific worth of which is claimed to be beyond doubt (www.triplep.net), seeks to ensure the security and safety of the family and society, whilst appearing to allow parents some degree of choice about the level at which they 'opt' into the programme. However, where the adolescent's behaviour is considered troublesome, the state takes a firmer hand and directs the parents towards a particular level of intervention. 'Parenting Orders' (Home Office Police and Justice Act 2006), the strand of law concerned with determining the care of individual children, including children whose parents have divorced, have been extended in the United Kingdom to increase the powers over parents to require them to control their children. The UK legislation has established a first-level, voluntary form of contractual agreement with parents, providing a 'formal structure' (Home Office Police and Justice Act 2006: 5).

Parenting contracts have two strands: the first is attendance at a parenting programme (which may be supplemented with other support) and a set of 'specific requirements', for example ensuring school attendance or avoiding contact with particular individuals. Parenting programmes, designed to

> develop parents' skills to reduce parenting as a risk factor and enhance parenting as a protective factor . . . include cognitive behaviour programmes, mentoring, parenting advice, individual family based therapy, functional family therapy, solution focussed (brief) therapy, family group conferencing and group based programmes.
>
> (Ministry of Justice, Department for Children, Schools and
> Families and the Youth Justice Board 2007: 2)

They are represented as 'not a punishment but a positive way of bolstering parental responsibility and helping parents develop their skills so they can respond more effectively to their child's needs' (p. 4). At the same time, they are a means of preventing youth offending and are thus a clear and incontrovertible security measure. If efforts to 'secure voluntary co-operation from parents' (p. 5) fail, a Parenting Order can be secured through the courts. With Parenting Orders comes a requirement, enforceable through law, for parents to attend a parenting programme. There are also specific requirements, which may include the parents ensuring that the young person attends school, attends a behaviour support programme, avoids certain contacts or presence in particular areas, remains at home at certain times at night and is effectively supervised (Ministry of Justice, Department for Children, Schools and Families and the Youth Justice Board 2007).

### Mechanisms of security

The measures involved in controlling, containing and governing individuals deemed to be dangerous amount to what Foucault (2009: 11) calls 'technologies

of security'. Foucault also suggests that these measures are essentially addressing an economic question of the relation between the cost of repression and
the cost of delinquency to society. These include whole-school approaches
to managing pupil behaviour, such as assertive discipline (Canter and Canter
1992) and improving the teacher's class control, through such strategies as were
outlined in Chapter 5 and which largely involve a high degree of structure and
the minimizing of uncertainty but also advocate the use of mechanisms for
commanding young people's attention and order, such as egg timers and bells.
External support from agencies is also advocated as a means of heightening the
security of the teacher (Gray and Panter 2000).

Current modes of practice also include forms of exile (Ball 2013) in behavioural units, which may be part of a mainstream school or in separate institutions, and there have been suggestions that their use is on the increase (Nordahl
and Hausstätter 2009; Slee 2011), a manifestation of the 'irresistible rise of the
SEN industry' (Tomlinson 2012: 267). Queensland, Australia is currently roll-
ing out a programme of intensive segregation of children with severe behavioural problems with a series of centres, called 'positive learning centres', which
are separated from mainstream or special schools, in one case by a 1.8 metre
fence and secure gate. A representative of the Queensland Teachers Union,
while welcoming the development of these centres and expressing a preference for them to be completely segregated from mainstream schools, denied
any allusion to prisons:

> It (a security fence) is extreme but we are also talking here about students
> that, in most circumstances, demonstrated an inability to operate in a nor-
> mal school setting . . . I would not draw any analogy between that and
> prison.
>
> (Fraser 2013)

One of the professionals we interviewed described helping young people with
strategies, including problem solving. Another described a form of training that
was involved:

> Some of the strategies are about helping young people to reflect on their
> own state, their own behaviour, and actually, you know, having a quiet
> corner that they can opt to go to, you know, rather than be sent to, and
> actually moderate, you know, monitoring their own performance, kind of
> know the times when that's what they want to do.
>
> (Professional 1, Educational Psychology, MCB Scotland)

The seemingly benign 'quiet corner', where individuals can apparently go to
collect their thoughts, regain their composure and avoid conflict, may have a
more ominous undertone of an incarceration of the soul. The public nature

of the 'corner' space means that any repair becomes a spectacle that has to be witnessed by the teacher and other students. The corner becomes the confessional, used by the student for 'hiding . . . madness, not expressing it, putting it from his mind, thinking of something else' (Foucault 2008b: 98), which can only be achieved by putting it on display.

## Desired consequences/outcomes

Much of the effort, in respect of mentally disordered adolescents, is initially directed at ensuring that the risks and dangers posed by these youngsters, to school and society, have been properly appreciated. This is achieved by practices which heighten awareness of the young people's degeneration, through a network 'on the borders of medicine and justice that serves both as a structure for the "reception" of abnormal individuals and as an instrument for the "defense" of society' (Foucault 2003a: 328). Thereafter the measures that are effected are concerned with quietening the excess associated with mental disorder; helping the young people towards better self-control; ensuring their parents are themselves able to control their child's behaviour; and introducing security measures which protect other children and teachers from children's excesses. There is little of the optimism that is seen in respect of primary aged children, where interventions seek to alter the child's persona and to wrest it from the grip of behaviour disorder. For the secondary aged young people, educational support is palliative, with an aspiration of making the patient, and those around him or her, more comfortable, and with less suffering for all concerned. Where there is some aspirational activity, it is in relation to minimizing the further risks to the individual, which come from the world of crime. A 'result' is thus for an individual to 'make it through' (Professional 12, Youth Justice, TNO England) to further education, employment or training, according to one professional, whose language of survival was particularly poignant.

# Chapter 7

# Colleges and universities

In the 2008 National College Health Assessment sponsored by the American College Health Association (ACHA-NCHA), more than one in three undergraduates reported *'feeling so depressed it was difficult to function'* at least once in the previous year.

(Hunt and Eisenberg 2010: 4, emphasis added)

Tertiary education students (those attending post-secondary school colleges and universities) are, as the above US report makes clear, a student group believed to be considerably affected by mental health issues. High rates of mental disorder and mental health issues in higher education students are also reported in countries such as the United Kingdom, where '29% of students [surveyed] reported clinical levels of psychological distress' (Royal College of Psychiatrists 2011: 23). According to the US National Institute of Mental Health, 'major depressive disorder is the leading cause of disability in the US for ages 15–44' with over 14.8 million or 6.7 per cent of the population affected (National Institute of Mental Health 2008). The rate for tertiary students is clearly significantly higher than in the general population. For this student cohort, depression is the mental disorder that incites the most concern, with reports that it has the highest prevalence rate amongst university students (Connell *et al.* 2007). A report on research conducted in Turkey demonstrates the extent of this concern, citing depression among university students as of widespread concern:

> Evidence that suggests that university students are vulnerable to mental health problems has generated increased public concern in Western societies. Previous studies suggest high rates of psychological morbidity, especially depression and anxiety, among university students all over the world.
>
> Psychological morbidity in undergraduate students represents a neglected public health problem and holds major implications for campus health services and mental policy-making. In terms of life quality, understanding the impact of this neglected public health phenomenon on one's educational attainment and prospective occupational success is very important.
>
> (Bayram and Bilgel 2008: 667)

Concern with depression and university students has been described in reports from a number of countries, including, Nigeria (Adewuya *et al.* 2006), Australia (Khawaja and Bryden 2006), Japan (Tomoda *et al.* 2000), Norway (Nerdrum *et al.* 2006), the United States (Hunt and Eisenberg 2010) and the United Kingdom (Stewart-Brown *et al.* 2000).

Contrasting with the potentiality of perfection stressed for very young children, in this student cohort the issue rests in their potentiality as threats to themselves (especially as failures in the academy) and to other students and the education institution. Concern with the latter (the troubled threatening student) has meant the identification of students has risen to prominence in higher education settings, particularly in the United States. Here this fear of the 'student as threat' has given rise to the demand for constant vigilance and the pursuit of ways to achieve early identification of troubled students. So great is the intensification of concern over the 'student as threat' that in this chapter we have elected to focus on this 'problem'. There is a second reason for this focus, namely that the intensification of this concern has seen transformations in the way in which depression, one of the most common mental disorders associated with university student mental health, is understood.

Violence is the key concern in this attention placed on the 'troubled' tertiary education student. This is evident in the rush to develop threat assessment protocols that occurred after the mass shootings at Virginia Tech, an event that has been referred to as 'Higher Education's 9/11' (Rinehart 2007). Although attention is given to other forms of student mental health problems, it is the spectre of the threatening student that dominates. This may at first seem at odds with findings such as those cited above. After all, the dominating issue is depression and not disorders that are commonly (and, we could argue, were previously) associated with violence, such as psychopathy (antisocial personality disorder). Unexpectedly, it seems depression is a disorder that has come to the fore, and this mental disorder has become intertwined in the depiction of the threatening student. This association between depression, troubled students and the potential for violence has become widespread, even implicit, in discourses about tertiary students and their mental health/ mental disorders.

Taking inspiration from a point made in *History of Madness* (Foucault 2006), the problem is not the matter of precision in definition of the troubled student university student; but rather, how this definition manifests. Made with reference to melancholy and the 'melancholic experience', the significance of this differentiation is driven home by Foucault in the following sentence:

> The key point is that this process did not go from observation to the construction of explanatory images, but that on the contrary images fulfilled the initial role of synthesis, and their organizing force made possible a structure of perception where symptoms could finally take on their significant value, and be organized into the visible presence of the truth.
>
> (Foucault 2006: 277)

Following this line of inquiry, the key point is that there are significant shifts in the way that the troubled student is conceptualized in higher education institutions. It is not the case that the depictions and descriptions of the troubled university student adhere to a logic born out of unsullied observation. Rather, it is an issue of grasping 'the structure of perception' at work in how this troubled student is understood.

Contemporary configurations of the troubled student position depression and dangerousness together. This has formed, to quote Foucault, a 'visible presence of truth' (2006: 277) that produces a compelling and, in the main, unquestioned account of the troubled student. However, the truths of the troubled student that are taken as facts are quite the contrary; they belong to what Hannah Arendt (1968b) describes as the domain of rational truths. Arendt's distinction between factual and rational truths supports an analysis of the truths told about tertiary students and their mental health. This distinction can facilitate deeper appreciation of the complexity of truths about depression and the troubled student, as well as assisting our recognition of the reluctance to subject these to critique.

Surprisingly, changing conceptualization of the troubled university student, and in particular the link made between depression and violence, remains bereft of commentary and critique. With the link to violence presented as unequivocally factual, depression poses threats that cannot afford to be questioned or ignored. This claim of the potency of depression, and, by extension, description of the troubled tertiary student, rests on the assumption that it is what Arendt (1968b) terms a factual truth. Contrary to this interpretation, the point of departure in this chapter is that perceptions of depression's violence and impotence are very far from factual truths.

## Points of arousal

Students enrolled in colleges and universities, as well as those who are to become enrolled, arouse the greatest suspicion of mental disorder. Concern has been raised regarding the backgrounds of different students, with the mental problems of those from backgrounds traditionally engaged in higher education considered to be of far less concern as compared to students from non-traditional backgrounds,

> One result of widening participation is that there is evidence to suggest that non-traditional entrants to higher education may make greater demands on support services. Meltzer et al. (2000) showed an increased incidence of mental disorders among children from working class families, those with less educated parents, larger families, lone parents and those experiencing poverty. Additionally, Smith and Naylor (2001) made a clear link between lower socioeconomic status and dropping out.
>
> (Royal College of Psychiatrists 2011: 36)

Concern with the mental health of the 'working classes' and the poor is not uncommon, as we discussed in Chapter 3. Undoubtedly, these concerns echo a trend that sees those who experience poverty as at much greater risk of mental health diagnoses. This is a practice that can effectively obscure the very real effects of experiencing disadvantages (Schram 2000).

Tertiary students (and here we might well pause and ask 'which' tertiary students) incite the greatest fear. It is difficult to overlook the powerful images of 'troubled' university or college students that have been conveyed throughout the news media. Stories such as the excerpt below depict violent events alongside descriptions of mental disorder and convey a sense of 'madness' in the individual.

> AURORA, Colo. – The text message, sent to another graduate student in early July, was cryptic and worrisome. Had she heard of 'dysphoric mania,' James Eagan Holmes wanted to know?
>
> The psychiatric condition, a form of bipolar disorder, combines the frenetic energy of mania with the agitation, dark thoughts and in some cases paranoid delusions of major depression . . .
>
> About two weeks later, minutes into a special midnight screening of 'The Dark Knight Rises' on July 20, Mr. Holmes, encased in armor, his hair tinted orange, a gas mask obscuring his face, stepped through the emergency exit of a sold-out movie theater here and opened fire. By the time it was over, there were 12 dead and 58 wounded.
>
> (Goode *et al.* 2012)

This tragic event occurred in Aurora, Colorado in July 2012. Holmes was then a PhD student in neuroscience at the University of Colorado, Denver. The event was quickly picked up by the US and international news media. Later reportage of the Holmes trial includes descriptions that he was 'socially awkward', had 'academic problems', was 'mentally ill' and was 'a quiet young man' (BBC 2013). A news report by Aljazeera describes Holmes' 'plea for not guilty by reason of insanity' as being accepted, explaining that 'Colorado law defines insanity as the inability to distinguish right from wrong caused by a diseased or defective mind' (Aljazeera 2013). The images conveyed of Holmes at the time of the event, the depiction of his appearance in the cinema and the later descriptions and images at his trial convey an individual different from the norm. At the same time, these news media reports also depict startlingly normal characteristics, such as his 'quietness'. One of the significant features of this point of arousal is precisely the issue of 'unknown mad amongst us' and the potential for harm created by the presence of the troubled-but-as-yet-unidentified-student.

The range of material that emerged following the massacre, the news media reports, blogs, footage and commentary released on the internet, through to the emerging artwork tends to draw together two threads: violence and the troubled student. Seven years prior to the mass shootings at Virginia Tech the

Federal Bureau of Investigation released *The School Shooter: a threat assessment perspective* (O'Toole 2000). Published shortly after the Columbine Massacre, this document provides 'a systematic procedure for threat assessment and intervention', but clearly states that it is 'not a profile of the "school shooter"' (O'Toole 2000: 1).[1] References to depression made in this document differ markedly from the way depression is linked with violence and the troubled student following the mass shootings at Virginia Tech. In *The School Shooter* depression is first discussed under the heading of 'pre-disposing factors'. These factors include 'underlying personality traits, characteristics, and temperament that predispose an adolescent to fantasize about violence or act violently' and mention 'underlying factors such as a student's vulnerability to loss and depression' (O'Toole 2000: 8). Although depression is implicated with violence in *The School Shooter*, this is done through 'predisposing factors', and not via a shift from a state limited by its own impotence to a state that is potent.

While references to depression and violent actions occur, it is the responses following the Virginia Tech mass shootings where the association becomes crystallized in a new form. Rumours about college student Seung Hui Cho's mental state promptly generated questions about connections between depression and violence. In the immediate aftermath of the mass shootings there were authoritative counter-narratives that advised against such conjecture. Consider, for example, the following excerpt from *CBS News* published two days after the Virginia Tech Massacre. The article poses the question, 'Might underlying depression be to blame?' (DeNoon 2007). Quoting a perceived medical expert (Robert Irvin, a medical doctor and director at Harvard's McLean Hospital), this association is then denied:

> 'People who are hopeless, who don't experience any joy or happiness, their thoughts are far more likely to tend toward self-harm than harm to anyone else,' Irvin says. 'If they are moved to violence, they are far and away more frequently the victims.'
>
> (DeNoon 2007)

This rebuttal refutes a direct link between depression and violence directed toward others and maintains the depressed individual as more likely to be a victim of violence than its perpetrator. This echoes what a reader of Burton's seventeenth-century *Anatomy of Melancholy* might find: where words such as violence occur, the action is in the main directed toward the self.

Some months later, however, following the release of *Mass Shootings at Virginia Tech*, discussion regarding a link between violence and depression had quietened. The emphasis seems to shift to being on the watch for people who have mental health problems, including, quite explicitly, depression. News media articles published after the release of the report rapidly fixed on the question of this new range of mental problems. For example, an article in *Medpage Today*, published the day of the release of *Mass Shootings at Virginia*

*Tech,* carried the title 'Virginia Tech Missed "Clear Warnings" of Shooter's Mental Instability' (Osterwell 2007). Here depression is treated as potency, a 'warning sign' that institutions need to be alert for, monitor and act upon. Here there is a tangible move from the vigorous defence of links between violence and depression to one where it is viewed as a 'red flag'. This turnabout casts depression at extremities, with the resultant loss of possibilities for depression to be imagined as complex, multi-faceted and particular.

### The Virginia Tech Massacre

The response to the Virginia Tech Massacre is a focal point for grasping the connection between dangerousness and mental disorders such as depression. In this discussion of Virginia Tech, the purpose is not to dissect this tragic event, nor to provide an analysis of the range of measures advocated in the report *Mass Shootings at Virginia Tech* (Virginia Tech Review Panel 2007). The intention is to contribute a critical perspective on the ways in which the troubled student is coming to be understood within higher educational institutions. This understanding differs markedly from the concerns raised about very young children, or children in primary schools or high schools, and it diverges from the once commonly accepted notion of depression and the depressed individual.

In April 2007 at Virginia Tech, Blacksburg, Virginia, Seung Hui Cho, a 23-year-old university student, perpetrated what has been claimed to be the worst mass shooting in the United States. In the period after this event sweeping changes occurred to US universities that have placed an emphasis on detecting troubled students. This detection pays particular attention to the identification of mental health problems in tertiary students and this atten-tion sustains an explicit link between depression and violence. Just days after this mass shooting, the Governor of Virginia, Timothy M. Kaine, convened a review panel that comprised nine 'nationally recognized individuals' across the disciplines of 'law enforcement, security, governmental management, mental health, emergency care, victims' services, the Virginia court system, and higher education' (Virginia Tech Review Panel 2007: viii). Six months after the shooting the panel published *Mass Shootings at Virginia Tech, April 16, 2007: Report of the Review Panel* (Virginia Tech Review Panel 2007). Together with detailed psychological analysis of Cho, the report issued rec-ommendations for threat assessment in higher education institutions. Almost 12 months after the shootings, the Government of Virginia instituted four new laws: 'Policies addressing suicidal students'; 'Institutional crisis and emergency management plan: review required'; 'Violence prevention com-mittee, threat assessment team'; and 'First warning and emergency notifica-tion system required' (Virginia General Assembly 2008: 28). Attending to key recommendations made in *Mass Shootings at Virginia Tech* (Virginia Tech Review Panel, 2007), the new laws included the mandate that all public higher education institutions in the State of Virginia establish threat assessment teams.

## Relations (networks of power)

Tertiary education institutions wield powerful effects over the discourses of the troubled tertiary student. These institutions have a variety of mechanisms that are brought into play. These include: counselling and guidance services; instruction on the identification of troubled students designed for faculty; identification and self-help promotional materials targeting students; and security measures (inclusive of personnel, protocols, surveillance and scanners for weapons). Authentication of such practices occurs through the truths that are conveyed about the troubled student. For instance, descriptions of students' inner mental states – and the consequent potentiality of these states – as a threat are treated as though simple observable facts. The problematic in this construct becomes clearer when, using Arendt's distinction between factual and rational truths, we analyse the presentation of truth in the case of the Virginia Tech Massacre.

The facts seem to be clear. As the opening statement of the report makes plain, 'On April 16 2007, Seung Hui Cho, an angry and disturbed student, shot to death 32 students and faculty of Virginia Tech, wounded 17 more, and then killed himself' (Virginia Tech Review Panel 2007: 1). While it is indisputable that Cho shot to death 32 students and faculty, wounded 17 more, and then killed himself, what needs to be called into question is how the depiction of Cho as 'angry and disturbed' is presented as fact. The reasoning for questioning this rests on the importance of grasping the use of the terms 'angry' and 'disturbed'. When these descriptions are cited as fact it is all too easy to overlook how meanings are attributed. For this reason it is helpful to accentuate the distinction between factual and rational truths.

Arendt placed careful emphasis on the necessity of factual truths and the importance of distinguishing these from rational truths. She offered the following as examples of a factual truth: 'in the night of August 4, 1914, German troops crossed the frontier of Belgium' and 'the earth moves around the sun' (Arendt 1968b: 239). Rational truths, by contrast, are typified by 'philosophical reflection' (Sharpe 2007: 101) or 'philosophical speculation' (Owens 2007: 269). This type of truth 'enlightens human understanding' (Arendt 1968b: 242), and includes 'mathematical, scientific or philosophical truth' (p. 231). Elaborating on the differences between the two types, Arendt depicts factual truths as 'seen and witnessed with the eyes of the body, and not the eyes of the mind' (1968b: 237). Relying on facts, factual truths are 'beyond agreement, dispute, opinion or consent' (1968b: 240); a point that Arendt underscores by citing Hugo Grotius, a seventeenth-century legal philosopher: 'even God cannot cause two times two should not make four' (Arendt 1968b: 240).

The correctness of facts is of great importance. For this reason it is vital that factual truths such as the frontier of Belgium example lack any form of appraisal of the individuals that crossed that frontier or of the events involved. In the Arendtian formulation, facts belong to the political realm, where they have a crucial function.

> Facts inform opinions, and various opinions, inspired by different interests and passions, can differ widely and still be legitimate so long as they respect factual truth. Freedom of opinion is a farce unless factual information is guaranteed and the facts themselves are not in dispute. In other words, factual truth informs political thought just as rational truth informs philosophical speculation.
>
> (Arendt 1968b: 238)

There is, then, much at stake should facts become confused. This is a key problem that affects the presentation of information about tertiary students and mental disorders or mental health. Arguably, too, this has resonance with how 'facts' are communicated in the other education sectors discussed in this book. For example, how are 'facts' about a primary school boy who 'misbehaves' communicated? We suggest that this is invariably done in a manner that presents rational truths as 'facts'. As such they are above question.

This issue with facts is stressed by Maurizio Passerin d'Entrèves: 'if opinions were not based on correct information and the free access to all relevant facts they could scarcely claim any validity' (2000: 257). This, as Mathew Sharpe points out, signals the need for a cautionary approach to the acceptance of facts: 'I suspect Arendt would counsel us to be hesitant in principle about political action based on conjectures whose factual basis at the time is impossible to establish or refute' (Sharpe 2007: 101). While Arendt does concede to using the distinction between factual and rational truth for 'convenience's sake without discussing its intrinsic legitimacy' (1968b: 231), her point is to draw attention to the difference of the two forms of truth. In so doing, she emphasizes the importance of each, as well as their place in the political realm. It is well worth asking whether any such distinction is made with regards to how mental issues and trouble are depicted with tertiary students.

When mental health problems and their consequences are presented as facts about the individual university student, the opportunity to identify the process of (to paraphrase Foucault (2006)) 'structuring perception' is confiscated. This is what occurs when the relationship between dangerousness, depression and the troubled tertiary student is presented as fact: we risk confusing rational and factual truth. From an Arendtian perspective, merging these types of truths has considerable implications for generating debate about the complex issues that affect tertiary education students and has serious implications for the prevention of campus violence. This is because when taken as fact our opinions (which rely on facts) are misinformed. There is also the sobering observation that the threat to facts is none other than lying (Arendt 1968b), which helps us to grasp why disputing interpretations of the troubled student is risky, given the stakes. Descriptions and mental health profiles of Cho following the Virginia Tech mass shooting in actuality confuse these types of truths. The intent in the discussion that follows is not to dive into analysis of the legitimacy of truths. Rather the objective is to work from Arendt's point of distinction to examine how these two forms of truth are confused and the consequences of blending these truths.

## Disorders of interest

Among the various mental disorders described as being diagnosable in tertiary students, depression (or symptoms of depression) is considered the most prevalent (Hunt and Eisenberg 2010; Royal College of Psychiatrists 2011). Variation occurs amongst disciplines, with depression in medical students reported in one study to be as high as 28 per cent (Mehanna and Richa 2006). Other mental disorders that are described in this population include bipolar disorder, eating disorders, schizophrenia, autism spectrum disorders and substance use disorder (alcohol and drug use) (Royal College of Psychiatrists 2011). Anxiety disorders are also described as a concern for this population and can be comorbid with depression (Royal College of Psychiatrists 2011).

Depression in tertiary students receives a good deal of interest, as is evident from the reportedly high prevalence rates. Such larger numbers have prompted questions of how depression is defined, and the ways in which it has become essentialized, with certain human experiences such as sadness becoming disordered (Horwitz and Wakefield 2007). A shift toward an association between depression and dangerousness raises newfound concerns about these issues. What is particularly problematic about this interest is the way it has become bound up with predictions and forensic explanations of the troubled student who commits acts of violence. These explanations are treated as straightforward facts, yet the connections made either predictively or retrospectively between depression and violence are a relatively new phenomenon. Melancholia, for instance, which is largely depicted as a historical precursor to depression, did not include acts of violence to others. Indeed, this mental problem, as well as previous iterations of depression, was far from 'active' or involving outwardly violent acts toward others. Current depictions of depression render it 'potent', while, in the main, a hallmark of depression was, arguably, its impotency.

Foucault's (2006: 277) emphasis on the 'structure of perception' enables the pursuit of a line of reasoning that takes as its object how depression and melancholia are perceived. While there is contention regarding the proposition that melancholy is the historical antecedent of depression, there is good justification for considering the cultural understanding attributed to the emblematic features of melancholy and depression. To consider these concepts together is not to stake a claim as to the continuity of melancholy or depression. The suggestion of a relationship between the concepts of melancholy and depression is rigorously analysed by Jennifer Radden (2003), who differentiates between the two on the basis of descriptive versus causal accounts, concluding that they are distinct. This view explicitly questions the attribution of melancholia as an historical precursor to contemporary depression.

### The impotency of melancholia and depression

For a very long time the image of physical lack has been pervasive as a signature of melancholy and, arguably, depression. This image is famously portrayed in Albrecht Dürer's engraving, *Melancholia I* (see Figure 7.1).

*Figure 7.1 Melancholia I* by Albrecht Dürer (1514)

© The Trustees of the British Museum

In *Melancholia I* the central figure sits limp and forlorn, lacking energy or motivation, and unable to move. In this woodcut engraving Dürer famously depicted the tension between 'melancholy, creativity, knowledge' (Sullivan 2008). Strewn aside, the tools and implements surrounding the figure of melancholia tell of the vanished creativity, and the star on the horizon is suggestive of the role of divine inspiration. Drawing on Hippocrates' humoral theory, Dürer's engraving portrays immobility; the figure's potency lost from within. This is an image that echoes across the interpretations of melancholy. Analysing a period that repeats the rational truth of melancholy's immobility, Foucault's *History of Madness* contributes instructive observations on melancholy. Based on his researches into seventeenth-century medicine, Foucault announces that 'melancholy never attains frenzy; it is a madness always at the limits of its own impotence' (2006: 266). This statement signals what has been a long-held assumption of melancholy and depression: both are 'limited by their own impotence'.

Coined in the mid-nineteenth century, and replacing melancholy, the term depression came from usage that was 'popular in middle nineteenth century cardiovascular medicine to refer to a reduction in function' (Berrios 1995: 386). Under this name, depression was characterized as 'reflected loss, inhibition, reduction, and decline' (Berrios 1995: 386). In *The Dictionary of Philosophy and Psychology* (Baldwin 1901) Joseph Jastrow defined depression as '[a] condition characterized by a sinking of spirits, lack of courage or initiative, and tendency to gloomy thoughts' (Jastrow 1901: 270). Here the word 'sinking' conjures the distinct image of deflation. The sense of impotence is brought to the fore when Jastrow distinguishes depression from dejection: 'depression refers more definitely to the lowered vitality of physical and mental life, dejection to the despondency of the mental mood' (Jastrow 1901: 270). In the *Anatomy of Melancholy*, first published in 1621, Robert Burton, who by his own admission busied himself writing his book as a means to avoid melancholy, describes the affliction as either 'disposition or habit' (Burton 2004: 83). Disposition refers to a

> Transitory melancholy which goes and comes upon every small occasion of sorrow, need, sickness, trouble, fear, grief, passion, or perturbation of the mind, any manner of care, discontent, or thought, which causeth anguish, dullness, heaviness and vexation of spirit.
>
> (Burton 2004: 218)

It is marked by its opposition to specific emotions, including feelings such as 'pleasure, mirth, joy, delight', and can cause 'frowardness in us, or a dislike' (Burton 2004: 219).[2] To describe melancholy of habit, Burton says, 'we call him melancholy that is dull, sad, sour, lumpish, ill disposed, solitary, any way moved, or displeased' (Burton 2004: 219). *The Anatomy of Melancholy*, encyclopaedic in its references across literature, mentions violence, but it is overwhelmingly violence directed upon the self. Instances of violence toward others are few; the picture of melancholy is one of impotence.

The idea that melancholy cannot attain the vigour possible in other ailments is clearly demonstrated in Foucault's recounting of the descriptions provided by the seventeenth-century anatomist and physician Thomas Willis (1672, 1683). Foucault describes Willis's account of melancholy, in which

> the spirits are carried away by an agitation, but a weak agitation that lacks power or violence, a sort of impotent upset that follows neither a particular path nor the *aperta opercula* [open ways] but traverses the cerebral matter constantly creating new pores.
>
> (Foucault 2006: 266, original emphasis)

The description draws a picture of movement without direction but with a telos of dissipation. In this movement, 'the spirits do not wander far on the new paths they create, and their agitation dies down rapidly, as their strength is quickly spent and motion comes to a halt' (Foucault 2006: 266). This 'melancholic experience' extends from the physiological to the soul, a view that prompts Jeremy Schmidt (2007) to conclude that, for Willis, the mind and the body are both involved in the melancholic condition. The melancholy described by Willis is one of diminishing strength, reduction in agitation. It is, again, one of impotence.

Essential to grasp in Foucault's account of Willis's analyses is not what we would now view as an extraordinary theory of causes (extraordinary certainly by twenty-first century medicine). What is necessary to contemplate is the emphasis on the conceptualization of experience. Thus in Foucault's words, for Willis the physician,

> the guiding principle mostly reflects the immediate qualities of melancholic illness: an impotent disorder, and the shadow that comes over the spirit with an acrid acidity that slowly corrodes the heart and the mind.
>
> (Foucault 2006: 267)

This comment is followed by a tremendously insightful observation: 'The chemistry of acids is not an explanation of the symptoms, but a qualitative option: a whole phenomenology of melancholic experience' (Foucault 2006: 267). What Foucault is directing our attention toward is the description of how the experience of melancholia is conceptualized. In this sense it is not the elaborate experiences that we need to dwell upon, but rather the efforts that are made to conceptualize these; an emphasis that draws our attention toward the processes of making these truths. Returning to our discussion of Arendt's distinction between rational and factual truths, Foucault's analysis assists with recognizing the processes that produce rational truths. This serves to upset the stability of concepts that, from an Arendtian point of view, might be at risk of being termed facts.

Surveying medical accounts of the eighteenth century from the work of English physician Robert James (1743) and Paris physician Anne-Charles Lorry

(1765), Foucault (2006) points out that while certain explanations vary and symptoms shift, there is a conceptual unity that writes the story of melancholy. What we have is an organizational apparatus that assembles symptoms, one that crafts explanations and faithfully portrays the idea of melancholy. This is, as outlined in the introduction to this chapter, a 'process' whereby an 'organizing force made possible a structure of perception where symptoms could finally take on their significant value, and be organized into the visible presence of the truth' (Foucault 2006: 277). The image of melancholy as impotent pervades, one of immobility, reduction and loss of power.

This particular structuring of perception that has held sway for so long is the very antithesis of the depression that has come to be associated with contemporary depictions of the troubled student. Foucault made the observation on melancholy's impotence with reference to the seventeenth century. While it is not the case that melancholy became, as it were, what was defined as depression in the later versions of the American Psychiatric Association's *Diagnostic and Statistical Manual of Mental Disorders* (*DSM III*, *DSM-III-R*, *DSM-IV*, *DSM-IV-TR*, *DSM-5*) (American Psychiatric Association 1980, 1987, 1994, 2000, 2013a), this characteristic of impotence is a point to labour upon. The kinship of melancholy and depression might be more usefully portrayed as their similar reliance on the idea of impotence. The two also share the status of being rational truths. They are truths that belong very much in the domain of speculation, of philosophical reflection, and of scientific deliberation.

### Depression, impotency and the DSM

In contemporary psychiatric knowledge depression is most authoritatively defined in the American Psychiatric Association's *DSM*, with *DSM-IV* including depression in the section on 'Mood Disorders' under the category 'Depressive disorders', which includes 'major depressive disorder', 'dysthymic disorder' and 'depressive disorder not otherwise specified' (American Psychiatric Association 2000). 'Major depressive episode' is the category with which the colloquial term 'depression' is most commonly associated. As enumerated in the *DSM*, for a major depressive episode to be diagnosed,

> Five (or more) of the following symptoms have been present during the same 2-week period and represent a change from previous functioning; at least one of the symptoms is either (1) depressed mood or (2) loss of interest or pleasure.
>
> (American Psychiatric Association 2000: 356)

Although the description for major depressive episode appears to place emphasis on an emblematic impotence, criteria for the specifier[3] 'psychotic features' includes either delusions or hallucinations (American Psychiatric Association 2000), and these may point toward violence to others. The specifier is differentiated into either 'mood-congruent psychotic features' or 'mood-incongruent psychotic features', with the latter defined as 'content [that] does not involve typical depressive themes of personal inadequacy, guilt disease, death, nihilism, or deserved punishment' but that does include 'persecutory delusions, thought insertion, thought broadcasting, and delusions of control' (American Psychiatric Association 2000: 413). Inclusion of persecutory delusions does render the possibility that, within a diagnosis of major depressive episode, there is scope for potency.[4] That said, this has been a less emphasized characteristic of depression. What remains to be seen is whether, if depression is linked more and more to dangerousness, this conceptualization comes to the fore.

A further point to note is that the *DSM* description of major depressive disorder departs in relation to children and adolescents. In 'prepubertal children', for example, 'Major Depressive Episodes occur more frequently in conjunction with other mental disorders (especially Disruptive Behavior Disorders, Attention-Deficit Disorders, and Anxiety Disorders) than in isolation' (American Psychiatric Association 2000: 354). In adolescents, the association between depression and other disorders is expanded to include the group of disruptive behaviour disorders as well as 'Anxiety Disorders, Substance-Related Disorders, and Eating Disorders' (American Psychiatric Association 2000: 354). Although it would appear that this link between depression and disruptive behaviour disorders signals potency, this would be a mistaken interpretation. While this is an association with what are considered potent disorders, it is not a definitional change in depression per se. This is a subtle yet essential distinction.

The lexicon of depression as it is defined in the *DSM* adheres to a tradition of generating knowledge as described by Foucault (2006). It is a 'structure of perception' (Foucault 2006: 277), discernible via the imagery of impotence. What perhaps earmarks depression as appearing as though it has a 'continuous history' (Foucault 1977), and thereby appearing as fact, is the association with recurring depictions of impotency. The heightened attention to depression/dangerousness shifts the imagery from that of impotency to that of potency.

## Modes of practice

The responses to the mass shootings at Virginia Tech have been influential across the United States (Fox 2009), so much so these can be taken as a turning point in the changing conceptualization of the troubled student. Numbers of threat assessment teams have risen to the point that Kaaryn Sanon, 'spokeswoman for the US National Association of Student Personnel Administrators' (Rushmann 2008), stated: 'You can't really go to a campus in this country post-Virginia Tech and not see a threat-assessment group' (Rushman 2008). In tandem with this impetus for threat assessment procedures there has been a concerted drive to manage troubled students.[5] The report *Mass Shootings at Virginia Tech* presses this point, stating that the shootings have forced all concerned organizations and individuals to reevaluate the best approach for handling troubled students . . . armed with accurate guidance, amended laws, and a new sense of direction, it is an ideal time to establish best practices for intervening in the life of troubled students.

(Virginia Tech Review Panel 2007: 70)

The growing numbers of threat assessment teams reveals the extent to which connecting the dots, a phrase that evocatively depicts the process for, and mandate for, detecting the troubled student, has reached into the fabric of higher educational institutions.

Higher education institutions contain several key means via which modes of practice can be directed at the tertiary student. That said, there is also a network of specialist services connected to these educational institutions that directly influence tertiary students via mechanisms such as mental health reporting. The effects of this network and how these influence higher education institutions becomes quickly transparent when we consider the development of modes of practice directed at the threat of the troubled tertiary student.

### Potency as a mode of practice

In the comic strip shown in Figure 7.2 Cho (the university student responsible for the Virginia Tech Massacre) is depicted in a psychiatric evaluation. The comic strip moves in a sequence from the psychiatrist's office to pills spilling from a bottle, and lastly to several live bullets in a pattern reminiscent of the pills. *Cho Seung Hui Comics 3* was originally published on 28 April 2007 on the website 'DeviantArt' (2009) by Carlos Latuff, and is available on The April 16 Archive, an online archive that 'collects and preserves the stories of the Virginia Tech tragedy' (CDDC and CHNM 2008).[6] While *Cho Seung Hui Comics 3* is one example of popular depictions of the coalescing of mental disorders, troubled students and violence, it is germane to this analysis as it provocatively underscores how the devices of psychiatric intervention, violence

*Figure 7.2 Cho Seung Hui Comics 3 by Carlos Latuff (2007)*

Permission to reproduce image granted by artist

and depression are brought together. It also represents the very real connection that can occur (and many maintain needs to be increased) between tertiary education institutions and mental health and allied services. Consequently it is appropriate to attend to the impacts and influences of popular culture in the production of discourses about psychopathologization (Harwood 2010a).

*Cho Seung Hui Comics 3* was commented on by 'OptikalIlluzion' on 7 May 2007, who wrote, 'The transformation of the pills into bullets was a brilliant statement. Wonderful work as always, Latuff' (deviantart 2009). Another comment by 'Catoninetails' commends Latuff 2's depiction of Cho:

> I had a class with Cho in my Sophomore year. You did a real good job of capturing his lack of expression and emotion. He looked like that every day.
>
> (deviantart 2009)

While the depiction of Cho as commented on by Catoninetails may have certain resemblance to Dürer's (1514) depiction of Melancholia, there is a startling difference. Although both may have their heads lowered, Cho is depicted in the first of three frames in a psychiatrist's office, which is then followed by the corollary of pills with bullets. This linking of pills with bullets evokes the debate concerning the relationship between selective serotonin uptake inhibitors (SSRIs) and violence, an issue discussed by Henry and Demotes-Mainard (2006). Dürer's Melancholia is a stark contrast to the depiction of Cho with pills and bullets. Melancholia is surrounded by the tools of creativity; forlorn yet appearing to await her creative inspiration. The depiction of Cho as depressed and violent is illustrative of the potency of depression that became familiar following the Virginia Tech mass shootings.

### Connecting the dots as a mode of practice

Detection is a key mode of practice associated with the higher education responses to depression being perceived as a harbinger of the potentially threatening troubled student. This drive to detect has been described as 'connecting dots'. The lack of this being accomplished has been held as an explanation for the failure to detect troubled students such as Cho. It has also been used (and continues to be) as a modus operandi for detecting threats and is thereby claimed to be preventing the violence enacted by students.

With the rise in shootings in higher education institutions there has been speculation that perpetrators of this form of violence 'have far more depth to their histories of mental illness' and that

> comparing the college cases post-2002 to the majority of the high school cases, we see that their more advanced age means they are much further along in the trajectory of developing serious psychiatric conditions.
>
> (Newman and Fox 2009: 1304)

This may well help to explain the increase in the reporting of psychiatric diagnosis, the subsequent attention to the range of disorders, and the pressing need to be vigilant and 'connect the dots' to detect troubled students. However, without a critical gaze such attention risks treating this phenomenon as a factual truth (Arendt 1968b). If it is positioned as factual, we are at risk of missing the crucial knowledge that these understandings are arrived at via speculation, that they are rational truths. Treating these as facts makes it difficult to discern how the 'structure of perception' (Foucault 2006) is implicated in the assembling of changing forms of knowledge. For this reason it is paramount to be, as Arendt (1968b) implores, cautious in our acceptance of facts, and, as is the case here, cautious of facts that would have us obey directives to connect the dots.

The report *Mass Shootings at Virginia Tech* has been central in prompting responses to prevent campus violence (Dunkle *et al.* 2008), responses that provoke questions as to the responsibility or 'duty' of higher education institutions for 'connecting the dots' (Williamson 2008). The idea, indeed the force of the mandate to 'connect the dots' relies on acceptance of the 'dots' as facts. This relationship is demonstrated in the following excerpt, which clearly situates them as facts and, as a consequence, states the need for action based on these facts. Reflecting on the use of the 'connecting the dots' approach, Gordon K. Davies, a member of the Virginia Tech Review Panel that produced the report, *Mass Shootings at Virginia Tech*, elaborated:

> One of the metaphors that recurred during the panel's discussions and in public testimony was that 'no one connected all the dots.' It is true that there were dots all over the map, but the way Virginia Tech is organized virtually ensured that no one ever was in a position to see them all and intervene in a potentially dangerous situation that eventually spiralled into disaster.
>
> (Davies 2008, n.p.)

'Connecting the dots' occurs prominently in *Mass Shootings at Virginia Tech*, and is mentioned in the 'Summary of the Key Findings' situated at the front of this extensive document. In discussing the 'numerous incidents' that 'were clear warnings of mental instability' the document draws a compelling conclusion: 'Although various individuals and departments within the university knew about each of these incidents, the university did not intervene effectively. No one knew all the information and no one connected all the dots' (Virginia Tech Review Panel 2007: 2). In other sections of *Mass Shootings at Virginia Tech* the dots are seen as 'red flags'. Chapter Four, entitled 'Cho's Mental Health History', includes commentary on the services involved with Cho. The document states that the Care Team at Virginia Tech 'was established as a means of identifying and working with students who have problems. That resource, however, was ineffective in connecting the dots or heeding the red flags that were so apparent with Cho' (Virginia Tech Review Panel 2007: 52). Failure is attributed to not connecting the dots; and to the problem of missing the red flags that, taken together, signify the troubled (depressed and dangerous) student.

The credible exercise of this metaphor implies two premises: first that the dots are facts, and second, that these facts can and must be drawn together in order to detect the troubled student. In relation to the first, situating depression alongside violence as a 'fact' (or, as it were, as one of the 'dots') renders depression potent. In the recommendations issued to Virginian higher education institutions, mental health assessment includes both assessment for, and treatment of, depression (Connell 2009). Depression is included in the list of problems along with 'psychotic symptoms', 'jealousy or mistreatment' and 'personality disorder' and included in reference to the 'prevention of interpersonal violence' (Connell 2009: 28). Locating depression in this list of problems instils potency in depression, linking depression with the potential for serious violence. Added to this, when a relationship between depression and violence is treated as a factual truth (as opposed to a rational one) we have set before us a 'fact'. Presented in this way we are not encouraged to question, but rather to comply, and to take responsibility for connecting the dots. This responsibility places the onus on educational institutions, one that gives rise to the imprimatur: do what is required to accomplish the collection and aggregation of the 'factual' dots.

## Threat assessment

Emphasis on connecting the dots has led to threat assessment in higher education being enshrined in legislation in the State of Virginia. Recommendations for implementation of this requirement place emphasis on 'threat assessment as violence prevention', where '[t]hreat assessment is a strategy for preventing violence through identification and evaluation of individuals or groups that pose a threat to harm someone, followed by intervention designed to reduce the risk of violence' (Connell 2009: 4). The document also distinguishes between threat assessment and criminal profiling. While the latter focuses on perpetrators, the former 'explicitly recognizes the diversity of individuals who may engage in a violent act and focuses on behavioral indications of preparation to carry out a violent act' (Connell 2009: 4).

Moves to connect the dots to prevent potential campus violence have been made beyond the State of Virginia, with institutions across the United States prompted to establish threat assessment teams (using this or a similar name) (Dunkle et al. 2008).[7] This spread is discussed in an article in the UK publication Times Higher Education titled 'Watching the disaffected' (Marcus 2008), which reports on threat assessment at Cornell University. The article quotes Kaaryn Sanon, a representative from a US higher education association, who states:'Many of these were in place prior to the more recent violent tragedies on various campuses, but they have been formalized and put in place almost everywhere that lacked such a system' (Marcus 2008).[8] The article also cites the director of counselling and psychological services at Cornell, who explains an important distinction: 'There aren't really profiles [of students prone to violence or suicide], but there are characteristics you can look at: depression, suspiciousness, grandiosity, social isolation' (Marcus 2008). Treated here as facts, these characteristics are taken as testimony to the factual truth of the relationship between depression and violence. This has the considerable effect of concealing their speculative nature and status as rational truths.

There are many cases of the new threat assessment team initiatives, and critical research is yet to be undertaken into this phenomenon. It is instructive to consider some examples of how threat assessment, depression, and the troubled student are discussed. For instance, Emory University in Atlanta, Georgia established a threat assessment team. Reporting on this initiative in the *Emory Report*, Amy Adelman, a member of the Threat Assessment Team (TAT), is cited explaining:

> Students lead diffuse lives, making it easier to miss a pattern of behavior that could indicate they are in crisis . . . A faculty member may see just one piece of the puzzle, while a roommate and a friend may see other pieces. The TAT is a way to bring the pieces together.
>
> (C. Clark 2008: 1)

At the University of Iowa, the Threat Assessment Team 'has two full-time threat assessment specialists' and 'signs of depression/severe mood swings' are included under the list of 'warning signs' in the section 'behavioural/physical clues' (HRWebTeam 2009). In 'Keeping our Campus Safe', a document provided by Rutgers Newark, the need for threat assessment explicitly references the Virginia Tech mass shootings. The document commences with the statement that 'the 2007 tragedy at Virginia Tech reminds all in higher education of the vulnerability of our college campuses' (Office of Student and Community Affairs 2008–9).

Members of the Rutgers Newark campus can refer a threat to the Threat Assessment Team by using a referral form that is available online. This form uses a list of 31 tick-box items divided into Section 1, 'Imminent Warning Signs' and Section 2, 'Troubling Behaviour'. Depression is item 29 in the second category. In this inventory, other items immediately precede depression. Numbers 21 to 29 are included below:

1    Inappropriate access, possession, use of firearms
2    Threats of violence (direct or indirect)
3    Talking about weapons or bombs
4    Ruminating over perceived injustices
5    Seeing self as victim of a particular individual
6    General statements of distorted, bizarre thoughts
7    Feelings of being persecuted
8    Obsession with particular person
9    Depression

(Rutgers Newark 2009)

Scrolling down this list of items it becomes apparent how the placement of depression alongside these other items can be generative for structuring our perceptions of the troubled student as both violent and depressed. The presentation of this material, together with the spread of threat assessment teams, points to the possibility of significant changes to how depression is understood as linked to violence. For instance, with threat assessment teams promoted as part of the normal structure of the university, the troubled student is increasingly described using terms that bring forth depression into a common parlance with violence prevention.

Measures to connect the dots include mandating which files are to be kept, lists of the behaviours to be on the alert for, people charged with administration of the threat assessment, and the induction and training of higher education staff for vigilance for troubled students. Staff members at US higher education institutions are obliged to keep on the lookout for the 'signs of trouble', where vigilance garners support precisely because it is seen to be in accord with the urgency to connect the dots. For instance, '[m]ore professors and others on campus are consulting with counseling centers about "students of concern" since Virginia Tech, according to 66% of center directors in a new survey of 272 colleges' (Elias 2008).

### Information sharing

In the State of Virginia the recent legislation has made it easier to share information between health, school and higher education authorities and has instigated measures that make it mandatory to report student mental health problems to parents (Kaine 2008). This effort to 'share information' creates new opportunities to track down young individuals in secondary school who are believed to have the potential to become troubled tertiary students. As stated above, this fundamentally shifts the concept of potentiality very far from that described in Chapter 4. Very young children have the potential by virtue of their age to be rendered 'clear' of mental problems. Mental disorder could be prevented for this cohort. By contrast, the individual who is pre-tertiary education (or early tertiary education), who is identified as potentially troubled (or troubled), will, by virtue of his or her history, always be so. These older students simply need to exhibit the requisite red flags and the dots get connected.

The need to connect the dots in this way led to amendments being made to FERPA, the Family Educational Rights and Privacy Act. These came into effect on 8 January 2009 and effectively provide for the sharing of information between education institutions.[9] Mental health records, with their detailed histories, are viewed as potentially revealing and therefore accessing them becomes wrapped in the momentum to initiate preventative action (Newman and Fox 2009). Access to such documents raises issues about student privacy and the vexed question of how much information about students' personal histories should be made available to institutions, within institutions, between institutions, and to parents.

Furthermore, such incursions into privacy are premised on the problematic of the degree of success of threat assessment, with threat assessment likely to yield far more false positives than true positives (Heilbrun *et al.* 2009; Fox 2009). This means that many students who are not violent are likely to experience intrusion on the premise of threat assessment. Such investigations may well have the effect of promoting and defining conceptualizations of dangerousness, which could, depending on how this is received, move in one of two possible directions. It could, for example, reinforce the attribution of dangerousness to depression, thereby influencing depictions of the troubled student. Conversely, the number of false positives could create a phenomenon of 'crying wolf', and lead to distrust in the processes that are designed to improve faith in campus safety. In either case, by linking depression and violence there remains the serious question of stigmatizing the human experience of depression in directions that link it to the spectre of extreme dangerousness.

## Desired consequences

Undeniably, the desired consequence of connecting the dots and establishing threat assessment protocols is to decrease risk and avoid tragic circumstances of student violence. The problem is that this effort and these modes of practice have served to connect a once impotent mental problem to one with substantial potency. Watching for the signs of the troubled student therefore becomes part of a mechanism of connecting the dots that, while it is directed at the laudable undertaking to prevent violence, at the same time gathers depression into a net that situates it in a relationship to violence.

What is especially problematic is the ways the new truths of depression are treated as fact. In her discussion of factual and rational truths, Arendt maintained that 'factual truth is so much less open to argument than philosophical [rational] truth' (1968b: 237). She also points to the vulnerability of these truths. When assumed to be factual, the only mode of opposition is 'neither error nor illusion nor opinion . . . but the deliberate falsehood or lie' (Arendt 1968b: 249). This effectively creates a non–refutable explanation of the trajectories and histories of mental illness as well as the duty to connect the dots. It also positions the opposition of factual truth in tricky terrain since challenging the new configurations of the troubled student will mean denying supposed facts. To question burgeoning practices such as surveillance, identification and reporting can imply betrayal of collective efforts in higher education to protect. The rationale that dots can *and must* be connected, together with reliance on these dots being 'facts', places the entire process above critique.

Factual truths are crucial for Arendt's conception of the political realm (1968b). We rely on facts to form our opinions, and in Arendt's vision, opinion is crucial for political dialogue – which is of ongoing importance for inclusive practices in education (Harwood 2010a, 2010b). From these factual truths we form opinions and can engage in debate. By drawing on Foucault, we can also inform our discussions with the knowledge of processes that formulate rational truths. That many people were killed at Virginia Tech is not in dispute; neither is the fact that it was committed by Cho. When we begin to interpret and explain, this is where we enter the realm of rational truths.

Alarmingly, when these truths are confused we run the risk of initiating actions that are bereft of the benefit of debate. Linda Zerilli (2006) mounts a persuasive case for reconsidering Arendt's analyses of truth, politics and opinion. For Zerilli, the point is not to 'be delivered of one's opinions, as if opinion were the opposite of truth . . . Rather it is to find, by means of public debate, what in one's opinions is true' (2006, para. 17). Given that opinion is vital to the political and factual truth is crucial for opinions, the implications of 'wrong facts' are considerable. Obfuscation of rational truths is thus a threat to the open dialogue required in order to develop responses to the problems of violence on campuses. To give an example, if debate over the troubled university student is premised on the assumption of factual truth, the very point that it is taken as fact will mean that the processes contributing to the making of the truth go unchallenged. This will make it all the more difficult to foster robust debate of the new practices of threat assessment in higher education institutions.

Drawing attention to the way these truths about the troubled student have been construed is, therefore, crucial to the effort to introduce balanced debate on the measures to prevent campus violence. In the event that an individual who has acted violently meets the diagnostic criteria for a major depressive episode, the need for balanced debate is not mitigated. While it may be the case that an individual can fit the *DSM* criteria, this does not provide a warrant to represent this as factual truth: we would be better positioned to treat it as a rational truth. This would involve paying close attention to how this truth is produced, the speculation that is involved and how our conceptualizations are drawn. For this reason, identifying the shift from impotency to potency demonstrates how the structuring of perception in turn structures depression, and this, importantly, clarifies that these are rational truths. Foucault's remark that the 'image fulfilled the initial role of synthesis' (2006: 277) tells us a great deal about how images of the troubled student affect what we have come to understand and how we now focus attention on threat assessment. It also gives pause to reconsider what Dodge calls the 'metaphors for youth violence' (2008: 573) and how these get taken up and drive interpretations of violent youth behaviour.

There are numerous consequences of the configuration of the troubled student in higher education as depressed and dangerous. This includes issues such as the lowering of privacy measures and the zealousness, regardless of good motivation, with which preventative measures are being taken up. For one, now that depression is considered one of the 'red flags' for the troubled student, we are forced to confront the paradox that the troubled student is inexorably like the rest of us, or like the young people around us. With depression listed amongst the signs that may warn of trouble or disturbance in higher education institutions across the United States, it now has the status of dangerousness. The sheer numbers of people diagnosed with depression, or the numbers of people prescribed antidepressant medication attests – if we are to take this seriously – to the scale of the numbers of people among us who are now harbouring potency (as opposed to impotence).

Returning to the urge to 'connect the dots', what indubitably drives much of this activity is the need for explanations of events. This brings to mind an observation made by Arendt, that

> the conviction that everything that happens on earth must be comprehensible to man can lead to interpreting history by commonplaces.
>
> (Arendt 1968a: viii)

This thought-provoking statement encourages us to consider an uncomfortable reality in the ready application of diagnostic categories such as depression to these types of problems of social consequence. Diagnosis may well be motivated by the understandable desire to render the world comprehensible. To think otherwise, to find what occurred incomprehensible, is unacceptable. To remain inexplicable in an age of diagnosis requires us to remain undiagnosed, and an outcome of non-diagnosis would be to remain without cure. This raises a fundamental question: is it this that is so uncomfortable and what propels forward a preparedness to ascribe to depression such a worrisome association? Perhaps the practice of mental health diagnosis is the vehicle via which comprehensibility can be wrought. And this is why depression has so effortlessly become potent.

To respond to Arendt's (1981) view of the necessity to be thinking, judging people, people who are engaged with the political, there is a genuine need to take careful account of the emerging concept of the troubled student in higher education. Recognition that what lies beneath these apparent facts are rational truths could open up the occasion for dialogue. It may well allow us to see the precariousness of the dots we are connecting as well as the folly of believing, too naively, that we will prevent disaster if we simply connect them.

## Notes

1 The report of the Virginia Tech Review Panel (2007), *The Mass Shootings at Virginia Tech*, provides a list of 42 fatal shootings in the United States, dating from 1966 to 2007. The majority of these events occurred at schools. The Columbine Massacre occurred on 20 April 1999: 'Students Eric Harris, 18, and Dylan Klebold, 17, killed 12 students and a teacher and wounded 23 others at Columbine High School. They had plotted for a year to kill at least 500 and blow up their school. At the end of their hour-long rampage, they turned the guns on themselves (Virginia Tech Review Panel 2007).

2 In the *Oxford English Dictionary* 'frowardness' is stated as having origins in Old English, meaning 'leading away from' (Soanes and Stevenson 2013).

3 In the *DSM* 'specifiers' are used to provide further detail for a diagnostic category, especially to designate subtypes of disorders.

4 The relationship between mental illness and violence is contentious. For analysis of the relationship, see Friedman (2006), and for critical analysis of discrimination and depression in US college settings, see Wolnick (2007).

5 Until the Virginia Tech mass shootings and the shootings at Northern Illinois University, this sector had not been faced with security threats of this nature.

6 The purpose of the website is stated as follows: 'The April 16 Archive uses electronic media to collect, preserve, and present the stories and digital record of the Virginia Tech tragedy of April 16, 2007' (CDDC and CHNM 2008).

7 Other names for threat assessment teams include: BART (Behavioral Assessment and Recommendation Team), Columbus State University; and BAIT (Behavior Assessment and Intervention Team), University of Dallas at Texas.

8 Sanon is 'a spokeswoman for the National Association of Student Personnel Administrators (NASPA), which represents university administrators in charge of student affairs' (Marcus 2008).

9 See Chapman (2009) for legal analysis of FERPA provisions.

# Chapter 8

# Professionals' interruptions

## Introduction

We have attempted to reveal the varied and varying dynamics, at different stages of schooling, which give rise to the pathologizing and medicalization of children's and young people's behaviour. As we have argued, various 'risk factors', including disadvantage and poverty as well as other markers of identity such as 'race', disability and gender, become intertwined in interpretations of children's behaviours – to the extent that diagnosis becomes inevitable. The period from the cradle to the crèche appears to be the most optimistic in respect of effecting some kind of rescue of the child from the grip of mental illness. This sanguine view continues through the primary stages of education, with substantial investments in interventions that assure a special – exalted – status for the 'behaviour-disordered' child within education. By the time the child has reached secondary age and has entered 'adolescence', however, hope has dwindled and efforts are shifted onto strategies of containment and ensuring that the needs and interests of other students, and the population as a whole, are protected from these troubling and troublesome individuals. Finally, within tertiary education, concern can be directed towards students who experience depression, less for its impact on their educational performance than for any associated threat that might result from individual students. The intensification of fear, and associated protocols for managing the 'student as threat', through a coupling of depression and violence (at least potentially), is a relatively recent phenomenon.

While, as we note in Chapter 1, there is debate regarding the attribution of diagnoses or behavioural interventions as medicalization, there are also ways in which disadvantage and poverty become intertwined in interpretations of children's behaviours – to the extent that contexts are exceeded by the attention to diagnosis. This, we suggest, creates striated spaces (Deleuze and Guattari 1987) that structure processes of understanding, especially in education and related services. However, such striated spaces may be challenged by what Deleuze and Guattari (1987) refer to as deterritorialization, a process of smoothing out of spaces and breaking existing codes and patterns. In this chapter we report on our analysis of practices undertaken by the professionals that we interviewed in Scotland. We have discussed some of their comments in earlier chapters. Here we focus on their reported practices, which differed from the approaches described by the professionals we interviewed in our work on medicalization and disadvantage in Australia, the United States and England. Although the Scottish study was developed to build on this project work we found something quite different: these professionals used practices that we term *medicus interruptus*. These practices interrupted, by braking and reversing, the flows towards a medically dominated interpretation of behaviour. The interruptions generated nuanced contextual interpretations of children's lives and their behaviours in schools and created opportunities for professionals to move in different ways. As we outlined in Chapter 1, our interviews with the professionals in Scotland comprised an exploratory study based in one of the areas in Scotland that is representative of lower rates of diagnosis of ADHD. An investigation of ADHD services over Scotland (National Health Service 2007) found an under-diagnosis of ADHD. This report found the Scottish rate of 0.6 per cent (4,539 children) to be well below accepted international prevalence rates of 1.5 per cent for the severe form hyper-kinetic disorder (HKD) and 5 per cent for ADHD (National Health Service 2007). Epidemiological rates for Scottish children are thus estimated to be 11,500 (HKD) and 38,000 (ADHD), indicating that very high numbers of Scottish children are under-diagnosed.

We begin by discussing how we use the work of Deleuze and Guattari to theorize the ways in which the medicalization of behaviour operated in striated spaces, and the professionals' interruptions of these striations and flows. We then present our analysis of *medicus interruptus* in terms of the linguistic, visual and affective strategies that were described by our interview respondents. These strategies were instrumental in undermining assumptions about a medical diagnosis of behaviour and provide one basis for our optimistic call, in the final chapter, for a privileging of pedagogy over pathology.

## From territorialization to deterritorialization: professionals' practices

Deleuze and Guattari (1987) depict organizational spaces as highly striated, with rigid lines of communication, authority and control. This appears helpful in understanding how the medicalization of behaviour arises and becomes irresistible (Allan 2008) within tightly defined and confined spaces, and with clear divisions, for example, between professional and client or between teacher and taught, and clear processes for diagnosing children's behavioural problems. In turn, as we have suggested, the intersections of disadvantage, poverty, 'race', disability and gender create a disposition towards seeing particular behaviours as pathological and warranting diagnosis and treatment. This establishes a territorializing effect, whereby positions of authority, routes of referral and pathways to diagnosis are rendered certain, but at the same time, as De Landa notes, '*lead to information explosions* which increase the overall amount of uncertainty' (1991: 66, original emphasis).

The professionals we interviewed recognized the striated spaces in which the behaviour of children in disadvantaged contexts was problematized and medicalized but they also revealed strategies for interrupting the lines of referral through which a medicalized diagnosis of behaviour was expected. They articulated ways in which they challenged, diverted and refused medicalized interpretations of children's behaviour and encouraged alternative understandings and practices in ways that could be read as acts of deterritorialization (Deleuze and Guattari 1987). The purpose of deterritorialization is to undo the 'processes of continuous control and instantaneous communication' (D. Smith 1998: 264) and to knock existing understandings and ways of acting into a different orbit or trajectory (Roy 2004). It is a performative breaking of existing codes, which is also a 'making' (Howard 1998: 115). That is, it is an escape from control, but in a positive sense, so that new intensities open up.

> The result is a return to a field of forces, transversing the gaps, puncturing the holes, and opening up the new world order to a quite different and new world of the multiple.
>
> (Howard 1998: 123-4)

Deterritorialization involves a smoothing out of spaces, interrupting the flow along expected lines of communication and creating a necessity for new ways of thinking and acting: 'once one ventures outside what's familiar and reassuring, once one has to invent new concepts for unknown lands, then methods and moral systems break down' (Deleuze 1995: 322). This seemed to be an appropriate depiction of the actions described by the professionals and of the language they used to convey how they halted flows through referrals, questioned the advance towards a medical diagnosis of behaviour and sought to redirect these flows towards other forms of interaction with the child or young person and their family.

Deterritorialization has the potential to attack the rigid, striated – or territorialized – spaces of professional engagement, replacing these with ones that are smooth and full of creative possibilities. Within these newly created spaces, 'life reconstitutes its stakes, confronts new obstacles, invents new paces, switches adversaries' (Deleuze and Guattari 1987: 500). Crucially, deterritorialization takes us from communication – through 'order-words' (Deleuze and Parnet 1987: 22), imperatives for others to act – to expression and it is a highly sophisticated process.

> The prudence required to guide this line, the precautions needed to soften, suspend, divert or undermine it, all point to a long process of labor directed not only against the State but against itself as well.
>
> (Deleuze and Guattari 1983: 95–6)

The interruptions by the professionals, what we are calling '*medicus interruptus*', were directed towards the processes of referral and diagnosis and were themselves sophisticated, involving a refusal of the inevitability of a medical diagnosis.

## Medicus interruptus

The influence of the classed striations and the potential for children and families from poorer backgrounds to become territorialized by classed-medicalization was something the professionals sought to interrupt. Their interruptions took place along three planes: linguistic, visual and affective, each creating opportunities to deterritorialize child behaviour and challenge the classed-medicalized striations that predominated perceptions of child behavioural problems. It is the very physical nature of the changes that were created through the interruptions – in how things were spoken about; how they were seen and what was felt about them; then the possibilities they provided to act differently – that distinguishes *medicus interruptus* from either simply critiquing medicalized naming and practices or engaging in social model analysis.

### Linguistic

> We've got to hijack speech. Creating has always been something different from communicating. The key thing may be to create vacuoles of noncommunication, circuit breakers, so we can elude control.
>
> (Deleuze 1995: 175)

Changing the language of child behaviour and the ways of talking to and about the children and families was a key way in which the professionals deterritorialized the classed-medicalized striations. This presented challenges because often families, children and the professionals who worked with them were experiencing considerable territorialization. While the professionals explained that they would work with people to assist them to recognize their perceptions, what especially stood out was the attention to language. Within one service this approach included ongoing efforts with the specialist education workers who work to support schools and teachers in the local area.

> We're trying to change the language and get people away from what they think is the bad child and helping people to understand that there's a context here, the reason we're getting the behaviour might be this experience or that experience.
>
> (Professional 3, Educational Psychology, MCB Scotland)

This attention to language had the effect of changing teachers' constructions of the behavioural assemblage of children experiencing poverty.

You might sit around the table and somebody would say, 'Oh he's being very aggressive, he's bringing weapons to school'; well actually he must be highly anxious if he's bringing weapons to school. You know, what can we do to stop him feeling quite so anxious? You know, how can we actually make him feel safer?

(Professional 2, Educational Psychology, MCB Scotland)

During these conversations support staff paid attention to words such as 'very aggressive' and would work to deterritorialize child behaviour by using other ways of describing the child. This resulted in

[teaching] staff being able then to actually not just react to the weapon and the aggression but 'right, actually I understand what he's all on about'. So if you know what he's all on about then you know how to change his environment to try and help him become *less* anxious so that he's less likely to be aggressive.

(Professional 2, Educational Psychology,
MCB Scotland, original emphasis)

This shift moved the emphasis from the territorializing language of poverty and medicalized behaviour and onto understanding the effects of trauma and of developmental attachment on children's behaviour. This meant that when 'critical events' occurred, 'rather than just seeing kids as you know behaving with difficulty, actually thinking, well this child's experience may [be a] house fire or you know two members of the family being killed or somebody's committed suicide or something' (Professional 2, Educational Psychology, MCB Scotland). By raising questions about context and trauma, classed-medicalization could be cast in a different light. This occurs in the comment below about classed diagnoses and the misdiagnosis of ADHD.

Perhaps some of the things that are diagnosed, medicated, isn't actually ADHD, it may be more to do with trauma and attachment, like you would see in other [social] classes, you know. I think there's a stigma attached to ADHD, but if you were in a kind of a more affluent area, you wouldn't want your child to have that diagnosis, whereas in other kind of social areas that isn't the case.

(Professional 6, Educational Support, MCB Scotland)

Trauma and misdiagnoses of ADHD were discussed by another professional who commented that 'there are times we're finding if we can actually pinpoint, particularly if it's been a single case trauma, with the young person . . . you can help their behaviour . . . all the symptoms that look like ADHD can . . . disappear' (Professional 2, Educational Psychology, MCB Scotland). This in turn raised questions as to whether it really is a medical diagnosis of ADHD and how 'the behaviours can look and the strategies that you might use might be very similar, but what might be underlying it might be a disordered attachment or trauma' (Professional 2, Educational Psychology, MCB Scotland). Recognizing disordered attachment or trauma enabled professionals to offer support for behaviour and to anticipate further behavioural problems in the future,

> Okay, what do we need to do for him because actually he's going to be difficult for the next while so rather than actually [saying] he's just being difficult [it is] recognizing we maybe need to put something in its place to stop him having behavioural difficulties further down the line. I think again our schools, the majority of them, are pretty on the alert to flag up to us when something happens so that they'll try to be a bit more proactive.
>
> (Professional 3, Educational Psychology, MCB Scotland)

In a sense it could be said that behavioural difficulties were normalized in a way that drew the attention from the behaviour and associated diagnostic striations. This practice supports the opportunity to disrupt the flows that construct 'aggression' in a way that overlooks the fears or anxieties that a child may have.

### Visual

Just as attention to language prompted a focus on how behaviour was named and children were described, attention to the way that the child was seen or viewed prompted understandings that could depart from the classed and medicalized assemblages of behaviour. One site where the emphasis on the visual came to the fore was with the professionals in the specialist mental health service that we interviewed. These individuals described the pressure on their service from the number of referrals and the expectations of psychiatric diagnosis.

> Sometimes we can have referrals of children or parents . . . very affluent people who are looking for reasons for antisocial behaviour that are a disorder [and] therefore explains [the] behaviour but we also have parents with children who are very impoverished and come from impoverished backgrounds emotionally and socio-economically and you know sometimes that disorder label can increase – well, it increases their benefits.
>
> (Professional 10, Child Mental Health, MCB Scotland)

This pursuit of diagnosis by impoverished people, driven by economic need, highlights the problems that can be caused by the medicalization of poverty (Schram 2000).

Professionals saw ways of interrupting the diagnosis sought by families and one of these was to not have a prescription pad, an object that was recognized as contributing to the process of medicalization.

Most people will know that I'm not able to prescribe, so as soon as the prescription pad is available then I think there's this pressure on the clinician to do that and I think because that is their first line of defence as well they're not able to go beyond that.

(Professional 10, Child Mental Health, MCB Scotland)

Expectations of medicalization, prompted by the prescription pad, could be challenged by turning to practices beyond the 'first line of defence', but professionals recognized the powerful striations and pull of the 'quick fix'.

Whereas [with] the psychology you don't have that as an option so you have to fall back on the ways that you have, what you've been trained in . . . You can see the dynamic happen, so I think it's both ways, it's the pressure of their training and also then I think the pressure of the individuals to have something fixed quickly because . . . it's probably quite difficult to live in a house with a child that's that active.

(Professional 10, Child Mental Health, MCB Scotland)

This dynamic could be taken to suggest that having access to the prescription pad means more than participating in a flow; it becomes part of the child behaviour assemblage. Being unable to access the prescription pad opened out other possibilities for the non-prescribing professionals, possibilities that could deterritorialize the child behaviour assemblage.

The encouragement of schools to pursue options other than a medical route interrupted the flow for children from poor backgrounds. For example, a professional commented that when schools with a number of 'youngsters from troubled families' are well supported 'in terms of strategies for dealing with difficult behaviour . . . they may be less likely to go down the medical route' (Professional 1, Educational Psychology, MCB Scotland). Other professionals who worked in a disadvantaged area explained:

We are aware that almost without exception the children who attend our primary and secondary behaviour support services . . . full time are children with significant histories of loss and trauma but they are children who could have diagnoses of, if you wanted to, ADHD, conduct disorder, personality disorder, opposition [oppositional defiant disorder].

(Professional 2, Educational Psychology, MCB Scotland)

Divergence from medicalized flows that may have resulted in diagnoses of psychiatric disorders such as conduct disorder was linked with the growth of knowledge of different ways of viewing the child and behaviour.

As knowledge has grown and people have felt more skilled without having to go to the medical model . . . I think for quite a long time it was felt that the knowledge and expertise about kids' emotional difficulties was invested in the clinical teams and I think that as the knowledge and expertise has grown elsewhere it hasn't felt like there was a need to go except in a few cases.

(Professional 3, Educational Psychology, MCB Scotland)

The consideration of the 'confidence of the teacher' was an important element in seeking to avoid a position of within-child-deficit and this also involved addressing perceived hierarchies of expertise. One professional described what he/she called the 'fried egg model' (Professional 1, Educational Psychology) that aimed to shift emphasis from 'expert' opinion to one that gathered perspectives from the range of people involved with the child:

My argument would be, you get all that information and you bring it back into the team around the child. It may be that [the] team continues to expand, but the kind of key decisions are not then made out here, you know, it's just the extra information gets brought in.

(Professional 1, Educational Psychology, MCB Scotland)

Awareness of the in-school context assisted in deterritorializing child behaviour by accentuating a range of perspectives that de-centred the collecting of knowledge and decision making away from 'out here', that is, in the realm of the specialists exterior to the school.

Another way the focus could be kept from moving 'out here' was to exert influence on the way that general practitioners made referrals to specialist mental health services. There were efforts by education support services to liaise with general practitioners that prompted the following comment: 'GPs will have their own ideas, and it would be interesting . . . to see what that kind of dialogue might look like' (Professional 1, Educational Psychology, MCB Scotland). One of the forays into dialogue with general practitioners was described by this professional in order to emphasize the challenges that could be experienced.

We were explaining that we had funding to work where there was a high level of deprivation and a concomitant high level of loss and trauma and what we intended to be doing about it. One of the GPs actually said, 'Well, what's the point, is that not just the way they are?'

(Professional 2, Educational Psychology, MCB Scotland)

Such descriptions point to how child behaviour is classed-medicalized as well as the difficulties that there can be in working to interrupt this flow.

We were also told how some services saw themselves as capable of acting without the requirement of diagnosis: 'We're very barrier-focussed and support-needs focussed . . . the child's communicating a need so we would prefer not to see it as a behaviour problem' (Professional 4, Educational Support, MCB

Scotland). This option, however, might not be used by all education services, with one possible reason being that some 'mainstream schools perhaps would be quite relieved to have their diagnosis because . . . it almost alleviates the blame that they're not doing the right thing' (Professional 6, Educational Support, MCB Scotland). It could be that the extent to which child behaviour is territorialized renders it difficult for other contexts and explanations to be pursued. In a territorialized landscape the child behaviour assemblage might be seen in a 'bipolar' way where non-diagnosis could come to imply fault. This could suggest that deterritorializing child behaviour is important as it provides a means to open up the possibilities for other contexts – and understandings – to be explored.

## Affective

Respondents reported their experience of fighting a difficult and intensive battle against the flows of judgement and referral, and at the heart of this was being able to distinguish 'between psychiatrically ill and psychological distress . . . all come through the same route' (Professional 10, Child Mental Health, MCB Scotland). The former would require a diagnosis but the latter would more than likely not, yet might be presented with the expectation of an ensuing medical diagnosis. Many of the children or young people presenting with the latter had experienced trauma in the early part of their lives or had difficult family circumstances that had contributed to their behavioural problems. The professionals recognized that values played a large part in making the distinction and indicated that it was more difficult to resist the pressure for diagnosis of behavioural problems in some geographical areas or in particular schools: 'There are no doubt pockets where there is still a very entrenched "this is a bad child"' (Professional 2, Educational Psychology, MCB Scotland). The professionals considered there to be much work to be done in changing the whole way in which children with behavioural problems were regarded and saw this partly as an affective process: 'There's the whole hearts and minds thing and it's about moving people away from the behaviours' (Professional 3, Educational Psychology, MCB Scotland). Respondents emphasized that their educational support service is not 'into the medicalization of behaviour, let's be honest' (Professional 3, Educational Psychology, MCB Scotland). This could be seen in the effort to avoid labels directed to the parents and carers of the children who were referred for behaviour problems. Increased knowledge of other options was a reason given for success in engaging parents and carers in the deterritorialization of child behaviour. In the following quote the professional describes a common diagnostic description for behaviour and then outlines the kinds of responses that the service may typically provide.

> I suppose as well as knowledge [having] increased it's possible to have dialogue
> with for example a carer or a parent who's saying, 'I want my child diagnosed

with ADHD' to actually say, 'Well, there are lots of other things that will make ADHD and you know that's okay, he's showing some of the symptoms that might be called ADHD but it might be this and it might be that and it might be the next thing and the important thing is what we do about it.'

(Professional 2, Educational Psychology, MCB Scotland)

A high value was placed by these professionals on their role in educating the community, and this was seen as one way to move away from the focus on medicalizing behavioural problems. Behaviour as an expression of unmet need was a key philosophy used in the service, with the educational support service working to 'enhance the knowledge of people who are working with children to understand the origins of behaviour . . . to help people see that children's behaviour is an expression of unmet need' (Professional 2, Educational Psychology, MCB Scotland). This stance viewed the behaviour of children who presented as a problem in schools in a way that sought not to medicalize.

I think we are moving towards a position where behavioural needs are treated as an additional support need and are treated, the child is treated for how they should be – as who they are rather than how they're presenting.

(Professional 2, Educational Psychology, MCB Scotland)

Affective interruptions involved considerable tenacity on the part of the professionals and refusals of diagnoses could incur the wrath of parents.

I think because people can obtain disability living allowance for having that diagnosis . . . if we don't diagnose children with it, the families, you know, are not happy with that.

(Professional 5, Child Mental Health, MCB Scotland)

Professionals were open to challenge, especially where there was a possibility that children or young people might have been masking symptoms on the initial assessment, but would ultimately be firm in their resolve where they felt the need to resist a diagnosis and invoked the finality of the drawn line.

Anybody's entitled to ask for a second opinion, and some of them do, occasionally we will revisit something if we think there's a good reason to . . . I suppose we're of a mind that it is or it isn't, then we've discussed it and we can justify what we're thinking and . . . we actually have to draw a line.

(Professional 5, Child Mental Health, MCB Scotland)

This particular professional declared herself uncomfortable with the entitlement to disability living allowance resulting from a medical diagnosis of a behaviour disorder and called for greater 'policing' of how any resources were spent, advocating more formal drawing of lines:

We do fill in the forms and there's some that I'm very happy to fill in because I think that you know certainly we make a big difference to the quality of that child's and that family's life if they were able to access a bit more financial resource . . . If [disability living allowance] is going to be used for a behavioural disorder there needs to be some policing of how it's spent . . . is it actually being used in a way that's going to address the child's difficulties or for the family to get a bit of extra support?

(Professional 5, Child Mental Health, MCB Scotland)

Seeking a medical diagnosis is, as McLaughlin (2005) and Goodley and Runswick-Cole (2011) have argued, a highly complex and uncertain process and disadvantage is just one of many factors which may have a bearing on parents' engagement with professional services.

Professionals sought to resist the easy, or at least most cost-effective, option of medicalization.

It's cost effective to hand out a prescription . . . and when you're dealing with this constantness of the referral, this kind of unrelenting and increased referral rate, it's cheaper to kind of opt for medication, you can see the argument for that, so sometimes it's power – you have to hold on to your values and it can feel quite difficult at times but we do it.

(Professional 9, Child Mental Health, MCB Scotland)

They saw their interruptions as successful or as having the potential for success.

I think for us there's a sense of . . . almost excitement that here's an opportunity to really pitch things at the mainstream . . . if you actually look into the attachment histories, for a lot of those young people, actually it would explain that . . . the way they might present themselves within a school, and I would ask [teachers to help them] learn to handle relationships and make school a safe place, in a way that life hasn't been before.

(Professional 1, Educational Psychology, MCB Scotland)

Professionals reported more willingness within schools than there had been in the past to seek to understand children's behaviour and to look to alter it, rather than expecting externally validated diagnoses, and this, for one participant, represented a significant affective shift towards a more negotiated position.

There was a stage in the past where schools wouldn't have looked to understand behaviour. And when the psychologist came in they would have given you the child to cure.

(Professional 1, Educational Psychology, MCB Scotland)

The professionals' interruptions along the affective plane seemed to create some significant effects in slowing down referrals and in some cases in stopping them, either through direct resistance or by providing other – and better – possibilities for the children and young people.

## Interrupting pathologies?

In the context of a global concern about an excessive and increasing pursuit of the medicalization of behaviour, albeit with the recognition of under-diagnosis within parts of Scotland and in Scotland as a whole, the findings from these interviews are surprising on a number of fronts. The professionals we encountered were acutely aware of the power of the striated space in which children and young people in disadvantaged contexts were likely to find their behaviour medicalized and to find themselves channelled towards diagnosis. Yet they sought to interrupt the inevitability of classed-medicalization through strategies that were linguistic, visual and affective and they often showed great tenacity in the face of expectations from parents and school staff that the diagnostic path would be followed. They described, not pathways to under-diagnosis, but judgements towards non-diagnosis. Resistance to the medicalization of obesity (Rich *et al.* 2010; Wright and Harwood 2009), childbirth (Arney 1982; Hunt and Symonds 1995) and homosexuality (Conrad and Stults 2008) has come from those most directly affected by it; in contrast, resistance to the medicalization of behaviour has come, not from young people and their families, but rather from the professionals working on their behalf and seeing the potentially negative impact of diagnosis on their future lives. Substantial deterritorialization of classed-medicalization appeared to have been achieved by these professionals, in some cases provoking the kind of compromises which Fair (2010) observed patients had achieved with doctors and in others creating a renewed recognition by teachers and schools of their capacities to manage difficult behaviour. It is important to remember Deleuze and Guattari's (1987) warning, however, that with deterritorialization can come reterritorialization, or a retrieval of control over space: 'not . . . returning to the original territory, but . . . the way in which deterritorialized elements recombine and enter into new relations in the constitution of a new assemblage or the modification of the old' (Patton 2000: 101–2). In other words, the desire to hunt down pathology and difference (Baker 2002) could well reassert itself, especially in difficult economic circumstances. However, as Land argues, even reterritorialization can be resisted if the will to do so is sufficiently strong: 'Always decode . . . believe nothing, and extinguish all nostalgia for belonging. Ask always where capital is most inhuman, unsentimental and out of control. Abandon all attachment to the state' (Land 1993: 67).

The Scottish professionals' success in deterritorializing the medicalization of children's behaviour, along linguistic, visual and affective planes, appeared to alter significantly how the behaviour of children, especially those in disadvantaged contexts, could be talked about, seen and experienced. Their work could be seen as constituting an ethics through which they are developing a 'people to come' (Deleuze and Guattari 1994: 218). Bennett (2001: 128) suggests that this arises from a kind of 'enchantment', whereby children are no longer defined by a series of pathologies, and 'other ways of connecting and perceiving become possible' (Malins 2011: 180). In this ethical work, 'part of the energy needed to challenge injustice comes from the reservoir of enchantment – including that derived from commodities' (Bennett 2001: 128). Whilst our data from this small study are limited only to the professionals, the effects that they speak of appear to have been far reaching and we think it is reasonable to speculate that the linguistic, visual and affective manoeuvres could enable classed assumptions about aggression and behavioural disorders to be challenged. The findings also help us to understand how, whilst managing the unpredictability of children's behaviour can be such an issue for education staff, it is paramount to remain alert to how concerns about chaos and disorganization can bring medicalization to the fore, obfuscating the experiences of poverty.

In the final chapter, we draw the arguments in each of the chapters together and explore the possibilities for putting pedagogy, including that directed at professionals, ahead of the reflex turn to pathology and diagnosis. This requires some substantial rethinking and we offer some theoretical resources that may be put to work effectively on interrupting psychopathologization.

# Chapter 9

# Conclusion
## Learning, teaching and the thrill of pedagogy

## Introduction

K: Me and my partner – he's 17 in a couple of weeks – we've been look-ing after Jye, his little younger brother for the last three years because his mother moved away to Queensland in the outback, in the bush, where they didn't even have a house to live in. They were in caravans with no running electricity and Jye has difficulties when he goes into a classroom, with trying to settle in with students and teachers.

I: How old is he?

K: Jye's 16 now and we thought it would be best to have him down here with us where we could slowly get him back into schooling.

I: So you're being a teacher?

K: Yes. Just slowly getting there because Jye's had a lot of trouble since he was a young boy. Since primary school – since the age of eight – Jye's been in and out of programmes – not actually mainstream. Schools for kids that have troubles being in classrooms where they might be really disruptive, get into trouble a lot or just didn't attend. He's been put into a lot of them and they've never worked out, sometimes because of other students – he doesn't get along – and he might get banned from there or he just might not attend.

Jye doesn't have a lot of confidence in himself; he thinks he can't read and write but he can. I've seen him – he can write fine on Facebook. That's when I say: 'You can read and write fine on Facebook; that means you can write and read a piece of paper. It's the same words, it's just not on a computer screen and it doesn't have Facebook written in the corner – it's just on a piece of paper.'

(Krissie, 17 years, IUE Interview South Australia, 2012)

In the above excerpt Krissie, a young Indigenous Australian, describes her care and teaching of her nephew Jye. She depicts the context of Jye's former home and his difficulties with school. She also explains how she challenged the dominant notion of reading/writing and recognized Jye's ability to write. Krissie's approach takes issue with 'paper-based definitions' of reading/ writing and establishes the opportunity to see writing and reading differently. In so doing she achieves what Comber and Kamler (2004) call 'pedagogies of reconnection', a worthy task that many a teacher might strive to achieve. Significantly, Krissie's efforts have occurred in a schooling context where Australian Indigenous children are much more likely to experience psychopathologization.

Compared to non-Indigenous Australian young people, mental health problems are at much higher rates for Aboriginal and Torres Strait Islander young people (AIHW 2011a; Williamson *et al.* 2010; Zubrick *et al.* 2005). The pattern of higher rates for Aboriginal and Torres Strait Islander young people is 2.7 times that for non-Indigenous people for mental and behavioural disorders (AIHW 2011a), and ADHD is more often diagnosed by paediatricians (16.9 per cent). In juvenile justice, incarceration is 15 times higher for Indigenous young people than for non-Indigenous young people (AIHW 2011b).

Linda Graham's (2012) analysis of the New South Wales public education system (the largest in Australia) reveals the extent of this issue. Citing research into enrolments into different Schools for Specific Purposes (SSPs) she reveals the differences in enrolment between 'Traditional SSPs', 'Mental Health SSPs' (MH SSP) and 'Juvenile Justice SSPs' (JJ SSP):

> It is important to note that while Indigenous students and non-Indigenous students face an equal risk of being in a Traditional SSP, their risk of being enrolled in an MH SSP is more than 5 times higher than that experienced by non-Indigenous students. Worryingly but somewhat predictably, given the high rates of incarceration of Indigenous youth (Cuneen, Luke, and Ralph 2006), Indigenous students face more than 14 times the risk of being in a JJ SSP than non-Indigenous students.
>
> (Graham 2012: 160–70)

The MH SSPs are for behavioural or emotional problems (Graham 2012), problems that, once ascribed, have the knack of concealing the contexts of peoples' lives. For instance, once in place, psychopathologizing descriptions such as these seem to quickly overshadow realities of poverty and racialized discrimination and relinquish problems within the education system. This effect can arguably be witnessed in the way that changes from psychopathologization of Indigenous young people have been resisted.

> Worryingly, the pervasiveness of deficit beliefs about Indigenous children and young people was noted in a major review of Indigenous education (NSW DET 2004) but, despite 71 recommendations, the identification and referral of Indigenous students to NSW government special schools has actually accelerated in the six years since (Sweller, Graham and Van Bergen, [2012]).
>
> (Graham 2012: 173)

It is hard to argue against the power and currency that psychopathological explanations of young people have over others ways of understanding school-based issues. It is haunting to pause to imagine what might have happened had Jye's lack of confidence been differently interpreted, or if pedagogies of reconnection had been developed that gave him the room to show his reading and writing, albeit in a different format.

The above questions bring pedagogy to the fore, and raise for us the proposition: what if the challenges met in the daily art of teaching were embraced as part and parcel of the thrill of pedagogy? Pedagogy here might be understood as a practice to be engaged with, to consider, to attempt, to try and, importantly, to retry.

What might it be like to conceive of educating as necessarily a challenge, perhaps as Bamford described it almost two centuries ago when he wrote, 'See even a boy of mild and diligent temper, who naturally desires to please, and study, *how he trembles in his run to school!*' (Bamford 1822: 16, emphasis added). When we cited this quote in Chapter 2 our aim was to emphasize a quite different view of schooling that was extant at that time – schooling as unnatural, as causing problems – and contrast this with contemporary views that to us seem to take the school as a natural starting point. Here we repeat this quote to not only signal a contrasting view, but to suggest that there might be a good deal of value in remembering that schools are not the natural places that many would like to believe.

## Psychopathology at school or the schooling of psychopathology?

We have outlined in this book how psychopathology is taken up and used in schooling; yet there is also the issue of the extent to which schooling is involved in the production of psychopathology. The title of this section is a provocation: is it the case that what we have covered in this book alerts us to how psychopathology has been, and continues to be, variously used in school contexts? Or is it the case that schools have a hand in the very production of the psychopathologies that would otherwise be attributed to twentieth- and twenty-first-century professions of the mind – namely psychiatry and psychology? In Chapter 1 we raised this concern, and we maintain that both are occurring. Schools are, as we have described throughout this book, key sites for the articulation of psychopathology and are also key sites in the production of psychopathology. Taking this point further, it is interesting to pose the hypothetical question: could ADHD in children and young people exist if schools did not exist? We suggest not. This inter-relationship flags how schools and schooling need to be reappraised.

Importantly though, we would be wise to remember that schools are, quite simply, strange places. They demand an assortment of things of children and young people (and teachers too), yet it seems that this was at its most recognizable in the nineteenth century. This observation seems to have simply vanished in the current century. Amongst all of the technology and spread of schooling we have forgotten one fundamental aspect of the school experience – it does things to people, and those things can be anticipated with a range of emotions such as worry, anticipation or excitement. Given the spread of the psychopathology industry into schooling (measuring hands, heads or labelling 'defectives', 'imbeciles' or the 'feebleminded') as the twentieth century commenced, it became all too easy to explain away problems as based on the individual. The school, and with it pedagogy, disappear from view and we begin our romance with pseudo-pedagogies such as 'behaviour management'.

The risk of psychopathologies – and these accompanying pseudo-pedagogies such as behaviour management – is greatest for certain groups. There is, as we have already pointed out, disproportionate representation of Indigenous Australians in specialist schools for mental health problems (Graham 2012). These young people meet with arguably the most severe of the pseudo-pedagogies: being placed in specialist units. The racialization of psychopathology at schools is, unfortunately, an issue not restricted to Australia's Indigenous population. As we discussed in Chapter 3, the problem is widespread with over-representation of black children in special educational needs in the United Kingdom (25 per cent) (Department for Education 2011a). In the United States the figures are similarly appalling, with black children over-represented in special education (Ferri and Connor 2005; Fitzgerald 2009). Risks are also associated with social class, where we see the medicalization of poverty occurring far too often. Under the shadow of psychopathologization, the effects of chaotic lives, the very contexts that need to be understood, are so easily smoothed away. Out of the chaos, as it were, comes the panacea of diagnosis/medication, a process that makes the disorderly orderly. Here again we see pseudo-pedagogy at work.

It is difficult to ignore how dangerous it is to be a boy, or at least a certain type of boy, in the era of psychopathologization. As we discussed, gender is one of the risk factors for diagnosis, yet it is so peculiarly accepted that more boys have behaviour disorders such as ADHD. Addressing any gendered problems with this imbalance appears to have been curiously accomplished by an outright 'gendering of ADHD'. Thus the feminine version is one of 'sluggishness and anxiety' and the masculine is one of aggression and marked disruption. While detailing these 'risk factors' for meeting with the psychopathologizing apparatus, we have cautioned the move to 'commatization' that is simply adding psychopathology to the list of 'issues' to be considered. Such gestures towards inclusion (described as 'intersectionality') are in danger of 'watering down' the complexity of issues that are at stake. Surely we need to understand these, as well as to understand how these may intersect?

One of the points we have tried to address is the way psychopathology is engaged in throughout the different 'phases' of schooling, and the way this engagement 'intensifies'. This intensification, or 'saturation' as Nealon

(2008) describes it, can be witnessed in education. The degree to which psychopathology has saturated education is a case in point, and a salutary wake-up call regarding the extent to which the psychopathological is now smeared across and throughout schooling. We analysed this intensification across four phases of schooling, considering for each of these the points of arousal, relations/networks of power, disorders of interest, modes of practice, and desired consequences/outcomes. Our analysis has indicated the extent to which the discourses of psychopathologization impose something akin to a 'temporal positioning' on children and young people. By this we are referring to how beliefs about the potential to be ideal (namely without psychopathology) are intricately linked to the temporality of the person. The younger the child is, the greater the enthusiasm for resolving mental health issues (or the risk of these). In Chapter 4 we described how this stance is operationalized under the rubric of 'intervention', with such interventions including those yet to be born. The link to the temporality of the child guides the actions taken, which can include intervening with parents in the name of their children's synapses. The feeling this period evokes is one of great attention and focus on 'wiring', with high stakes at play if opportunities for 'wiring' are squandered.

By primary school the wholesale attention to intervention has changed. While we are not suggesting there is no intervention as children get older and enter primary school, what we are proposing is that there is a palpable change from the intense desire to 'act while we can' to one where there is the acceptance that things have now been 'set on course'. It is difficult to deny the degree of influence that synapse discourse holds over such beliefs. In this regard we might be wise to be alert to how attention on the young and very young child as a site of possible 'immaculate change' reverberates to the fixed conceptions of the older child. In Chapter 5 we discussed how the disorderly primary school child is treated with 'exaltation' and, more often than not, placed on a path for special treatment. At the primary school psychopathologization is supported by a network of experts with the mandate to address the condition of the child. Here, it is no longer the case of gently directing behaviours so as to optimize the development of synapses; but rather, engaging in practices such as recognizing the extant 'breaks in brain circuitry' and applying treatments (whether these be medication or behavioural). The primary years are consequently periods where practices – such as separation (separate schools, classrooms), pharmaceutical treatments and training programmes (for parents; within schools) – swing into full-scale operation.

In the secondary years, as we outlined in Chapter 6, while this operation is evident, it, to us, has taken a more sombre tone; one that is ever more concerned with 'ameliorating' problems believed to be 'entrenched'. Intensification in secondary school consequently has a much greater concentration on what could be described as a 'palliative focus'. While we acknowledge that there are exceptions to this approach, we contend that, in the main, the approach is one of resignation to a belief in the fixity of the young person's problem, and this unfortunately guides the actions taken to train, discipline or corral that young person. The secondary school aged student is thus exposed to a form of governmentality wielded to control a condition and minimize its impacts.

Discussion of psychopathology at the crèche, the primary or the secondary school is generally bereft of any depiction of the school as a problematic or strange place. A delicately forceful means to govern the child and young person is required to be instituted. These governing actions are 'delicately forceful' since, as they rule bodies, they do so in ways that, in the name of psychopathology, are considered to be appropriately helpful. Under this ideology, it becomes possible to have, without question, exceedingly high numbers of minority youth in special education systems. This is occurring, as Graham (2012) has shown, with Indigenous Australians in the Mental Health or Juvenile Justice Schools for Specific Purposes in NSW. Justified in this way, these actions are not subjected to questioning about over-representation, racism or classism. Neither are the gendered distributions called into question; rather it is simply the case that ADHD in 'males' and 'females' differs. Again, the influence of psychopathology means that such interpretations are not only justified, but actually smother other possible explanations. This has dire consequences for children as they 'age', moving along a continuum of decreasing potential.

It is not, however, only this temporal effect that has concerned us in this book. We have also sought to draw attention to how embracing psychopathology as a rationality in education has influenced our understandings of what it means to be a human who learns. This is an issue for children who are deemed less and less able to partake in all that education can offer. It is also an issue where recourse to particular readings of psychopathology can actually lead to shifts in how human behaviours are understood. This issue was the point of Chapter 7, where, in our discussion of colleges and universities, we paid particular attention to the making of 'the potency of depression'. Here we outlined how psychopathology has become linked with the troubled student – but not in any simplistic manner (for instance, identifying the troubled student as a psychopath). Rather, the troubled student becomes linked with depression, rendering depression not only potent, but those described as experiencing depression now having, by association, a dangerous potential for potency. Surprisingly, then, we see at the 'end' of the phases of schooling the rising once more of potential. This time, however, it is not the potential of the baby or the very young child to be optimal, but rather, the potential to be dangerous.

We have acknowledged that while the 'regime of psychopathology' might seem overpowering, not everyone is overpowered. In Chapter 8 we described how health, education and welfare professionals working with children interrupted the pressure to psychopathologize children experiencing poverty. Their efforts are noteworthy, providing ideas for how others might do the same.

This is because, while psychopathology has been so effective in smothering and territorializing schooling, it is conceivable to interrupt these processes and deterritorialize.

## The use of theory

Lyotard (1986) reminds us that, in a world in which success is equated with saving time, theory, and thinking itself, reveals its fundamental flaw to be its capacity to waste time. Value has replaced values (Peters *et al.* 2003) and both theory and thinking struggle to prove their 'worth', while, as Latour (2004: 225) suggests, critique has 'run out of steam'. This reluctance for theory, and indeed thinking, is most evident among governments.

> Governments, and some within the scholarly community itself, seem to be seeking to turn educational research into a technology that can be applied to solving short-term educational problems, rather than a system of enquiry that might help practitioners and policymakers think more productively about the nature of the problem and how it might be addressed.
>
> (Torrance 2008: 522)

As Torrance (2007) points out, 'Globalized policy developments chase each other around the world as governments eschew "theory" in favour of identifying and borrowing "what works".' Furthermore, policymakers seem keen to borrow from theories of change without acknowledging these as theories. As we have argued, the plethora of resources promising to help teachers manage the behaviour of 'unruly' pupils, or assist parents in dealing with their 'difficult' children, are constituted from a mixture of incompatible and semi-formed theories and appear to be endorsed by governments and national agencies. They are also much sought after by anxious teachers and parents seeking immediate solutions to the problems apparently caused by mental disorder.

The removal or reduction of theory from teacher education has been noted across the globe but Dennis Beach (2012) draws on Basil Bernstein to illustrate the negative impact this has had on beginning teachers' thinking. Bernstein (1999) distinguishes between a horizontal, everyday, discourse, linked to commonsense understandings and often tacit, oral and context specific, and a vertical discourse, produced within universities and which offers, 'a scientific "know why" discourse' (Bernstein 1999: 6). The erosion or the removal of the vertical discourse (through a move away from an emphasis on scientific praxis or the removal of philosophy of education) could, Bernstein suggests, be part of a move to undermine the knowledge interests of a professional discourse and open them up to influences. But, as others have argued (Apple 2001; Beach 2012; Sleeter 2008; Lauder *et al.* 2009; Oancea and Bridges 2009), the erosion of the vertical discourse removes the capacity of beginning teachers to think critically and to understand the global influences on their profession and their selves, precisely at a time when the effects are considerable. Furthermore, the absence of this discourse, and the criticality that comes with it, may leave teachers less able to recognize the competing demands of equity and choice and therefore find a balance between them (Alexandersson 2011) and make them in turn more at risk of political manipulation and economic exploitation (Sleeter 2008).

Latour (2004: 225) calls urgently for progress towards 'a fair position' and for the development of 'new critical tools' to work positively and constructively towards social change. The theory that we have made use of in this book – from the work of Foucault, Arendt, and Deleuze and Guattari – has, in our view, the potential to assist us in progressing towards a fair position. Their work provides the critical tools necessary to deliver acceptable and appropriate critique, identify possibilities for change and elaborate the mechanisms and relationships for that change, 'acting counter to our time and thereby acting on our time and, let us hope, for the benefit of a time to come' (Nietzsche 1983: 60). We expand on this potential below.

### Foucault

> We have to imagine and to build up what we could be to get rid of this kind of political 'double bind', which is the simultaneous individualization and totalization of modern power structures.
>
> (Foucault 1982: 216)

Michel Foucault, as many other researchers have demonstrated, helps us to read the history of our present as something other than we might have hitherto understood it. His invitation to step out of causality, refusing questions of *why* we have become what we are, and to be curious instead about *how* things have emerged, is liberating. It allows us to see things that might have seemed to us to be ordinary, as remarkable. In this book, we have, through a genealogical analysis, been able to trace patterns in psychopathologization that seem to us to be remarkable. Thus we have a clearer idea of the concerns about the risks schooling has posed to children and young people over the last century and of the ways in which 'race', class and gender become imbricated as 'risk' factors and heighten the exposure of children and young people to psychopathologization. We have also been able to interpret shifts in the focus of psychopathologization through different phases of education, from a hope of salvation to an explicit representation of the mentally disordered student as a threat, as an artefact of shifts in power relations and of different positioning of the individual child or young person in relation to the state.

As Foucault himself contended, the point of such knowledge is to make it possible to resist it: 'Maybe the target nowadays is not to discover what we are but to refuse what we are' (1982: 216). Simons and Masschelein (2006) suggest that we should not be concerned with resisting such things as governance, but should instead resist the subjectification of the self that goes with it. They advocate what they call a 'creative ontology' (2006: 302), which involves finding new words or phrases that do theoretical work or at least remind policy and policymakers of the '*impossible* domain' of educational policy because it seeks to govern that which is to come. As Hacking (2002: 8) suggests, 'With new names, new objects come into being. Not quickly. Only with usage, only with layer after layer of usage.' The theoretical work done by a creative ontology could also limit inequality by constantly reminding us, in Foucault's words, 'not that everything is bad but that everything is dangerous . . . If everything is dangerous, then we always have something to do' (1984: 343). It also enables individuals to see themselves as the main source of transformation, rather than waiting for a more substantial structural or material change and leads 'not to apathy but to a hyper- and pessimistic activism' (Foucault 1984: 343).

### Arendt

Hannah Arendt's work also helps to orient us towards action, but additionally provides us with an impetus – and even an imperative – for thinking and critique. Arendt's work, with its clearly established link between critique and political action (1968b), has enabled us to see how psychopathologization is politicized and to understand the political ends intended by specific practices. Furthermore, Arendt alerts us to the dangers of silence as signalling a descent into depoliticized ground. The resources Arendt offers are in the practice of critique and, in particular, recognizing the distinction between factual truths and rational truths (1968b). The distinction is a crucial one, and again understanding how the two become confused may be liberating. Factual truths, seen literally with the eyes (Arendt 1968b) and involving undisputable truths, differ in nature from rational truths, which involve philosophical reflection and even speculation. But Arendt's warning, that 'All truths – not only the various kinds of rational truth but also factual truth – are opposed to opinion in their mode of asserting validity' (1968b: 239), is salutary. With this distinction and caveat in mind, we were able to demonstrate how the mentally ill student in higher education, presenting as depressed, becomes dangerous, and his or her potency becomes established as a factual truth. This in turn serves as the justification for a whole set of practices which verify the (potential) risk and danger of the individual and provide protection and security for the higher education community and society. It also gives rise to a new domain of knowledge which is recognized as 'joining the dots', consisting of piecing together so-called 'warning signs', that are individually speculative, but which together are legitimized as a factual truth.

Arendt inspires us to act, by first finding spaces for public action. These may be anywhere, according to Arendt, who invokes the *polis* as meaning the 'space of appearance' and a space for political action:

> The *polis*, properly speaking, is not the city-state in its physical location; it is the organization of the people as it arises out of acting and speaking together, and its true space lies between people living together for this purpose, no matter where they happen to be.
>
> (Arendt 1958: 198)

Arendt also urges us to exercise political judgement through the exercise of 'representative' thinking, always considering the viewpoint or perspective of others.

> Political thought is representative. I form an opinion by considering a given issue from different viewpoints, by making present to my mind the standpoints of those who are absent; that is, I represent them . . . The more people's standpoints I have present in my mind while I am pondering a given issue, and the better I can imagine how I would feel and think if I were in their place, the stronger will be my capacity for representative thinking and the more valid my final conclusions, my opinion.
>
> (Arendt 1968b: 241)

It is easy to see how such thinking could enable the recognition of how particular 'truths' become established, their validity to be questioned and alternative spaces and ways of knowing to be put in place.

### Deleuze and Guattari

Giles Deleuze and Félix Guattari, like Hannah Arendt, are spatial thinkers and their significant contribution to thinking and critique is to demonstrate the deeply controlling and constraining nature of institutional spaces. Recognizing spaces such as schools as territorialized (Deleuze and Guattari 1987) enables us to understand how the powerful striations and lines of communication direct action along specific flows, create a sense of rules of engagement and produce particular kinds of order. It alerts us to the purpose of such organizations as producing 'meaning in the service of power' (Thompson 1984:7) on behalf of the state, but allows us also to see how iniquities arise as individuals with particular markers of 'risk', such as 'race', class and gender, become further locked into the striations of schooling and become destined for diagnosis of mental disorders. The concept of territorialization was useful to us in understanding the patterns of higher rates of referral among disadvantaged children and how they were both so entrenched and so recognizable to professionals in the field.

Yet with Deleuze and Guattari's notion of territorialization comes deterritorialization, the act of smoothing out the rigid institutional spaces, and this helped to explain the efforts made by the professionals in the Scottish study to interrupt the flow towards diagnosis. The possibilities for deterritorialization appear to be multiple, but require four specific practices. The first of these is a requirement that we become foreigners in our own tongue, experiencing the world around us as new, a 'becoming-intense' of language (Roy 2004: 310). This allows us to question taken-for-granted understandings, such as those associated with psychopathology, and to confront existing certainties by inserting a doubt 'blow by blow' (Deleuze and Guattari 1994: 76). The second element of deterritorialization is a refusal of essences or of signifieds, effecting instead what Roy calls a 'de-*monstration* which replaces the Idea' (2004: 310; original emphasis). Thus, we refuse the artefact of the mentally abnormal child and ask instead how this notion has surfaced. Creative subtraction represents a third element of deterritorialization and involves a calculated loss, rather than an acquisition.

> It is an ascetic practice, an awareness of the movement of sense and non-sense as well as the paradoxicalities of language, and that subtracts in a creative manner in order to make openings for new becomings.
>
> (Roy 2004: 311)

The final element of deterritorialization is an acceptance that there is no one behind expression. Individuals may be part of expression, but not the authors of it: 'there is no individual enunciation. There is not even a subject of enunciation' (Deleuze and Guattari 1987: 79). Instead, individuals may be 'interpellated' into 'the currents and cross-currents of this infinitely dispersed discourse' (Haraway, cited in Roy 2004: 309) and any identity that is revealed is 'essentially fortuitous' (Deleuze 1990: 178). This frees them up to contribute to new combinations of expression, without worrying about their own implication in these forms.

The particular strands of theory, considered above and put to work in our analysis of psychopathology, constitute important resources for finding new ways of thinking about, and practising with, mental disorder. They have also provoked some ideas about new possibilities for action and we discuss these below.

## What can be done?

> There are times in life when the question of knowing if one can think differently than one thinks, and perceive differently than one sees, is absolutely necessary if one is to go on looking and reflecting at all.
>
> (Foucault 1985: 8)

Much of what we have identified as psychopathologization is a cause for concern. While we have sought to avoid normative judgements about the various patterns and trajectories we have uncovered, our sense of injustice is, we hope, clear. We have also indicated our concerns about what appear to be exponential rises in psychopathologization – at least for some children and young people. We think that things needn't be as they are and we propose three modes of action. These involve a return to questions of education, asserting the importance of pedagogy over matters of individual pathology; engagement in public discourse and debate in order to change the conversation; and the training of teachers and other professionals in ways that are educational.

## Privileging pedagogy over pathology

> Education is the point at which we decide whether we love the world enough to assume responsibility for it and by the same token to save it from that ruin which, except for renewal, except for the coming of the new and the young, would be inevitable. And education, too, is where we decide whether we love our children enough not to expel them from our world and leave them to their own devices . . .
>
> (Arendt 1968b: 196)

We have argued that one of the significant consequences of psychopathologization is that diagnosis obscures other interpretations of children and their behaviour. It also detracts from considerations of what is best, educationally, for individual children. Once a diagnosis is in place, or even while there is a suspicion that a diagnosis might be warranted, attention is deflected from how to educate and onto how to *manage* the child. Biesta argues that we have deviated from matters of education more generally, as a result of a fixation on learning, and consequently, 'something has been lost' (2006: 14). While we recognize these more generic effects, we contend that the consequences for children subjected to the panoply of diagnostic apparatuses are more dire.

We echo the call made in the first volume of the series, *Theorizing Education*, to which this book belongs, for a return to questions of education beyond concerns with the child and school (Allan *et al.* 2013) and endorse Biesta's (2006) argument for inventing a new language for education to cope with today's challenges. This involves reconsidering theorizing as practices within the world rather than being simply thinking about the world (Edwards 2011) but might also entail some work on undoing the theories behind psychopathology.

## Discourse demos-tration: Changing the conversation

O:  . . . yes, a couple of days ago my friends got picked on because people were calling them 'racist' because they're black. I had a go at them but then again, I've got something wrong with me – I got ADHD or whatever you want to call it – really badly and whatever I do, I can listen to Bec but I won't listen to anyone else to be honest, if I get angry. It's like if I have say . . . who can I put as an example? If I had . . . one of the girls that bashed me up and she was in my personal, I'll knock them out.

I: Oh, so you're quite violent you reckon?

O: I'm not violent. I don't like people in my personal space and I'm really angry and I've got ADHD and I can't really handle it. That's why I've got Lou to help me with it.

I: Oh, the youth worker here?

O: Yes.

(Odette, 13 years old, Newcastle, Australia, IUE, 2012)

We have suggested that much of psychopathology goes on without question or challenge and without consideration of the consequences for children and families. Yet the professionals in the Scottish study surprised us with their intent to interrupt assumed patterns of referral and diagnosis, and the children and young people in the Australian study often gave striking displays of awareness of the impact of having a 'thing' on their identities.

There is a need to increase understanding of psychopathology, to recognize its consequences and to develop the means of challenging it, and each of these is a political task. Critchley usefully advocates a kind of demonstration as 'demos-tration', with an emphasis on the original Greek meaning of the 'common people', to denote a process of 'manifesting the presence of those who do not count' (2007: 130). They involve naming and privileging particular voices and identities, described usefully by Rancière (2008) as a process of making a discourse of that which has formally been a noise and as a process of rupture which renders certain identities visible:

> For me a political subject is a subject who employs the competence of the so-called incompetents or the part of those who have no part, and not an additional group to be recognised as part of society. 'Visible minorities' means exceeding the system of represented groups, of constituted identities . . . It's a rupture that opens out into the recognition of the competence of anyone, not the addition of a unit.
>
> (Rancière 2008: 3)

Critchley argues that the scope for political action has been reduced by the disarticulation of names which are inherently political, such as the 'proletariat' or the 'peasant', and we could add to that the mentally disordered child. Critchley cites the examples of 'indigenous' peoples achieving the status of a force for change in Mexico and Australia, and we might envisage mobilized groups of 'families with diagnoses' engaging to similar effect. The academic has an important role in mobilizing people and discourses, exemplifying – and inviting – critique to encourage parents, professionals and even children to become readers of power, and generating alternative responses. The political tasks that are invoked here are both productive and creative, involving 'setting fire to the unjust state of things instead of burning the things themselves, and restoring life to primary life' (Deleuze and Guattari 1986: 108).

### *Professional training that is educational*

We have discussed how the engagement of teachers, both experienced and novice, with children diagnosed with mental disorder is shrouded in anxiety. Aside from the fears that young people, particularly those of secondary age or in higher education, may pose a danger, teachers worry that they do not know enough about particular disorders or that they may fail to 'spot the signs' that would necessitate diagnosis. Beginning teachers are particularly controlled by this anxiety and remain 'in perpetual training' (Deleuze 1992: 5), never finished with education, in the sense of not yet having proved themselves as competent, and 'in debt'.

There is a need to interrupt the systems, structures and processes of training teachers and other professionals and to break into assumptions that pathology offers credible explanations for student failure. Teachers and professionals in health and social care can be exposed to, and engaged in, the kind of demostration described above, and can be invited to think and speak within the vertical discourses proposed by Bernstein. They can also be encouraged, through their training, to turn away (Hickey-Moody 2009) from psychopathology and from what is known about mental disorders, but this will involve some toughness on the part of teacher educators in order to refuse to allow beginning teachers to pursue their 'often well intentioned hunt for disability' (Baker 2002: 665); a hunt that, arguably, stems from preservice teachers' propensity to deploy 'if–then' (or diagnosis-contingent) pedagogies; that is, they tend to base their pedagogical decisions on the logic, 'if a child has this, then I teach like that' (McMahon 2012, 2013). Explorations with student teachers of the damaging consequences of psychopathologization, and of the inadequacy of the resources for behaviour management, together with the promise of constituting pedagogy for all children as thrilling, which we discuss in the final section of this chapter, could quell their anxieties. Such a turning away from psychopathology will enable new teachers to develop new beginnings, and new becomings, and it involves a kind of training – or rather education – that is creative, inventive and even playful.

> Creativity is always a becoming, a reterritorialization and an establishment of new affective systems of relation. One cannot become-other unless there is something from which one turns away.
>
> (Hickey-Moody 2009: 178)

We end this book with some reflections on what it might take to revive and recover some of the thrill of pedagogy, such that psychopathology may be rendered inconsequential.

## Thinking differently and differently thinking: the thrill of pedagogy

I am a happy teacher, I am a teacher who thrives on my work, *the thrill of pedagogy* and the constant opportunity to improve, trial, create motivates me hugely and I adore what I do. I am lucky, so lucky and so humble because I am reflective and self aware and I know why I love my work so much. I know why I can cope with my workload and my other commitments.

(the human teacher 2013, emphasis added)

When we typed in the phrase 'thrill of pedagogy' into a Google search there were only two results. Both results came from a blog by thehumanteacher, a secondary school teacher working in the United Kingdom. We've included her reference to this phrase, where in referring to the thrill of pedagogy, other activities are described, namely 'the constant opportunity to improve, trial, create' (the humanteacher 2013). While we are certainly surprised by the few results yielded by our search, we are buoyed by these comments since they articulate the idea that teaching engages with all manner of challenges that require imaginative responses. In our view, this activity is highly likely to be compromised when the recourse is always to the default position of psychopathology. One simply is not required to think otherwise.

In closing this book, we want to encourage a move away from this default position, as it is a dangerous stance to adopt in education. It threatens to replace the art of teaching and thinking with the mechanistic apparatus that not only invokes diagnosis, management, separation and medication but instils temporal value onto the bodies and minds of children and young people. Receding optimism for the resolution of mental problems is not restricted to those who are diagnosed, but carries a weight of influence that can inform how children and young people are perceived. This has reverberations for those who are at greater risk of being psychopathologized, such as those experiencing disadvantage. Suddenly it becomes possible to conceive of certain children and young people as uneducable, and, as our research in Australia has shown, this can have devastating consequences.

It is possible to make pedagogy exquisite, to embrace it as edgy. It is also possible to incite teachers, especially our teachers in training, to view challenges as part and parcel of teaching. We need teachers who can see what Krissie saw in Jye, teachers who can say, 'He thinks he can't read and write but he can' (IUE Interview South Australia, 2012). This is by far preferable to the situations that Jye had experienced in schooling where he was banned or just 'didn't turn up'. Jye needed to be engaged, to have, as Comber and Kamler describe, the opportunity to experience 'turn around pedagogies' (2004: 295), where his teachers turn around themselves and develop understanding of the student. Reflecting on their research they explain: 'in every case, teachers needed to move outside of deficit discourses to move ahead to be able to engineer pedagogic redesigns that made a difference' (Comber and Kamler 2004: 307). The great danger with psychopathology is the way it functions as a deficit discourse so powerfully, obscuring other interpretations of children's lives.

It is important that such knowledge and skills are conveyed to teachers during their professional training. These new teachers need to be given the opportunity to be excited about difference (as opposed to being scared about behaviour). We have suggested some ways forward for engaging in pedagogy as a thrill. One important lesson is to not turn away from schooling's history and to remember that schools are strange places. How many fewer diagnoses might there be if this principle was enacted? Surely it would give pause to the default reaction of psychopathology as the explanation for children's reactions in school environments. Another key action is to have professionals who have the knowledge and capacity to interrupt the flows to diagnosis of psychopathology. It is also important to recognize how optimism for change is constructed and how this can affect beliefs and attitudes about students (as well as the students themselves). These suggestions are not simplistic, but are about 'thinking differently', involving activities such as invoking history, or interrupting a pattern in order to re-engage in the thrill of pedagogy. All this relies on conceptual work, rather than a type of practical list of 'to dos'. Martin Luther King wrote of the purpose of education:

> To think incisively and to think for one's self is very difficult. We are prone to let our mental life become invaded by legions of half truths, prejudices, and propaganda . . . The function of education is to teach one to think intensively and to think critically. Intelligence plus character – that is the goal of true education.
>
> (King 1947: n.p.)

In this respect teaching necessitates thinking critically. It requires the teacher to think for his or her self, to be able to sift through the 'half truths' – or the truths that tend to obscure. These are vital if teachers are to educate their students. In this sense there is much more at issue with the use of psychopathology in schools. It is not simply a matter of a minority of children getting diagnosis and medication. Rather, we risk losing the opportunity to experience pedagogy as a thrill and rejoicing in the activity of thinking intensively.

# List of legislation cited

The Education Act of 1870 (§ 36), UK Government. Available HTTP: http://www.parliament.uk/about/living-heritage/transformingsociety/livinglearning/school/overview/1870educationact (accessed 26 March 2013).

Family Educational Rights and Privacy Act (FERPA) (20 U.S.C. § 1232g; 34 CFR Part 99), US. Available HTTP: http://www.ed.gov/policy/gen/guid/fpco/ferpa/index.html (accessed 10 July 2013).

Home Office Police and Justice Act 2006 (Chapter 48), UK. Available HTTP: http://www.legislation.gov.uk/ukpga/2006/48/contents (accessed 20 September 2013).

# References

Achenbach, T.M. (1998) 'Diagnosis, assessment, taxonomy and case formulations', in T.H. Ollendick and M. Herson (eds) *Handbook of Child Psychopathology*, 3rd edn, New York: Plenum Press.

Achenbach, T.M. and Rescorla, L.A. (2000) *Manual for the ASEBA preschool forms and profiles: an integrated system of multi-informant assessment*, Burlington, VT: University of Vermont Department of Psychiatry.

Adewuya, A.O., Ola, B.A., Olutayo, O.A., Mapayi, B.M. and Oginni, O.O. (2006) 'Depression amongst Nigerian university students. Prevalence and socio-demographic correlates'. *Social Psychiatry and Psychiatric Epidemiology*, 41: 674–8.

Akinbami L.J., Liu, X., Pastor, P.N. and Reuben, C.A. (2011) 'Attention deficit hyperactivity disorder among children aged 5–17 years in the United States, 1998–2009', NCHS data brief, no. 70, Hyattsville, MD: National Center for Health Statistics. Available HTTP: http://www.cdc.gov/nchs/data/databriefs/db70.pdf (accessed 2 March 2013).

Alban-Metcalfe, J., Cheng-Lai, A. and Ma, T. (2002) 'Teacher and student teacher ratings of attention-deficit/hyperactivity disorder in three cultural settings', *International Journal of Disability, Development and Education*, 49(3): 281–99.

Alexander, F.G. and Selesnick, S.T. (1967) *The History of Psychiatry: an evaluation of psychiatric thought and practice from prehistoric times to the present*, London: George Allen and Unwin Ltd.

Alexandersson, M. (2011) 'Equivalence and choice in combination: the Swedish dilemma', *Oxford Review of Education*, 37: 195–214.

Aljazeera. (2013). 'Colorado shooter's insanity plea accepted', *Aljazeera*, 4 June 2013. Available HTTP: http://www.aljazeera.com/news/americas/2013/06/201364161536157158.html (accessed 19 July 2013).

Alkon, A., Ramler, M. and MacLennan, K. (2003) 'Evaluation of mental health consultation in child care centers', *Early Childhood Education Journal*, 31(2): 91–9.

Allan, J. (2008) *Rethinking Inclusive Education: the philosophers of difference in practice*, Dordrecht: Springer.

Allan, J. (2010) 'The sociology of disability and the struggle for inclusive education', *British Journal of Sociology of Education*, 31(5): 603–19.

Allan, J., Edwards, R. and Biesta, G. (2013) 'Towards an agenda for theoretical interventions in education', in G. Biesta, J. Allan and R. Edwards (eds) *Making a Difference in Theory: the theory question in education and the education question in theory*, London: Routledge.

Allan, J. and Harwood, V. (2013) 'Medicus interruptus in the behaviour of children in disadvantaged contexts in Scotland', *British Journal of Sociology of Education*, published online 27 April. DOI:10.1080/01425692.2013.776933.

Allin, M.P.G. (2010) 'Preterm babies grown up: understanding a hidden public health problem', *Psychological Medicine*, 40(1): 5–7.

Allin, M.P.G., Rooney, M., Cuddy, M., Wyatt, J., Walshe, M., Rifkin, L., Murray, R. (2006) 'Personality in young adults who are born preterm', *Pediatrics*, 117(2): 309–16.

Amaral, O.B. (2007) 'Psychiatric disorders as social constructs: ADHD as a case in point', *American Journal of Psychiatry*, 164(10): 1612.

American Psychiatric Association. (1980) *Diagnostic and Statistical Manual of Mental Disorders (DSM-III)*, 3rd edn, Washington DC: American Psychiatric Association.

American Psychiatric Association. (1987) *Diagnostic and Statistical Manual of Mental Disorders*, 3rd edn, revised (*DSM-III-R*), Washington DC: American Psychiatric Association.

American Psychiatric Association. (1994) *Diagnostic and Statistical Manual of Mental Disorders*, 4th edn (*DSM-IV*), Washington DC: American Psychiatric Association.

American Psychiatric Association. (2000) *Diagnostic and Statistical Manual of Mental Disorders*, 4th edn, text revision (*DSM-IV-TR*), Washington DC: American Psychiatric Association.

American Psychiatric Association. (2013a) *Diagnostic and Statistical Manual of Mental Disorders (DSM-5)*, Washington DC: American Psychiatric Association.

American Psychiatric Association. (2013b) *DSM-5 Development*. Available HTTP: www. dsm5.org (accessed 8 June 2013).

American Psychiatric Association Committee on Nomenclature and Statistics. (1952) *Diagnostic and Statistical Manual of Mental Disorders*, 1st edn *(DSM-I)*, Washington DC: American Psychiatric Association Committee on Nomenclature and Statistics.

American Psychiatric Association Committee on Nomenclature and Statistics. (1968) *Diagnostic and Statistical Manual of Mental Disorders*, 2nd edn *(DSM-II)*, Washington DC: American Psychiatric Association Committee on Nomenclature and Statistics.

Amini Virmani, E., Masyn, K.E., Thompson, R.A., Conners-Burrow, N.A. and Whiteside Mansell, L. (2013) 'Early childhood mental health consultation: promoting change in the quality of teacher-child interactions', *Infant Mental Health Journal*, 34(2): 156–72.

Andre, L. (2009) 'Study shows kids in lesbian families well-adjusted', *Mothering*, March/April: 32.

Anon. (1732) *An account of several work-houses for employing and Maintaining the POOR, setting forth the rules by which they are Governed, their great usefulness to the publick and in particular to the parishes where they are erected. As also several Charity schools for promoting work, and labour*, London: Joseph Downing.

Anon. (1822) 'Article XV. Bamford on school discipline', *The British Review and London Critical Journal*, XX: 316–36.

Anticich, S.A.J., Barrett, P.M., Silverman, W., Lacherez, P. and Gillies, R. (2013) 'The prevention of childhood anxiety and promotion of resilience among preschool-aged children: a universal school based trial', *Advances in School Mental Health Promotion*, 6(2): 93–121.

Appadurai, A. (2009) 'The shifting ground from which we speak', in J. Kenway and J. Fahey (eds) *Globalizing the Research Imagination*, Oxford: Routledge.

Apple, M.W. (2001) 'Markets, standards, teaching, and teacher education', *Journal of Teacher Education*, 52: 182–96.

Applegate, B., Lahey, B.B., Hart, E.L., Biederman, J., Hynd, G.W., Barkley, R.A. and Shaffer, D. (1997) 'Validity of the age-of-onset criterion for ADHD: a report from the DSM-IV field trials', *Journal of the American Academy of Child and Adolescent Psychiatry*, 36: 1211–21.

Arendt, H. (1958) *The Human Condition*, Chicago: University of Chicago Press.

Arendt, H. (1968a). *The Origins of Totalitarianism*, New York: Harvest Book, Harcourt Inc.

Arendt, H. (1968b) *Between Past and Future: eight exercises in political thought*, New York: Penguin Books.

Arendt, H. (1981) *The Life of the Mind, One/Thinking, Two/Willing*, one vol. edn, New York: Harcourt.

Arendt, H. (2003) 'Some questions of moral philosophy', in J. Kohn (ed.) *Responsibility and Judgement*, New York: Shocken Books.

Armstrong, D. (1995) *Power and Partnership in Education*, London: Routledge.

Arney, W. (1982) *Power and the Profession of Obstetrics*, London: The University of Chicago Press.

Arthur, R. (2005) 'Punishing parents for the crimes of their children', *Howard Journal*, 44(3): 233–53.

Artiles, A. (1998) 'The dilemma of difference. Enriching the disproportionality discourse with theory and context', *Journal of Special Education*, 32: 32–6.

Artiles, A. (2004) 'The end of innocence: historiography and representation in the discursive practice of LD', *Journal of Learning Disabilities*, 37(6): 550–5.

Artiles, A., Kozleski, E.S., Trent, S.T., Osher, D. and Ortiz, A. (2010) 'Justifying and explaining disproportionality, 1968–2008: a critique of underlying views of culture', *Exceptional Children*, 76(3): 279–99.

Artiles, A., Trent, S. and Juan, L. (1997) 'Learning disabilities empirical research on ethnic minority students: an analysis of 22 years of studies published in selected refereed journals', *Learning Disabilities Research and Practice*, 12: 82–91.

Ashley, M. (2009) 'Time to confront Willis's lads with a ballet class? A case study of educational orthodoxy and white working-class boys', *British Journal of Sociology of Education*, 30: 179–91.

Association of Teachers and Lecturers. (2011) 'Boys' behaviour at school is still more challenging than that of girls, but the behaviour of both is getting worse', Press Release. Available HTTP: http://www.atl.org.uk/Images/15%20April%202011%20-%20Boys%20behaviour%20still%20more%20challeging%20than%20girls%20but%20behaviour%20of%20both%20is%20getting%20worse%20-%20ATL%20annual%20conf%20final.pdf (accessed 30 July 2012).

Atkinson, M. and Hornby, G. (2002) *Mental Health Handbook for Schools*, London/New York: RoutledgeFalmer.

Attention Deficit Disorder Information and Support Service (ADDISS). (2006) *Families Survey August 2006*. Available HTTP: http://www.addiss.co.uk (accessed 15 January 2010).

Australian Bureau of Statistics (ABS). (2001) *Census of Population and Housing: socio-economic indexes for areas, Australia, 2001*, Canberra: ABS.

Australian Institute of Health and Welfare (AIHW). (2011a) 'The health and welfare of Australia's Aboriginal and Torres Strait Islander people, an overview 2011', Cat. no. IHW 42, Canberra: AIHW.

Australian Institute of Health and Welfare (AIHW). (2011b) 'Aboriginal and Torres Strait Islander child safety', Cat. no. IHW 50, Canberra: AIHW.

Averill, L.A. (1928) *The Hygiene of Instruction – a study of the mental health of the school child*, London: George G. Harrap & Company.

Azevedo, P., Caixeta, L., Andreda, L. and Bordin, I. (2010) 'Attention deficit hyperactivity disorder symptoms in indigenous children from the Brazilian Amazon', *Arquivos de neuro-psiquiatria*, 68 (4), 541–4.

Baby Brain Box. (2013a). *Brain Wiring Facts.* Available HTTP: http://www.babybrainbox. com/productdetails.asp (accessed 11 December 2013).

Baby Brain Box. (2013b). *Brain Wiring Facts.* Available HTTP: http://www.babybrainbox. com/brainWiringFacts.asp (accessed 11 December 2013).

Bagley, C. (2006) 'From Sure Start to Children's Centres: capturing the erosion of social capital', *Journal of Education Policy*, 26(1): 95–113.

Baker, B. (1998) '"Childhood" in the emergence and spread of U.S. public schools', in T. Popkewitz and M. Brennan (eds) *Foucault's Challenge: discourse, knowledge and power in education*, New York: Teachers College Press.

Baker, B. (2002) 'The hunt for disability: the new eugenics and the normalization of school children', *Teachers College Record*, 104(4): 663–704.

Baker, B. (2007) 'The apophasis of limits: genius, madness, and learning disability', *International Journal of Inclusive Education*, 11(1): 33.

Baldwin, J.M. (ed.). (1901–5) *Dictionary of Philosophy and Psychology*, New York: Macmillan.

Baldwin, S. (2000) How should ADHD be treated?, *The Psychologist*, 13(12): 598–602.

Ball, S. (2013) *Foucault, Power and Education*, London: Routledge.

Bamford, R.W. (1822) *Essays on the Discipline of Children, Particularly as Regards their Education*, London: Baldwin, Cradock & Joy.

Barkley, R.A. (1997) *ADHD and the Nature of Self-Control*, New York: Guilford Press.

Barkley, R.A. (1998) 'Attention-deficit hyperactivity disorder', *Scientific American*, 3(3): 66.

Barkley, R.A. and Biederman, J. (1997) 'Towards a broader definition of the age-of-onset criterion for attention deficit hyperactivity disorder', *Journal of the American Academy of Child and Adolescent Psychiatry*, 36: 1204–10.

Barkley, R.A., DuPaul ,G.J. and McMurray, M.B. (1990) 'A comprehensive evaluation of attention deficit disorder with and without hyperactivity', *Journal of Consulting and Clinical Psychology*, 58: 775–89.

Barkley, R. *et al.* (2002) 'International consensus statement on ADHD', *Clinical Child and Family Psychology Review*, 5: 89–111.

Barnes, M., Chanfreau, J. and Tomaszewski, W. (2010) *Growing Up In Scotland: the circumstances of persistently poor children*, Edinburgh: National Centre for Social Research.

Bauermeister, J., Matos, M., Reina, G., Salas, C., Martinez, J., Cumba, E. and Barkley, R. (2005) 'Comparison of the DSM-IV combined and inattentive types of ADHD in a school-based sample of Latino/ Hispanic children', *The Journal of Child Psychology and Psychiatry*, 46: 166–79.

Baumeister, A.A, and Hawkins, M.F. (2001) 'Incoherence of neuroimaging studies of attention deficit hyperactivity disorder', *Clinical Neoropharmacology*, 24(6): 2–10.

Bayram, N. and Bilgel, N. (2008) 'The prevalence and socio-demographic correlations of depression, anxiety and stress among a group of university students', *Social Psychiatry and Psychiatric Epidemiology*, 43(8): 667–72.

BBC. (2013) 'Profile: Aurora cinema shooting suspect James Holmes', *BBC News US & Canada*, 1 April 2013. Available HTTP: http://www.bbc.co.uk/news/world-us-canada-18937513 (accessed 17 April 2013).

Beach, D. (2012) 'Sixty years of policy development in teacher education in Sweden: changing professional discourses in teacher education policy', keynote address at the International Conference on the Transformation of School and Teacher Professionalism, Gothenburg, 26–27 April 2012.

Bean, P.T., Bingley, I., Bynoe, A. and Faulkner, A. (1991) *Out of Harm's Way*, London: MIND.

Béhague, D. (2009) 'Psychiatry and politics in Pelotas, Brazil: the equivocal quality of conduct disorder and related diagnoses', *Medical Anthropology Quarterly*, 23(4): 433–82.

Behaviour.Adviser.com (undated) 'Dr Mac's behaviour management site'. Available HTTP: http://www.behavioradvisor.com (accessed 25 March 2013).

Bennett, J. (2001) *The Enchantment of Modern Life: attachments, crossings, and ethics*, Princeton: Princeton University Press.

Bernstein, B. (1999) 'Vertical and horizontal discourse: an essay', *British Journal of Sociology of Education*, 20(2): 157–73.

Berrios, G.E. (1995) 'Mood disorders', in G.E. Berrios and R. Porter (eds) *A history of Clinical Psychiatry: the origin and history of psychiatric disorders*, London: Athlone Press.

Berubé, M. (1997) 'The cultural representation of disabled people affects us all', *Higher Education Chronicle*, May: 85.

Berubé, M. (2002) 'Foreward: side shows and back bends', in L. Davis (ed.) *Bending Over Backwards: disability, dismodernism and other difficult positions*, New York/London: New York University Press.

Biesta, G. (2006) *Beyond Learning: democratic learning for a human future*, Boulder, CO: Paradigm Publishers.

Bilkey, T. (2013) 'ADHD in adolescence: a focus on impulsivity', *Psychology Today*, 16 May 2013. Available HTTP: http://www.psychologytoday.com/blog/fast-minds/201305/adhd-in-adolescence-focus-impulsivity (accessed 10 June 2013).

Birrell, B., Healy, E., Edwards, D. and Dobson, I. (2008) *Higher Education in Australia: demand and supply issues, Report for the Review of Higher Education*. Melbourne: Monash University.

Bolten, M. (2013) 'Infant psychiatric disorders', *European Child & Adolescent Psychiatry*, 22(1): 69–74.

Bonnie, R.J. (1990) 'Soviet psychiatry and human rights: reflections on the report of the U.S. delegation', *Law, Medicine and Health Care*, 18(1–2): 123–31.

Bowlby, J. (1969) *Attachment*, New York: Basic Books.

Bowlby, J. (1998) *Attachment and loss, Volume 2: Separation, anger and anxiety*, London: Random House.

Brah, A. and Phoenix, A. (2004) 'Ain't I a woman? Revisiting intersectionality', *Journal of International Women's Studies*, 5(3): 75–86.

Brantlinger, E. (2004) 'Confounding the needs and confronting the norms: an extension of Reid and Valle's essay', *Journal of Learning Disabilities*, 37(6): 490–9.

Brantlinger, E. (2006) 'Winners need losers: the basis for school competition and hierarchies', in E. Brantlinger (ed.) *Who Benefits from Special Education? Remediating [fixing] other people's children*, Mahway, NJ: Lawrence Erlbaum.

Brantlinger, P. (2011) 'Educating the Victorians', in S. Ledger and H. Furneaux (eds) *Charles Dickens in Context*, Cambridge: Cambridge University Press.

Breggin, P.R. (1999) 'Psychostimulants in the treatment of children diagnosed with ADHD: risks and mechanism of action', *International Journal of Risk and Safety in Medicine*, 12(1): 3–35.

Brooks, R.A. (2000) 'Official madness: a cross-cultural study of involuntary civil confinement based on "mental illness"', in J. Hubert (ed.) *Madness, Disability and Social Exclusion: the archaeology and anthropology of 'difference'*, London: Routledge.

Bruer, J. (1999) *The Myth of the First Three Years*, New York: The Free Press.

Burnham, W.M. (1924) *The Normal Mind: an introduction to mental hygiene and the hygiene of school instruction*, New York: D. Appleton and Company.

Burton, R. (2004) *The Anatomy of Melancholy* [1624]. Available HTTP: http://www. gutenberg.org/files/10800/10800-h/ampart1.html (accessed 29 June 2012).

Bussing, R., Schoenberg, N.E., Rogers, K.M., Zima, B.T. and Angus, S. (1998) 'Explanatory models of ADHD: do they differ by ethnicity, child gender, or treatment status?', *Journal of Emotional and Behavioral Disorders*, 6(4): 233–42.

Cabinet Office. (2008) 'Getting on, getting ahead. A discussion paper analysing the trends and drivers of social mobility', London: The Cabinet Office Strategy Unit.

Campaign Against Living Miserably (CALM). (2010) 'Exclusion – a boys problem'. Available HTTP: http://www.thecalmzone.net/2010/11/exclusion-a-boys-problem-around-80-of-students-permanently-excluded-from-schools-are-boys/ (accessed 21 September 2012).

Cannon, M., Jones, P.B. and Murray, R.M. (2002) 'Obstetric complications and schizophrenia: historical and meta-analytic review', *American Journal of Psychiatry*, 159: 634–8.

Canter, L. and Canter, M. (1992) *Lee Canter's Assertive Discipline: positive behaviour management for today's classroom*, Santa Monica, CA: Canter and Associates.

Cantwell, D. (1996) 'Attention deficit disorder: a review of the past 10 years', *Journal of the American Academy of Child Adolescccent Psychiatry*, 35: 978–87.

Caplan, P. (1995) *They Say You're Crazy: how the world's most powerful psychiatrists decide who's normal*, New York: Addison-Wesley Publishing Co.

Carmichael, M. (2008, 26 May). 'Welcome to Max's world; Bipolar Disorder is a mystery and a subject of medical debate. But for the Blakes, it's just reality', *Newsweek*, 3: 151.

Carr, E.G., Dunlap, G., Horner, R.H., Koegel, R.L., Turnbull, A.P., Sailor, W., Anderson, J. L., Albin, R.W., Koegel, L.K. and Fox, L. (2002) 'Positive behavior support: evolution of an applied science', *Journal of Positive Behavior Interventions*, 4: 4–16.

Carter, A.S., Briggs-Gowan, M., Jones, S.M. and Little, T.D. (2003) 'The Infant-Toddler Social and Emotional Assessment (ITSEA): factor, structure, reliability and validity', *Journal of Abnormal Child Psychology*, 3: 495–514.

Carter, A., Briggs-Gowan, M. and Davies, N. (2004) 'Assessment of young children's social-emotional development and psychopathology: recent advances and recommendations for practice', *Journal of. Child and Adolescent Psychiatry*, 45: 109–34.

Castenda, C. (2002) *Figurations: child bodies*, Durham, NC: Duke University Press.

Center for Digital Discourse and Culture Virginia Polytechnic Institute and State University, and Center for History and New Media George Mason University (CDDC and CHNM). (2008) 'The April 16 Archive'. Available HTTP: http://www.april16archive. org (accessed 29 November 2008).

Centers for Disease Control and Prevention (CDC). (2011) 'Increasing prevalence of parent-reported attention-deficit/hyperactivity disorder among children – United States, 2003 and 2007'. Available HTTP: http://www.cdc.gov/mmwr/preview/mmwrhtml/ mm5944a3.htm (accessed 6 July 2012).

Centre for the Developing Brain. (2013) 'Perinatal imaging'. Available HTTP: http:// www.kcl.ac.uk/medicine/research/divisions/imaging/centres/cdb/research/perinatal/ index.aspx (accessed 18 December 2013).

Chapman, K. (2009). 'A preventable tragedy at Virginia Tech: Why confusion over FERPa's provisions prevents schools from addressing student violence', *The Boston University Public Interest Law Journal*, 18 (Spring): 349–85.

Charach, A., Yeung, E., Climans, T. and Lillie, E. (2011) 'Childhood attention-deficit/ hyperactivity disorder and future substance use disorders: comparative meta-analyses', *Journal of the American Academy of Childhood and Adolescent Psychiatry*, 50(1): 9–21.

Child Guidance Council. (1937) *Proceedings of the Child Guidance Inter-Clinic Conference of Great Britain*, London: Child Guidance Council.

Chilcott, T. (2012) 'High school teacher speaks out on learning problem affecting well behaved pupils'. *The Courier-Mail*, 28 August 2012. Available HTTP: http://www. couriermail.com.au/news/queensland/high-school-teacher-speaks-out-on-learning-problem-affecting-well-behaved-pupils/story-e6freoof-1226459362713 (accessed 12 June 2013).

Clarizio, H.F. and McCoy, G.F. (1970) *Behaviour Disorders in School-Aged Children*, Scranton: Chandler Publishing Company.

Clark, A. (2011) 'New school year gives Shire sales a boost', *The Times.*, 29 October 2011. Available HTTP: http://www.thetimes.co.uk/tto/business/industries/health/article3209883.ece (accessed 11 December 2013).

Clark, C. (2008) 'Team formed to balance safety, privacy', *Emory Report*. 23 June 2008. Available HTTP: http://www.emory.edu/EMORY_REPORT/erarchive/2008/June/June23/ThreatAssessmentComm.htm (accessed 7 July 2009).

Clarke, A.M., Clarke A.D.B. and Berg, J.M. (1985) 'Preface', in A.M. Clarke, A.D.B. Clarke and J.M. Berg (eds) *Mental Deficiency: the Changing Outlook*, London: Methuen and Co.

Cohen, E. and Kaufman, R. (2005) *Early Childhood Mental Health Consultation*, Rockville MD: Center for Mental Health Services, Substance Abuse and Mental Health Services Administration.

Coldstream, J. (1856) *The Education of the Imbecile, and the Improvement of Invalid Youth: home school for invalid and imbecile children*, Edinburgh: Home and School for Invalid and Imbecile Children.

Comber, B. and Kamler, B. (2004) 'Getting out of deficit: pedagogies of reconnection', *Teaching Education*, 15(3): 293–310.

Committee for Promoting the Royal Lancasterian System for the Education of the Poor. (1810) *Address of the Committee for Promoting the Royal Lancasterian System for the Education for the Poor*, London: Author.

Connell, D. (2009) *Recommended Practices for Virginia College Threat Assessment*, Virginia: Virginia Department of Criminal Justice Services.

Connell, J., Barkham, M. and Mellor-Clark, J. (2007) 'CORE-OM mental health norms of students attending university counselling services benchmarked against an age-matched primary care sample', *British Journal of Guidance and Counselling*, 35(1): 41–57.

Conrad, P. (2007) *The Medicalization of Society: on the transformation of human conditions into treatable disorders*, Baltimore: Johns Hopkins University Press.

Conrad, P. and Stults, S. (2008) 'Contestation and medicalization', in P. Moss and K. Teghtsoonian (eds) *Contesting Illness: processes and practices*, Toronto: University of Toronto Press Incorporated.

Cooksey, E. and Brown, P. (1998) 'Spinning on its axes: DSM and the social construction of psychiatric illness', *International Journal of Health Services*, 28(3): 525–54.

Costello, E.J., Worthman, C., Erkanali, A., and Angold, A. (2007) 'Prediction from low birth weight to female adolescent depression: a test of competing hypotheses', *Archives of General Psychiatry*, 64: 338–44.

Crenshaw, K. (1994) 'Demarginalizing the intersection of race and sex: a black feminist critique of antidiscrimination docrine, feminist theory, and antiracist politics', in A. Jagger (ed.) *Living with Contradiction: controversies in feminist social ethics*, Boulder: Westview.

Critchley, J. (2007) *Infinitely Demanding: ethics of commitment, politics of resistance*, London and New York: Verso.

Crone, D. and Horner, R. (2003) *Building Positive Behavior Support Systems in Schools: functional behavioral assessment*, New York: The Guildford Press.

Cuneen, C., Luke, G. and Ralph, N. (2006) *Evaluation of the Aboriginal Over-representation Strategy*, Sydney: Institute of Criminology, The University of Sydney.Daley, D., Sonuga-Burke, E.J.S., Thompson, T. and Chen, W. (2008) 'Gene social environment interplay in relation to attention deficit hyperactivity disorder', *Psychiatry*, 7: 520–4.

Daniels, H. and Porter, J. (2007) 'Learning needs and difficulties among children of primary school age: definition, identification, provision and issues', *Primary Review* Research Briefings 5/2. Available HTTP: http://www.primaryreview.org.uk/downloads/Int_Reps/4.Children_development-learning/Primary_Review_5-2_briefing_Learning_needs_difficulties_071214.pdf (accessed 9 August 2012).

Daniels, H., Visser, J., Cole, T. and de Reybekill, N. (1999) *Emotional and Behavioural Difficulties in Mainstream Schools*, Sudbury: Department for Education and Employment.

Daniels, H., Visser, J., Cole, T. and de Reybekill, N. (1999) *Emotional and Behavioural Difficulties in Mainstream Schools*, Sudbury: Department for Education and Employment.

Davies, G.K. (2008) 'Connecting the dots: lessons from the Virginia Tech shootings', *Change, the Magazine of Higher Learning*, 40(1) January–February: 8–15.

Davis, L. (2002) *Bending Over Backwards: disability, dismodernism and other difficult positions*, New York/London: New York University Press.

De Landa, M. (1991) *War in the Age of Intelligent Machines*, New York: Zone Books, MIT Press.

Del Giudice, M. (2012). 'Fetal programming by maternal stress: Insights from a conflict perspective', *Psychoneuroendocrinology*, 37(10), 1614–1629.

Deleuze, G. (1990) *The Logic of Sense*, New York: Columbia University Press.

Deleuze, G. (1992) 'Postscript on the Societies of Control', *October*, 59: 3–7.

Deleuze, G. (1995) *Negotiations*, trans. M. Joughin, New York: Columbia University Press.

Deleuze, G. and Guattari, F. (1983) *Anti-Oedipus: capitalism and schizophrenia*, Minneapolis: University of Minnesota Press.

Deleuze, G. and Guattari, F. (1986) *Kafka: toward a minor literature*, trans. D. Polan, Minneapolis: University of Minnesota Press.

Deleuze, G. and Guattari, F. (1987) *A Thousand Plateaus: capitalism and schizophrenia*, London: The Athlone Press.

Deleuze, G. and Guattari. F. (1994) *What is Philosophy*, trans. G. Burchell and H. Tomlinson, London: Verso.

Deleuze, G. and Parnet, C. (1987) *Dialogues*, trans. H. Tomlinson and B. Habberjam, New York: Columbia University Press.

Delgado-Bernal, D. (2002) 'Critical race theory, Latino critical theory, and critical raced-gendered epistemologies: recognising students of color as holders and creators of knowledge', *Qualitative Inquiry*, 8(1): 105–26.

Demos. (2009) *Building Character*, London: Demos.

DeNoon, D. (Producer) (2007) 'V.A. Tech Gunman Warning Signs?', *CBS News*, 18 April 2007. Available HTTP: http://www.cbsnews.com/2100-500368_162-2698905.html (accessed 20 June 2013).

d'Entrèves, M.P. (2000) 'Arendt's theory of judgment', in D.R. Villa (ed.) *The Cambridge Companion to Hannah Arendt* (pp. 245–60), Cambridge: Cambridge University Press.

Department for Education (DFE) (1994) *Pupils with Problems, Circulars 8–13/94*, London: Her Majesty's Stationery Office.

Department for Education. (2011a) 'Special educational needs in England: January 2011'. Available HTTP: http://www.education.gov.uk/rsgateway/DB/SFR/s001007/index. shtml (accessed 6 July 2012).

Department for Education (2011b) *Support and Aspiration: a new approach to special educational needs and disability*, Norwich: The Stationery Office.

Department for Education (2012a) 'Getting the simple things right: Charlie Taylor's behaviour checklists'. Available HTTP: http://www.education.gov.uk/a00199342/getting-the-simple-things-right-charlie-taylors-behaviour-checklists (accessed 25 March 2012).

Department for Education (2012b) *Teachers' Standards*, Available HTTP: http://media.education. gov.uk/assets/files/pdf/t/new%20teachers%20standards.pdf (accessed 22 February 2013).

Department for Education and Children's Services (DECS). (2010) 'ICAN: Innovative community action networks'. Available HTTP: http://www.ican.sa.edu.au/pages/aboutus/ (accessed 15 January 2010).

deviantart. (2009) 'Cho Seung Hui comics 3'. Available HTTP: http://latuff2.deviantart. com/art/Cho-Seung-Hui-comics-3-54219309 (accessed 10 September 2009).

Dewey, J. (1934) *Art as Experience*, New York: Capricorn Books.

Dickens, C. (1850) *The Personal History and Experience of David Copperfield the Younger.* ebooks@Adelaide (University of Adelaide).

Disanto, G., Morahan, J.M., Lacey, M.V., DeLuca, G.C., Giovannoni, G., Ebers, G. C. and Ramagopalan, S.V. (2012) 'Seasonal distribution of psychiatric births in England', *PLoS One*, 7(4): e34866.

Dodge, K.A. (2008) 'Framing public policy and prevention of chronic violence in American youths', *American Psychologist*, 63(7): 573–90.

Donnelly, K. (2007). *Dumbing Down: outcomes-based and politically correct – the impact of the culture wars on our schools*, Prahran: Hardie Grant Books.

Doshi, J., Hodgkins, P., Kahle, J., Sikirica, V., Cangelosi, M., Setyawan, J., Erder, M. and Neumann, P. (2012) 'Economic impact of childhood and adult attention-deficit/ hyperactivity disorder in the United States', *Journal of the American Academy of Child Adolescent Psychiatry*, 51(10): 990–1002.

Dudley-Marling, C. (2001) 'Reconceptualizing learning disabilities by reconceptualizing education', in L. Denti and P. Tefft-Cousin (eds) *New Ways of Looking at Learning Disabilities*, Denver: Love.

Dukes, C. (1887) *Health at School: Considered in its Mental, Moral and Physical Aspects*, London: Cassell & Company Ltd.

Dunkle, J.H., Silverstein, Z.B. and Warner, S.L. (2008) 'Managing violent and other troubling students: the role of threat assessment teams on campus', *Journal of College and University Law*, 34(3): 585–636.

Durand-Fardel, M. (1885) *Étude sur le Suicide chez les Enfants*, Paris: Annales Médico-psychologiques.

Dürer, A. (Artist) (1514). *Melancholia I* [engraving].

Dwivedi, K. and Banhatti, R.G. (2005) 'Attention deficit hyperactivity disorder and ethnicity', *Archives of Disease in Childhood*. Available HTTP: http://adc.bmj.com/content/90/suppl_1/i10.full.pdf (accessed 6 July 2012).

Edwards G., Barkley R.A., Laneri M., Fletcher, K. and Metevia, L. (2001) 'Parent–adolescent conflict in teenagers with ADHD and ODD', *Journal of Abnormal Child Psychology*, 29: 557–72.

Edwards, R. (2011) 'Theory matters: representation and experimentation in education', *Educational Philosophy and Theory*, 44: 522–34.

Egan, M. (2006) 'The manufacture of mental defectives. Why the number of mental defectives increased in Scotland 1857–1939', in P. Dale and J. Melling (eds) *Mental Illness and Learning Disability Since 1850: Finding a place for mental disorder in the United Kingdom*, Oxford: Routledge.

Egger, H.L. (2009) 'Psychiatric assessment of young children', *Child Adolescent Psychiatric Clinic North America*, 18: 559–80.

Elias, M. (2008) 'Colleges put out safety nets', *USA Today*, April 15 2008. Available HTTP: http://www.usatoday.com/news/health/2008-04-15-college-safety_N.htm (accessed 15 May 2008).

Ellingsen, P. (2001). 'Drugging away the pain of youth', *The Age*, 12 March 2001: 1.

Emde, R., Bingham, R. and Harmon, R. (1993) 'Classification and the diagnostic process in infancy', in C.H. Zeanah (ed.) *Handbook of Infant Mental Health*, 2nd edn, New York: Guilford Press.

Erevelles, N. (2005) 'Signs of reason: Rivière, facilitated communication and the crisis of the subject', in S. Tremain (ed.) *Foucault and the Government of Disability*, Ann Arbor, MI: University of Michigan Press.

Erevelles, N. (2010) 'Unspeakable offenses: untangling race and disability in discourses of intersectionality', *Journal of Literary and Cultural Disability Studies*, 4(2): 127–45.

Errington, M. (1987) '"Mental illness" in Australian legislation', *The Australian Law Journal*, 61: 182–91.

Eryigit-Madzwamuse, S. and Barnes, J. (2013) 'Is early center-based child care associated with tantrums and unmanageable behavior over time up to school entry?', *Child and Youth Care Forum*, 42(2): 101–17.

European Commission. (2011) 'Family literacy in Europe: using parental support initiatives to enhance early literacy development', Brussels: European Commission. Available HTTP: http://ec.europa.eu/education/more-information/doc/2011/literacy_en.pdf (accessed 29 March 2012).

Fair, B. (2010) 'Morgellons: contested illness, diagnostic compromise and medicalisation', *Sociology of Health and Illness*, 32: 597–612.

Ferri, B. (2004) 'Interrupting the discourse: a response to Reid and Valle', *Journal of Learning Disabilities*, 37(6): 509–15.

Ferri, B.A. and Connor, D.J. (2005) 'In the shadow of Brown', *Remedial and Special Education*, 26(2): 93–100.

Fife-Yeomans, J. (2007) 'The Ritalin generation: top judge condemns ADHD explosion', *The Daily Telegraph*, 28 April 2007: 1, 4.

Fitzgerald, T.D. (2009) 'Controlling the black school-age male', *Urban Education*, 44: 225–47.

Fontana, A. (1975) 'The intermittences of rationality', in M. Foucault (ed.) *I, Pierre Rivière, Having Slaughtered my Mother, my Sister, and my Brother: a case study of parricide in the nineteenth century*; trans F. Jellinek, Lincoln: University of Nebraska Press.

Foucault, M. (1970) *The Order of Things: an archaelogy of the human sciences*, London: Tavistock Publications.

Foucault, M. (1976) *History of Sexuality*, vol. 1, Harmondsworth: Penguin.

Foucault, M. (1977) 'Nietzsche, genealogy, history', in D.F. Bouchard (ed.) *Language, Counter-Memory, Practice: selected essays and interviews*, Ithaca, NY: Cornell University Press.

Foucault, M. (1979) *Discipline and Punish*, New York: Pantheon Press.

Foucault, M. (1980a) 'Two lectures', in C. Gordon (ed.) *Power/Knowledge: selected interviews and other writings 1972–1977*, New York: Pantheon.

Foucault, M. (1980b). 'The confession of the flesh', in C. Gordon (ed.) *Power/Knowledge: selected interviews and other writings 1972–1977*, New York: Pantheon.

Foucault, M. (1980c) 'Truth and power', in C. Gordon (ed.) *Power/Knowledge: selected interviews and other writings 1972–1977*, New York: Pantheon.

Foucault, M. (1980d) 'Questions of geography', in C. Gordon (ed.) *Power/Knowledge: selected interviews and other writings 1972–1977*, New York: Pantheon.

Foucault, M. (1982). 'The subject and power', in H.L. Dreyfus and P. Rabinow (eds), *Michel Foucault: beyond structuralism and hermeneutics*, Chicago: University of Chicago Press.

Foucault, M. (1983). 'The subject and power', in H.L. Dreyfus and P. Rabinow (eds), *Michel Foucault: beyond structuralism and hermeneutics*, 2nd edn, Chicago: University of Chicago Press.

Foucault, M. (1984) 'On the genealogy of ethics: an overview of work in progress', in P. Rabinow (ed.) *The Foucault Reader*, New York: Pantheon.

Foucault, M. (1985) *The History of Sexuality: The Use of Pleasure*, New York: Pantheon.

Foucault, M. (1988) 'Truth, power, self: an interview with Michel Foucault', in L.H Martin, H. Gutman and P. Hutton (eds) *Technologies of the Self*, Amherst, MA: The University of Massachusetts Press.

Foucault, M. (1989) *Foucault Live: interviews*; trans J. Johnson, ed. S Lotringer, New York: Semiotext(e).

Foucault, M. (1997a) 'Subjectivity and truth', in S. Lotringer and L. Hochroth (eds) *The Politics of Truth: Michel Foucault*, New York: Semiotext(e).

Foucault, M. (1997b) 'What is critique?', in S. Lotringer and L. Hochroth (eds) *The Politics of Truth: Michel Foucault*, New York: Semiotext(e).

Foucault, M. (1998) 'Structuralism and post-structuralism', in J.D. Fabion (ed.) *Aesthetics, Method, and Epistemology. The essential works of Michel Foucault*, vol. 2, New York: The New Press.

Foucault, M. (2000) 'Truth and power', in J.D. Faubion (ed.) *Power, The Essential Works of Michel Foucault*, vol. 3, New York: The New Press.

Foucault, M. (2001) *Madness and Civilisation*, London: Routledge.

Foucault, M. (2003a) *Abnormal: lectures at the Collège de France 1974–75*; trans. G. Burchell, London: Picador.

Foucault, M. (2003b) *Society Must be Defended: lectures at the Collège de France 1975–1976*; trans. D. Macey, eds M. Bertani and A. Fortana, New York: Picador.

Foucault, M. (2006) *History of Madness*; trans. J. Murphy and J. Khalfa, Abingdon, Oxon: Routledge.

Foucault, M. (2008a) *Psychiatric Power: lectures at the Collège de France 1973–74*, trans. G. Burchell, London: Palgrave Macmillan.

Foucault, M. (2008b) *The Government of the Self and Others: lectures at the Collège de France, 1982–1983*; trans. G. Burchell, New York: Palgrave Macmillan.

Foucault, M. (2009) *Security, Technology, Population: lectures at the Collège de France 1977–1978*, London: Palgrave Macmillan.

Fox, J.A. (2009) 'Mass murder goes to college', *American Behavioral Scientist*, 52(10): 1465–85.

Fox, N.J. and Ward, K.J. (2011) 'What are health identities and how may we study them?', *Sociology of Health and Illness*, 30(7): 1007–21.

Frances, A. (2012) 'Diagnosing the D.S.M.', *New York Times* (opinion), 11 May 2012. Available HTTP: http://www.nytimes.com/2012/05/12/opinion/break-up-the-psychiatric-monopoly.html (accessed 1 April 2013).

Fraser, K. (2013) 'Queensland school to have "behavioural hub" to segregate unruly students from peers behind 2m-high security fence', *news.com.au*, 5 May 2013. Available HTTP:

http://www.news.com.au/national-news/queensland-school-to-have-behavioural-hub-to-segregate-unruly-students-from-peers-behind-2m-high-security-fence/story-fncynjr2-1226635167405 (accessed 5 May 2013).

Friedman, R.A. (2006). 'Violence and mental illness: how strong is the link?', *New England Journal of Medicine*, 355(20), 2064–6.

Garth, T. (1919) 'Racial differences in mental fatigue', *Journal of Applied Psychology*, 4: 235–44.

Garth, T. (1931) *Race Psychology: a study of racial mental differences*, New York: McGraw-Hill.

Gentschel, D. and McLaughlin, T. (2000) 'Attention deficit hyperactivity disorder as a social disability: characteristics and suggested methods of treatment', *Journal of Developmental and Physical Disabilities*, 12(4): 333–47.

Gillborn, D. (2008) *Racism and Education: coincidence or conspiracy?*, London: Routledge.

Gilliam, W.S. (2005). *Pre-kindergarteners Left Behind: expulsion rates in state pre-kindergarten systems*, New Haven, CT: Yale University Child Study Center.Gilliam, W.S. and Shahar, G. (2006) 'Preschool and child care expulsion and suspension: rates and predictors in one state', *Infants and Young Children*, 19(3): 228–45.

Gillies, V. (2005) 'Raising the "meritocracy": parenting and the individualization of social class', *Sociology*, 39(5): 835–53.

Glover, V. and O'Connor, T. (2002) 'Effects of antenatal stress and anxiety: implications for development and psychiatry', *British Journal of Psychiatry*, 180: 389–91.

Goode, E., Kovaleski, S.F., Healy, J. and Frosch, D. (2012) 'Before gunfire, hints of "bad news"', *The New York Times*, 26 August 2012. Available HTTP: http://www.nytimes.com/2012/08/27/us/before-gunfire-in-colorado-theater-hints-of-bad-news-about-james-holmes.html (accessed 24 September 2013).

Goodley, D. and Runswick-Cole, K. (2011) 'Problematising policy: conceptions of "child", "disabled" and "parents" in social policy in England', *International Journal of Inclusive Education*, 15: 71–85.

Goodman, A. and Gregg, P. (2010) *Poorer Children's Educational Attainment: how important are attitudes to behaviour*, York: Institute for Fiscal Studies, Joseph Rowntree Foundation.

Goodman, S., Rouse, M., Connell, A., Broth, M., Hall, C. and Heyward, D. (2011) 'Maternal depression and child psychopathology: a meta-analytic review', *Clinical Child and Family Psychology Review*, 14(1): 1–27.

Gorard, S. (2010) 'Education can compensate for society – a bit', *British Journal of Studies in Education*, 58(1): 47–65.

Gorard, S. and Smith, E. (2010) *Equity in Education: an international comparison of pupil perspectives*, London: Palgrave.

Gradín, C. (2007) *Why is poverty so high among Afro-Brazilians? A decomposition analysis of the racial poverty gap*, Bonn: Institute for the Study of Labor.

Graham, L.J. (2008) 'Drugs, labels and (p)ill-fitting boxes: ADHD and children who are hard to teach', *Discourse: studies in the cultural politics of education*, 29(1): 85–106.

Graham, L.J. (2012) 'Disproportionate over-representation of Indigenous students in New South Wales government special schools', *Cambridge Journal of Education*, 42(2): 163–76.

Gray, P. and Panter, S. (2000) 'Exclusion or inclusion? A perspective on policy in England for pupils with emotional and behavioural difficulties', *Support for Learning*, 15(1): 4–7.

Gros, F. (2008) 'Course context', in F. Gros (ed.) *The Government of Self and Others*, New York: Palgrave Macmillan.

Guardian. (2008) 'Male teachers are crucial role models for boys, suggests research', *The Guardian*, 30 September 2008. Available HTTP: http://www.guardian.co.uk/education/2008/sep/30/primaryschools.malerolemodels (accessed 30 September 2008).

Hack, M., Flannery, D., Schluchter, M., Cartar, L., Borawski, E. and Klein, N. (2002) 'Outcomes in young adulthood for very-low-birth-weight infants', *New England Journal of Medicine*, 346: 149–57.

Hackett L. and Hackett R.J. (1993) 'Parental ideas of normal and deviant behaviour: a comparison of two ethnic groups', *British Journal of Psychiatry*, 162, 353–7.

Hacking, I. (2002) 'Inaugural lecture: Chair of Philosophy and History of Scientific Concepts at the Collège de France, 16 January 2001', *Economy and Society*, 31: 1–14.

Hanks, P. (ed.) (1981) *Collins Dictionary of the English Language*, Sydney: Collins.

Harpin, V. (2005) 'The effect of ADHD on the life of an individual, their family, and community from preschool to adult life', *Archives of Disease in Childhood*, 90 (Suppl I): i2–i7.

Harwood, V. (2004) 'Subject to scrutiny: taking Foucauldian genealogy to narratives of youth oppression', in M. Rasmussen, S. Talburt and E. Rofes (eds) *Youth and Sexualities: pleasure, subversion, and insubordination in and out of schools*, New York: Palgrave.

Harwood, V. (2006) *Diagnosing 'Disorderly' Children: a critique of behaviour disorder discourses*, Oxford: Routledge.

Harwood, V. (2010a) 'Mobile asylums: psychopathologisation as a personal portable psychiatric prison', *Discourse: studies in the cultural politics of education*, 31(4): 437–51.

Harwood, V. (2010b). 'The new outsiders: ADHD and disadvantage', in L.J. Graham (ed.) *(De)Constructing ADHD: Critical guidance for teachers and teacher educators* (pp. 119–142). New York: Peter Lang.

Harwood, V. (2011) 'Connecting the dots: threat assessment, depression and the troubled student', *Curriculum Inquiry*, 41(5): 586–609.

Harwood, V. and Rasmussen, M.L. (2013) 'Practising critique, attending to truth: the padagogy of discriminatory speech', *Educational Philosophy and Theory*, 45(8): 874–84.

Heginbotham, C. (1987) *The Rights of Mentally Ill People*, London: Minority Rights Group.

Heilbrun, K., Dvoskin, J. and Heilbrun, A. (2009) 'Toward preventing future tragedies: mass killings on college campuses, public health and threat/risk assessment', *Psychological Injury and the Law*, 2(2): 93–9.

Heinemann, H.A. (1870) *Loss of Health and Beauty caused by Ordinary School Life: a lecture on seats and tables, delivered at the Royal College of Preceptors, London*, London: Asher & Co.

Helpguide.org (undated) 'Expert, ad-free resources to help you resolve health challenges'. Available HTTP: http://www.helpguide.org (accessed 2 March 2013).

Henry, C. and Demotes-Mainard, J. (2006) 'SSRIs, suicide and violent behaviour: is there a need for a better definition of the depressive state?', *Current Drug Safety*, 1(1): 59–62.

Hickey-Moody, A. (2009) 'Becoming-dinosaur: collective process and movement aesthetics', in L. Cull (ed.) *Deleuze and Performance*, Edinburgh: Edinburgh University Press.

Hillen, T., Gafson, L., Drage, L. and Conlan, L.M. (2012) 'Assessing the prevalence of mental health disorders and mental health needs among preschool children in care in England', *Infant Mental Health Journal*, 33(4): 411–20.

Hjörne, E. and Säljö, R. (2004) '"There is something about Julia" – symptoms, categories and the process of invoking ADHD in the Swedish school', *Journal of Language, Identity and Education*, 3(1): 1–24.

HM Treasury and DFES. (2007) *Policy Review of Children and Young People: a discussion paper*, Norwich: Her Majesty's Stationery Office.

Hoffman, H. (2004) *Struwwelpeter: merry tales and funny pictures*, Project Gutenberg. Available HTTP: http://www.gutenberg.org/files/12116/12116-h/12116-h.htm (accessed 3 July 2012).

Hogget, B. (1990) *Mental Health Law*, 3rd edn, London: Sweet and Maxwell.

Horwitz, A.V. and Wakefield, J. (2007) *The Loss of Sadness: how psychiatry transformed normal sorrow into depressive disorder*, New York: Oxford University Press.

House, A.E. (2002) *DSM-IV Diagnosis in the Schools – Updated 2002*, New York: The Guilford Press.

Howard, J. (1998) 'Subjectivity and space: Deleuze and Guattari's BwO in the new world order', in E. Kaufman and K.J. Heller (eds) *Deleuze and Guattari: new mappings in politics, philosophy and culture*, Minneapolis/London: University of Minnesota Press.

HRWebTeam. (2009) 'Threat assessment team (TAT)'. Available HTTP: http://www.uiowa.edu/hr/tat/tat_program.html (accessed 19 November 2009).

Hunt, J. and Eisenberg, D. (2010) 'Mental health problems and help-seeking behavior among college students', *The Journal of Adolescent Health: official publication of the Society for Adolescent Medicine*, 46(1): 3–10.

Hunt, S. and Symonds, A. (1995) *The Social Meaning of Midwifery*, Basingstoke: Macmillan.

Hyman, S (2010) 'The diagnosis of mental disorders: the problem of reification', *Annual Review of Clinical Pschology*, 6(12): 1–25.

Indredavik, M.S., Vik, T., Heyerdahl, S., Kulseng, S. and Brubakk, A.M. (2005) 'Psychiatric symptoms in low birth weight adolescents, assessed by screening questionnaires', *European Child and Adolescent Psychiatry*, 14: 226–36.

Infant Mental Health. (2012) 'Infant Mental Health', *Premie Press: a quarterly publication for those interested in the development of premature babies and children*, 13(1): 10–13.

Ireland, W.W. (1877) *On Idiocy and Imbecility*, London: J & A Churchill.

Ireland, W.W. (1898) *The Mental Affections of Children, Idiocy, Imbecility and Insanity*, London: J & A Churchill.

Isaacs, D. (2006) 'Attention-deficit/hyperactivity disorder: are we medicating for social disadvantage?', *Journal of Paediatrics and Child Health*, 42: 544–7.

Jacob, J.I. (2009) 'The socio-emotional effects of non-maternal childcare on children in the USA: a critical review of recent studies', *Early Child Development and Care*, 179(5): 559–70.

James, R. (1743). *A medicinal dictionary, including physic, surgery, anatomy, chymistry, and botany, in all their branches relative to medicine*. London: T. Osborne.

Jastrow, J. (1901) 'Depression', in J.M. Baldwin (ed.) *Dictionary of Philosophy and Psychology*. Available HTTP: http://psychclassics.yorku.ca/Baldwin/Dictionary/defs/D1defs.htm (accessed 30 August 2011).

Jenkins, R.L. (1973) *Behavior Disorders of Childhood and Adolescence*, Springfield, IL: Charles C. Thomas Publishers.

Johnston, J., Foxx, R., Jacobson, J., Green, G. and Mulick, J. (2006) 'Positive behavior support and applied behavior analysis', *Behavioral Analysis*, Spring 29(1): 51–74.

Jones, D., Dodge, K., Foster, E.M. and Nix, R. (2002) 'Early identification of children at risk for costly mental health service use', *Prevention Science*, 3(4): 247–56.

Kagan, J. (1998) *Three Seductive Ideas*, Cambridge, MA: Harvard University Press.

Kaine, T. (2008) 'Governor Kaine signs legislation in response to Virginia Tech shootings – legislation includes bills to reform and fund mental health services, adjust legal commitment criteria, and improve campus security' (media release, April 9 2008). Available HTTP: http://www.huliq.com/56597/governor-kaine-signs-legislation-response-virginia-tech-shootings (accessed 18 December 2013).

Kaiser, S. and Sachser, N. (2009) 'Effects of prenatal social stress on offspring development: pathology or adaptation?', *Current Directions in Psychological Science*, 18(2): 118–21.

Khawaja, N.G. and Bryden, K.J. (2006) 'The development and psychometric investigation of the university student depression inventory', *Journal of Affective Disorders*, 96: 21–9.

Kimmins, C.W. (1927) *The Mental and Physical Welfare of the Child*, London: Partridge.

King, M.L. (1947) 'The purpose of education', *The Maroon Tiger*, January–February. Available HTTP:    http://mlk-kpp01.stanford.edu/index.php/encyclopedia/documentsentry/doc_470200_000 (accessed 15 September 2013).

Kirk, S.A. and Kutchins, H. (1992) *The Selling of the DSM: the rhetoric of science in psychiatry*, New York: Aldine De Gruyte.

Knoster, T., Anderson, J., Carr, E.G., Dunlap, G. and Horner R. (2003) 'Emerging challenges and opportunities: introducing the Association for Positive Behavior Support', *Journal of Positive Behavior Interventions*, 5:183–6.

Kope, T. and Lansky, P.S. (2007) 'Infant mental health part 1: clincial concerns', *British Columbia Medical Journal*, 49(3): 114–15.

Kurtz, Z., Thornes, R. and Wolkind, S. (1995) *Services for the Mental Health of Young People in England: assessment of needs and unmet need. Report to the Department of Health*, London: Department of Health.

Ladson-Billings, G. (2006) 'From the achievement gap to the educational debt: understanding achievement in US schools', *Educational Researcher*, 35(7): 3–12.

Lancaster, J. (1806) *Improvements in Education, as it respects the industrious classes of the community, containing among other important particulars, an account of the Institution for the Education of One Thousand Poor Children, Borough Road, Southwark; and of the new system of education on which it is conducted*, 4th edn, London: J. Lancaster.

Lancet (2010) 'Editorial: DSM-5: diagnosis of medical disorders', *The Lancet*, 376(9739): 390.

Land, N. (1993) 'Making it with death: remarks on Thanatos and desiring production', *Journal of the British Society for Phenomenology*, 24: 66–76.

Lapage, C.P. (1911) *Feeblemindedness in Children of School-Age*, Manchester: Manchester University Press.

Lareau, A. (2003) *Unequal Childhoods: class, race, and family life*, Berkeley, CA: University of California Press.

Latour, B. (2004) 'Why has critique run out of steam? From matters of fact to matters of concern', *Critical Inquiry*, 30: 225–48.

Latuff, C. (Artist) (2007) *Cho Seung Hui comics 3 by Latuff2* [comic]. Available HTTP: http://latuff2.deviantart.com/art/Cho-Seung-Hui-comics-3-54219309 (accessed 26 November 2007).

Lauder, H., Brown, P. and Halsey, A.H. (2009) 'Sociology of education: a critical history and prospects for the future', *Oxford Review of Education*, 35: 569–85.

Laurence, J. and McCallum, D. (2006) 'The myth or reality of attention deficit disorder: a genealogical approach', *Discourse*, 19(2): 183–200.

Lee, S., Humphreys, K., Flory, K., Lieu, R. and Glass, K. (2011) 'Prospective association of childhood attention-deficit/hyperactivity disorder (ADHD) and substance use and abuse/dependence: a meta-analytic review', *Clinical Psychology Review*, 31(3): 328–41.

Lee, Y.A. and Goto, Y. (2013) 'The effects of prenatal and postnatal environmental interaction: prenatal environmental adaptation hypothesis', *Journal of Physiology – Paris*, 107(6): 483–92.

Lemke, T. (2001) '"The birth of bio-politics": Michel Foucault's lecture at the Collège de France on neo-liberal governmentality', *Economy and Society*, 30(2): 190–207.

Levy, D.M. (2006) 'Child psychiatry', in M.A. Beg and S.G. Beg (eds) *Global Encyclopedia of the Theoretical Psychology*, vol. 1, New Delhi: Global Vision Publishing House.

Li, D., Sham, P.C., Owen, M.J. and He, L. (2006) 'Meta analysis shows significant association between dopamine system genes and attention deficit hyperactivity disorder', *Human Molecular Genetics*, 15(4): 2276–84.

Lloyd, G., Cohen, D. and Stead, J. (eds) (2006) *Critical New Perspectives on ADHD*, Oxford: Routledge.

Loe, I. and Feldman, H. (2007) 'Academic and educational outcomes of children with ADHD', *Ambulatory Pediatrics*, 7: 82–90

Lords Hansard. (2007) 'Health: Ritalin', 14 November (column 471–2), London: UK House of Lords.

Lorry, A.-C. (1765) *De Melancholia et morbis melancholicis*, Paris: G. Cavelier.

Lyotard, J. (1986) *The Postmodern Explained to Children: correspondence 1982–1985*, Sydney: Power Publications.

Macbeath, J., Galton, M., Steward, S., Macbeath, A. and Page, C. (2006) *The Costs of Inclusion*, report prepared for the National Union of Teachers. Available HTTP: http://www.teachers.org.uk/node/2269 (accessed 18 December 2013).

McCartney, K., Burchinal, M., Clarke-Stewart, A., Bub, K.L., Owen, M.T. and Belsky, J. (2010) 'Testing a series of causal propositions relating time in child care to children's externalizing behavior', *Developmental Psychology*, 46(1): 1–17.

McCracken, J.T., Smalley, S.L., McGough, J.J., Crawford, L., Del'Homme, M., Cantor, R.M., Liu, A. and Nelson, S.F. (2000) 'Evidence for linkage of a tandem duplication polymorphism upstream of the dopamine D4 receptor gene (DRD4) with attention deficit hyperactivity disorder (ADHD)', *Molecular Psychiatry*, 5(5): 531–6.

McDowell, L. (2003) *Redundant Masculinities? Employment change and white working class youth*, London: Blackwell.

McGee, R., Silva, P. and Williams, S. (1983) 'Parents' and teachers' perceptions of behaviour problems in seven-year-old children', *The Exceptional Child*, 30(2): 151–61.

McGrath, P., Rawson-Huff, N. and Holewa, H. (2012) 'Building babies' brains: a mental health program for promoting parenting skills of "at risk" children', *International Journal of Psychosocial Rehabilitation*, 16(2): 106–13.

McKay, R. (2006) 'At school with looked after children', unpublished EdD thesis, University of Stirling.

Mackie, D. (2004) EIS Presidential Address, Edinburgh: Educational Institute of Scotland.

McKinney, F. (1947) *The Psychology of Personal Adjustment*, New York: John Wiley & Sons.

McLaughlin, J. (2005) 'Exploring diagnostic processes: social science perspectives', *Archives of Disease in Childhood*, 90: 284–7.

McMahon, S. (2012) 'Doctors diagnose, teachers label: the unexpected in pre-service teachers' talk about labelling children with ADHD', *International Journal of Inclusive Education*, 16(3): 249–64.

McMahon, S. (2013). 'Mapping the epistemological journeys of five preservice teachers: the reconstruction of knowledge of challenging behaviour during Professional Experience', unpublished PhD thesis, University of Wollongong.

MacNaughton, G. (2005) *Doing Foucault in Early Childhood Studies: applying poststructural ideas*, London: Routledge.

Malins, P. (2011) 'An ethico-aesthetics of heroin chic: art, cliché and capitalism', in L. Guillaume and J. Hughes (eds) *Deleuze and the Body*, Edinburgh: Edinburgh University Press.

Mandel, S. (1934) *Mental Hygiene and Education*, New York: Longman, Green & Co.

Maniadaki, K., Sonuga-Barke, E.J.S. and Kakouros, E. (2003) 'Trainee nursery teachers' perceptions of disruptive behaviour disorders; the effect of sex of child on judgements of typicality and severity', *Child: Care, Health and Development*, 29(6): 433–40.

Marcus, J. (2008) 'Watching the disaffected', *Times Higher Education*, 31 July 2008. Available HTTP: http://www.timeshighereducation.co.uk/story.asp?storyCode=402971&sectioncode=26 (accessed 13 July 2012).

Marmot, M. (2004) *Status Syndrome: how our position on the social gradient affect longevity and health*, London: Bloomsbury.

Martin, J. and Clausing. J. (2012) 'Police handcuff tantrum-throwing six-year-old', *Stuff.co.nz*, 18 April 2012. Available HTTP: http://www.stuff.co.nz/world/americas/6762749/Police-handcuff-tantrum-throwing-six-year-old (accessed 19 June 2012).

Marwick, H., Doolin, O., Allely, C.S., McConnachie, A., Johnson, P., Puckering, C., Golding, J., Gillberg, C. and Wilson, P. (2012) 'Predictors of diagnosis of child psychiatric disorder in adult, infant social-communicative interaction at 12 months', *Research in Developmental Disabilities*, 34(1): 562–72.

Mehanna, Z. and Richa, S. (2006) 'Prevalence of anxiety and depressive disorders in medical students: transversal study in medical students in the Saint-Joseph University of Beirut', *Encephale*, 32(6/1): 150–6.

Meltzer, H., Gatward, R., Goodman, R., and Ford, T. (2000) *The Mental Health of Children and Adolescents in Great Britain*, Office for National Statistics, London: The Stationery Office.

Mental Health Foundation. (2012) 'Mental health statistics'. Available HTTP: http://www.mentalhealth.org.uk/help-information/mental-health-statistics/ (accessed 6 February 2012).

Miller, D., Derefinko, K.T., Lynam, D.R., Milich, R. and Fillmore, M.T. (2011) 'Impulsivity and attention deficit-hyperactivity disorder: subtype classification using the UPPS impulsive behaviour', *Journal of Psychopathological Behavior Assessment*, 32(3): 323–32.

Miller, G. (2008) 'Growing pains for fMRI', *Science*, 320: 1412–14.

Miller, R. (undated) 'Negatives of disruptive behaviour in the classroom'. Available HTTP: http://www.ehow.co.uk/info_7879979_negatives-disruptive-behavior-classroom.html (accessed 13 June 2012).

Miller, T. and Leger, M.C. (2003) 'A very childish moral panic: Ritalin', *Journal of Medical Humanities*, 24(1/2): 9–33.

Ministry of Education. (1955) *Report of the Committee on Maladjusted Children*, London: Her Majesty's Stationery Office.

Ministry of Justice, Department for Children, Schools and Families and the Youth Justice Board. (2007) *Parenting Orders and Contracts Guidance*. Available HTTP: http://dera.ioe.ac.uk/7949/7/parenting-contracts.pdf (accessed 10 September 2012).

Multimodal Treatment Study for Attention-Deficit Hyperactivity Disorder (MTA) Cooperative Group. (1999) '14 months randomised clinical trial of treatment strategies for Attention Deficit Hyperactivity Disorder', *Archive of General Psychiatry*, 56(12): 1073–86.

Muncie, J. (1999) *Youth and Crime: a critical introduction*, London: Sage.

Mundasad, S. (2013). 'Babies' brains to be mapped in the womb and after birth', *BBC News Health*, 10 April 2013. Available HTTP: http://www.bbc.co.uk/news/health-21880017 (accessed 14 April 2013).

Murthy, R.S. and Wig, N.N. (1993) 'Evaluation of the progress in mental health in India since independence', in P. Mane and K.Y. Gandevia (eds) *Mental Health in India: issues and concerns*, Bombay: Tata Institute of Social Sciences.

Myttas, N. (2001) 'Understanding and recognizing ADHD', *Practice Nursing*, 12(7): 278–80.

National Collaborating Centre for Mental Health. (2009) *Attention Deficit Hyperactivity Disorder: diagnosis and management of ADHD in children, young people and adults*, Leicester/London: The British Psychological Society and the Royal College of Psychiatrists.

National Council for Special Education. (2012) '*The Education of Students with Challenging Behaviour arising From Severe Emotional Disturbance/Behavioural Disorders*', NCSE Policy Advice Paper: Trim, Co. Meath. Available HTTP: http://www.ncse.ie/uploads/1/EBDPolicyReport_1.pdf (accessed 1 March 2013).

National Health Service. (2007) *ADHD: Services over Scotland. A report of the service profiling*, Edinburgh: NHS Scotland.

National Institute of Mental Health. (2008) 'The numbers count: mental disorders in America', 5 June 2008. Available HTTP: http://www.nimh.nih.gov/health/publications/the-numbers-count-mental-disorders-in-america/index.shtml (accessed 17 June 2008).

Nature. (2013) 'Web focus – telomere biology', *Nature*. Available HTTP: http://www.nature.com/nature/focus/telomerebiology/ (accessed 11 August 2013).

Nealon, J. (2008) *Foucault Beyond Foucault: power and its intensification since 1984*, Stanford, CA: Stanford University Press.

Nerdrum, P., Rustøen, T. and Rønnestad, M.H. (2006) 'Student psychological distress: a psychometric study of 1750 Norwegian 1st year undergraduate students', *Scandinavian Journal of Educational Research*, 50(1): 95–109.

New South Wales Department of Education and Communities (NSW DEC). (undated) 'Professional Learning and Leadership Development'. Available HTTP: https://www.det.nsw.edu.au/proflearn/areas/nt/resources/bm01.htm (accessed 22 February 2013).

New South Wales Department of Health. (2002) 'Trends in the prescribing of stimulant medication for the treatment of Attention Deficit Hyperactivity Disorder in children and adolescents in NSW'. Available HTTP: http://www.health.nsw.gov.au/pubs/2002/pdf/ADHD2002sup.pdf (accessed 30 July 2012).

New South Wales Department of Education and Training (NSW DET). (2004) *Review of Aboriginal Education*, Sydney: NSW DET.

New South Wales Department of Education and Training (NSW DET). (2009) *Enforcement of Compulsory School Attendance*. Sydney, NSW: NSW DET.

Newman, K. and Fox, C. (2009) 'Repeat tragedy: rampage shootings in American high school and college settings, 2002–2008', *American Behavioral Scientist*, 52: 1286–1308.

Nietzsche, F. (1983) 'On the uses and disadvantages of history for life', in *Untimely Meditations;* trans. R.J. Hollingdale, Cambridge: Cambridge University Press.

Nordahl, T. and Hausstätter, R.S. (2009) *Spesialundervisningens Forutsetninger, Innsatser og Resultater* ('Special teaching: Assumptions, predictions and results'), Hamar: Høgskolen i Hedmark.

O'Brien Caughy, M., O'Campo, P.J. and Muntaner, C. (2004) 'Experiences of racism among African American parents and the mental health of their preschool-aged children', *American Journal of Public Health*, 94(12): 2118–24.

O'Dowd, C. (2012) 'ADHD guidelines: flaws in the literature and the need to scrutinise the evidence', *Australian Family Physician (AFP)*,41(3): 87–8. Available HTTP: http://www.racgp.org.au/afp/2012/march/adhd-guidelines (accessed 30 July 2012).

O'Neil, S. and Stephenson, J. (2010) 'The use of functional behavioural assessment for students with challenging behaviours: current patterns and experience of Australian practitioners', *Australian Journal of Educational and Developmental Psychology*, 10: 65–82.

O'Regan, F. (2010) 'Exclusion from school and attention deficit/hyperactivity disorder', *The International Journal of Emotional Education*, 2(2): 3–18.

O'Toole, M.E. (2000) *The School Shooter: a threat assessment perspective*, Quantico: Federal Bureau of Investigation (FBI). Available HTTP: http://www.fbi.gov/stats-services/publications/school-shooter (accessed 11 December 2013).

Oancea, A. and Bridges, D. (2009) 'Philosophy of education in the UK: the historical and contemporary tradition', *Oxford Review of Education*, 35: 553–68.

Office of Student and Community Affairs. (2008–9) *Keeping our Campus Safe*, Newark: Rutgers Newark.

Olssen, M. (1993) 'Science and individualism in educational psychology: problems for practice and points of departure', *Educational Psychology*, 13(2): 155–72.

Osterwell, N. (2007). 'Virginia Tech missed "clear warnings" of shooter's mental instability', *Medpage Today*, 30 August 2007. Available HTTP: http://www.medpagetoday.com/Psychiatry/AnxietyStress/6546 (accessed 11 December 2013).

Owens, P. (2007) 'Beyond Strauss, lies, and the war in Iraq: Hannah Arendt's critique of neoconservatism', *Review of International Studies*, 33(2): 265–83.

Paperson, L. (2010) 'The postcolonial ghetto: seeing her shape and his hand', *Berkeley Review of Education*, 1(1). Available HTTP: http://www.escholarship.org/uc/item/3q91f9gv#page-5 (accessed 25 September 2013).

Parker, G., Mahendran, R., Koh, E.S. and Machin, D. (2000) 'Season of birth in schizophrenia: no latitude at the equator', *British Journal of Psychiatry*, 176: 68–71.

Paton, G. (2012) 'Bad behaviour in schools fuelled by over-indulgent parents', *The Telegraph*, 30 March 2012. Available HTTP: http://www.telegraph.co.uk/education/educationnews/9173533/Bad-behaviour-in-schools-fuelled-by-over-indulgent-parents.html (accessed 30 July 2012).

Patton, P. (2000) *Deleuze and the Political*, London: Routledge.

Pelham, W., Foster, M. and Robb, J. (2007) 'The economic impact of attention-deficit/hyperactivity disorder in children and adolescents', *Measuring Outcomes in Attention Deficit Hyperactivity Disorder*, 7(1): 121–31.

Perry, D., Dunne, M.C., McFadden, L. and Campbell, D. (2008) 'Reducing the risk for preschool expulsion: mental health consultation for young children with challenging behaviors', *Journal of Child and Family Studies*, 17(1): 44–54.

Peters, M., Lankshear, C. and Olssen, M. (2003) *Critical Theory: founders and praxis*, New York: Peter Lang.

Polanczyk, G., de Lima, M.S., Horta, B.L., Biederman, J. and Rohde, L.A. (2007) 'The worldwide prevalence of ADHD: a systematic review and metaregression analysis', *American Journal of Psychiatry*, 164(6): 942–5.

Power, S. and Gewirtz, S. (1999) 'Reading Education Action Zones', paper presented at the British Educational Research Association Conference, Brighton, September 1999.

Prosser, B. and Reid, R. (2009) 'Changes in use of psychostimulant medication for ADHD in South Australia (1990–2006)', *Australian and New Zealand Journal of Psychiatry*, 43(4): 340–7.

Pruitt, D. (2000) *Your Adolescent*, New York: Harper Collins.

Quinn, P. (2005) 'Treating adolescent girls and women with ADHD: gender-specific issues', *Journal of Clinical Psychology*, 61(5): 579–87.

Quinn, P. and Wigal, S. (2004) 'Perceptions of girls and ADHD: results from a national survey [online]', *Medscape General Medicine*, 6(2): 2.

Radden, J. (2003) 'Is this dame melancholy? Equating today's depression and past melancholia', *Philosophy, Psychiatry and Psychology*, 10(1): 37–52.

Ramani, D. (2009) 'The brain seduction: the public perception of neuroscience', *Journal of Science and Communication*, 8(4): 1–8.

Rancière, J. (2008) 'Jacques Rancière and indisciplinarity: an interview', *Art and Research*, 2(1): 1–10.

Rappley, M.D. (2005) 'Attention deficit hyperactivity disorder', *The New England Journal of Medicine*, 352(2): 165–73.

Ream, R.K., Ryan, S.M. and Espinoza, J.A. (2012) 'Reframing the ecology of opportunity and achievement gaps: why "no excuses" reforms have failed to narrow student group differences in educational outcomes', in T.B. Timar and J. Maxwell Jolly (eds) *Narrowing the Achievement Gap: perspectives and strategies for challenging times*, Cambridge, MA: Harvard Education Press.

Reavis, W.C. (1926) *Pupil Adjustment in Junior and Senior High Schools. A treatment of the problems and methods of educational counselling and guidance with examples from actual practice*, Boston: D.C. Heath and Company.

Reid, K. and Valle, J. (2004) 'The discursive practice of learning disability: implications for instruction and parent-school relations', *Journal of Learning Disabilities*, 37(6): 466–81.

Reid, M.J., Webster-Stratton, C. and Beauchaine, T.P. (2002) 'Parent training in Head Start: a comparison of program response among African American, Asian, Caucasian, and Hispanic mothers', *Prevention Science*, 2(4): 209–27.

Reiner Foundation. (1997) *The First Years Last Forever: I am your child*, Ottawa: Reiner Foundation, Canadian Institute of Child Health.

Reti, I.M., Samuals, J.P., Eaton, W.W., Bienvenu, O.J.I., Costa, P.T.J. and Nestadt, G. (2002) 'Influences of parenting on normal personality traits', *Psychiatry Research*, 111: 55–64.

Rich, E.L., Monaghan, F. and Aphramor, L. (eds) (2010). *Debating Obesity: critical perspectives*, Basingstoke: Palgrave Macmillan.

Rinehart, K.A. (2007) 'Higher education's 9/11: crisis management', *University Business: Solutions for Higher Education Management*, December. Available HTTP: http://www.universitybusiness.com/article/higher-educations-911-crisis-management (accessed 20 August 2013).

Rivlin, H.N. (1936) *Educating for Adjustment: the classroom applications of mental hygiene*, New York: Appleton & Co.

Roberts, S. (2012) 'I just got on with it: the educational experiences of ordinary, yet overlooked, boys', *British Journal of Sociology of Education*, 33(2): 203–21.

Robinson, K. (2006) 'Schools kill creativity', *TED Talks*. Available HTTP: http://www.ted.com/talks/ken_robinson_says_schools_kill_creativity.html (accessed 30 July 2012).

Rohde, A.L. (2002) 'ADHD in Brazil: the DSM-IV criteria in a culturally different population', *Journal of the American Academy of Child Psychiatry*, 14(9): 1131–3.

Roithmayr, D. (2003) 'Locked in inequality: the persistence of discrimination', *Michigan Journal of Race and Law*, 9: 31–75.

Rose, N. (1996) 'Psychiatry as a political science: advanced liberalism and the administration of risk', *History of the Human Sciences*, 9: 1–2.

Rose, N. (1999) *Powers of Freedom: reframing political thought*, Cambridge: Cambridge University Press.

Rose, N. (2010). '"Screen and intervene": governing risky brains', *History of the Human Sciences*, 23(1): 79–105.

Roy, K. (2004) 'Overcoming nihilism: from communication to Deleuzian expression', *Educational Philosophy and Theory*, 36: 297–312.

Royal Australasian College of Physicians. (2009) *Draft Australian Guidelines on Attention Deficit Hyperactivity Disorder (ADHD)*, Sydney: Royal Australasian College of Physicians.

Royal College of Psychiatrists. (2011) *Mental Health of Students in Higher Education*, London: Royal College of Psychiatrists.

Rushmann, A. (2008) 'Threat Assessment Groups cropping up nationwide', *Minnesota Daily*, 4 April 2008. Available HTTP: http://www.mndaily.com/2008/04/04/threat-assessment-groups-cropping-nationwide (accessed 12 May 2009).

Rutgers Newark. (2009) 'Threat Assessment Referral Form'. Available HTTP: www.newark.rutgers.edu/files/threatreferral.pdf (accessed 2 June 2013).

Ryan, C.W. (1938) *Mental Health Through Education*, New York: The Commonwealth Fund.

Ryan, J. (1991) 'Observing and normalizing: Foucault, discipline and inequality in schooling', *The Journal of Educational Thought*, 25(2): 104–19.

Said, E. (2002) 'Excerpt from *Orientalism*', in C. Harrison and P.J. Wood (eds) *Art in Theory 1900–2000: an anthology of changing ideas*, 2nd edn, London: Wiley-Blackwell.

Saigal, S. and Doyle, L.W. (2008) 'An overview of mortality and sequalae of preterm birth from infancy to adulthood', *Lancet*, 371: 261–9.

Sameroff, A.J., McDonnought, S.C. and Rosenblum, K.L. (2004) *Treating Parent-infant Relationship Problems: strategies for intervention*, New York: Guilford Press.

Sandiford, P. (1913) *The Mental and Physical Life of School Children*, London: Longmans, Green & Co.

Sawyer, M.G., Rey, J., Graetz, B.W., Clark, J.J. and Baghurst, P.A. (2002) 'Use of medication by young people with attention-deficit/hyperactivity disorder', *Medical Journal of Australia*, 177(1): 21–5.

Scheffler, R.M., Hinshaw, S.P., Modrek, S. and Levine, P. (2007) 'The global market for ADHD medications: the United States is an outlier among developed countries in its high usage rates of these medications among children', *Health Affairs*, 26(2): 450–7.

Schlotz, W. and Phillips, D.I.W. (2009) 'Fetal origins of mental health: evidence and mechanisms', *Brain, Behavior and Immunity*, 23(7): 905–16.

Schmidt, J. (2007) *Melancholy and the Care of the Soul: religion, moral philosophy and madness in early modern England*, Aldershot: Ashgate Publishing.

Schram, S.F. (2000) 'In the clinic: the medicalization of welfare', *Social Text*, 18(1): 81–107.

Science Daily. (2010) 'One in five children meets criteria for a mental disorder across their lifetime, national US study shows', *Science Daily*, 13 October 2010. Available HTTP: http://www.sciencedaily.com/releases/2010/10/101013121606.htm (accessed 3 January 2012).

Seale, C., Boden, S., Williams, S., Lowe, P. and Steinberg, D. (2007) 'Media constructions of sleep and sleep disorders: a study of UK national newspapers', *Social Science and Medicine*, 65: 418–30.

Sellgren, K. (2013) 'Disruptive behaviour rising, teachers say', *BBC News: Education and Family*, 23 March 2013. Available HTTP: http://www.bbc.co.uk/news/education-21895705 (accessed 17 December 2013).

Senellart, M. (2009) 'Course context', in M. Foucault, *Security, Technology, Population: lectures at the Collège de France 1977–1978*, London: Palgrave Macmillan.

Shakespeare, T. (2005) 'For whom the school bell tolls', *BBC – Ouch!*, 27 June 2005. Available HTTP: http://www.bbc.co.uk/ouch/opinion/for_whom_the_school_bell_tolls.shtml (accessed 11 December 2013).

Sharpe, M. (2007). 'A question of two truths? Remarks on parrhesia and the "politicalphilo sophical'difference"', *Parrhesia*, 2, 89–108.

Sibley, M., Waxmonsky, J., Robb, J. and Pelham, W. (2013) 'Implications of changes for the field: ADHD', *Journal of Learning Disabilities*, 46(1): 34–42.

Siegler, M. and Osmond, A. (1966) 'Models of madness', *British Journal of Psychiatry*, 112: 1193–203.

Simmons, T., Novins, D. and Allen, J. (2004) 'Words have power: (re)-defining serious emotional disturbance for American Indian and Alaska Native children and their families', *American Indian and Alaska Native Mental Health Journal*, 11(2): 59–64.

Simons, M. and Masschelein, J. (2006) 'The permanent quality tribunal in education and the limits of educational policy', *Policy Futures in Education*, 4(3): 292–305.

Singh, I. and Rose, N. (2009) 'Biomarkers in psychiatry', *Nature*, 460(7252): 202–7.

Skounti, M., Philalithis, A. and Galanakis, E. (2007) 'Variations in prevalence of attention deficit disorder worldwide', *European Journal of Pediatrics*, 166(2): 117–23.

Slee, R. (2011) *The Irregular School: exclusion, schooling and inclusive education*, London and New York: Routledge.

Sleeter, C. (2008) 'Equity, democracy, and neo-liberal assaults on teacher education', *Teaching and Teacher Education*, 24: 1947–57.

Smith, D. (1998) 'The place of ethics in Deleuze's philosophy: three questions of immanence', in E. Kaufman and K.J. Heller (eds) *Deleuze and Guattari: New Mappings in Politics, Philosophy and Culture*, Minneapolis/London: University of Minnesota Press.

Smith, J. (2011) 'Global study tracks pediatric mental illness incidence, treatment', *Clinical Psychiatry News*, 16 October 2011. Available HTTP: http://www.clinicalpsychiatrynews.com/news/more-top-news/single-view/global-study-tracks-pediatric-mental-illness-incidence-treatment/52fd203bc2.html (accessed 30 October 2011).

Smith, J. and Coldstream, J. (1857) *First Report: the home school for invalid and imbecile children, Edinburgh*, Edinburgh: Thomas Constable.

Smith, J. and Naylor, R. (2001) 'Determinants of degree performance in UK universities: a statistical analysis of the 1993 student cohort', *Oxford Bulletin of Economics and Statistics*, 63: 29–60.

Soanes, C. and Stevenson, A. (2013). 'Definition of froward in English', *Oxford Dictionaries Online*. Available HTTP: http://oxforddictionaries.com/definition/english/froward (accessed 3 August 2013).

Soja, E. (1996). *Thirdspace: journeys to Los Angeles and other real-and-imagined places*, Oxford: Blackwell.

Solórzano, D.G and Yosso, T.J. (2002) 'Critical race methodology: counter-storytelling as an analytical framework for education research', *Qualitative Inquiry*, 8(1): 23–44.

Sonuga-Barke, E.J.S., Daley, D., Thompson, M., Laver-Bradbury, C. and Weeks, A. (2001) 'Parent-based therapies for preschool attention-deficit/hyperactivity disorder: a randomized, controlled trial with a community sample', *Journal of the American Academy of Child and Adolescent Psychiatry*, 40(4): 402–8.

Sroufe, L.A. (2012) 'Ritalin gone wrong' *New York Times*, 28 January 2012. Available HTTP: http://www.nytimes.com/2012/01/29/opinion/sunday/childrens-add-drugs-dont-work-long-term.html (accessed 4 February 2012).

Stehlik, T.P. (2006) *Levels of Engagement: report of findings of the School Retention Action Plan action research project*. Adelaide: University of South Australia.

Stein, A., Malmberg, L.E., Leach, P., Barnes, J. and Sylva, K. (2012) 'The influence of different forms of early childcare on children's emotional and behavioural development at school entry', *Child: Care, Health and Development*, 39(5): 676–87.

Stevenson, G.S. and Smith, G. (1934) *Child Guidance Clinics, a quarter century of development*, New York: The Commonwealth Fund.

Stewart-Brown, S., Evans, J., Patterson, J., Petersen, S., Doll, H., Balding, J. and Regis, D. (2000) 'The health of students in institutes of higher education: an important and neglected public health problem?', *Journal of Public Health*, 22(4): 492–9.

Still, G. (1902) 'Goulstonian lectures', presented to the Royal College of Physicians. Available HTTP: http://adhd-npf.com/history-of-adhd-1902-sir-george/ (accessed 3 July 2012).

Stoughton, E. (2006) 'Marcus and Harriet: living on the edge in school and society', in E. Brantlinger (ed.) *Who Benefits from Special Education? Remediating (fixing) other people's children*, Mahwah, NJ: Lawrence Erlbaum Associates.

Strahan, S.A.K. (1893) *Suicide and Insanity: a physiological and sociological study*, London: Swan Sonnenschein.

Strand, S. (2010) 'The limits of social class in explaining ethnic gaps in educational attainment', *British Educational Research Journal*, 37(2): 197–229.

Stromberg, C.D. and Stone, A.A. (1983) 'A model state law on civil commitment of the mentally ill', *Harvard Journal on Legislation*, 20: 275–396.

Sullivan, E. (2008). 'The art of medicine: melancholy, medicine and the arts', *The Lancet*, 372(9642): 884–5.

Sweller, N., Graham, L.J. and Van Bergen, P. (2012) 'The minority report: disproportionate representation in Australia's largest education system', *Exceptional Children*, 79(1): 107–25.

Symonds, B. (1998) 'The philosophical and sociological context of mental health care legislation', *Journal of Advanced Nursing*, 27: 946–54.

Thehumanteacher. (2013) 'Why we leave the profession in the first 5 years'. Available HTTP: http://thehumanteacher.wordpress.com (accessed 10 September 2013).

Thomas, G. (2007) 'Theory and the construction of pathology', paper presented at the American Educational Research Association, New York, 24–28 March.

Thomas, G. (2013) 'A review of thinking and research about inclusive education policy, with suggestions for a new kind of inclusive thinking', *British Educational Research Journal* 39(3): 473–90. Available HTTP: http://dx.doi.org/10.1080/01411926.2011.652070 (accessed 5 April 2013).

Thompson, J. (1984) *Studies in the Theory of Ideology*, Cambridge: Polity; Berkeley: University of California Press.

Thorndike, E. L. (1910) *Educational Psychology* (2nd edn), New York: Teachers College, Columbia University (original work published 1903).

Throsby, K. (2012) 'Obesity surgery and the management of excess: exploring the body multiple', *Sociology of Health and Illnes*, 34(1): 9–15.

Thwing, C.F. (1892) 'A too-long vacation', *The North American Review*, 154(427): 761–2.

Timimi, S. (2008) 'Child psychiatry and its relationship with the pharmaceutical industry: theoretical and practical issues', *Advances in Psychiatric Treatment* 14(1): 3–9.

Timimi S. and Taylor E. (2004) 'ADHD is best understood as a cultural construct', *British Journal of Psychiatry*, 184: 8–9.

Tizard, B., Blachford, P., Burke, J., Farquar, C. and Plewis, L. (1988) *Young Children at School in the Inner City*, Hove: Lawrence Erlbaum.

Todd, R.D. and O'Malley, K. (2001) 'The dopamine receptor DRD4 gene: are duplications distracting?', *Trends in Pharmacological Sciences*, 22(2): 612–16.

Tomlinson, S. (2012) 'The irresistible rise of the SEN industry', *Oxford Review of Education*, 38(3): 267–86.

Tomoda, A., Mori, K., Kimura, M., Takahashi, T. and Kitamura, T. (2000) 'One-year prevalence and incidence of depression among first-year university students in Japan: a preliminary study', *Psychiatry and Clinical Neurosciences*, 54(5): 583–8.

Torrance, H. (2007) 'Correlation, causation and intervention: policy as a special case of theory', paper presented at the American Educational Research Association Conference, New York, 24–28 March.

Torrance, H. (2008) 'Building confidence in qualitative research: engaging the demands of policy', *Qualitative Inquiry*, 14: 507–27.

Triple P. (undated) 'Positive parenting programme'. Available HTTP: http://www.triplep. net/glo-en/home (accessed 1 February 2013).

Troyna, B. (1994) 'The "everyday" world of teachers? Deracialised discourses in the sociology of teachers and the teaching profession', *British Journal of Sociology of Education*, 15(3): 325–39.

Tubic, T. (2013) 'El efecto del ejercicio fisico en la salud mental de los ni?os de edad preescholar' ('Exercise effects on mental health of preschool children'), *Anales de Psicología*, 29(1): 249.

Tyre, P. (2006) 'The trouble with boys', *Newsweek*, 29 January 2006. Available HTTP: http://www.thedailybeast.com/newsweek/2006/01/29/the-trouble-with-boys.html (accessed 30 July 2012).

Unwin, C. (1988) *Child Psychotherapy, War and the Normal Child: selected papers of Margaret Lowenfield*. London: Free Association Books.

Upshur, C., Wenz-Gross, M. and Reed, G. (2009) 'A pilot study of early childhood mental health consultation for children with behavioral problems in preschool', *Early Childhood Research Quarterly*, 24(1): 29–45.

Van Acker, R. (2007) 'Antisocial, aggressive, and violent behaviour in children and adolescents within alternative education settings: prevention and intervention', *Preventing School Failure*, 51(2): 5–12.

Vaughan, B., Fox, L., Lentini, R. and Blair, K.-S. (2009) *Creating Teaching Tools for Young Children with Challenging Behavior: user's manual*, Tampa: University of South Florida. Available HTTP: http://www.ecmhc.org/ttyc/documents/A%20User%27sManual/ Users%20Manual%20Rev1209.pdf (accessed 1 March 2013).

Verhulst, F. and Akkerhuis, G. (1989) 'Agreement between parents' and teachers' ratings of behavioural/emotional problems of children aged 4–12', *Journal of Child Psychology*, 30(1): 123–36.

Vincent, C. (2000) *Including Parents? Education, citizenship and parental agency*, Buckingham/ Philadelphia: Open University Press.

Vincent, C., Rollock, N., Ball, S. and Gillbourn, D. (2012) 'Being strategic, being watchful, being determined: black middle-class parents and schooling', *British Journal of Sociology of Education*, 33(3): 337–54.

Vinson, T. (2007) *Dropping Off the Edge: the distribution of disadvantage in Australia*, Richmond, Victoria: Jesuit Social Services/Catholic Social Services.

Virginia General Assembly. (2008) *Violence Prevention Committee: threat assessment team*, Richmond: Government of Virginia.

Virginia Tech Review Panel. (2007) *Mass Shootings at Virginia Tech, April 16, 2007: Report of the Review Panel*, Virginia: Commonwealth of Virginia.

Visser, J. and Jehan, Z. (2009) 'ADHD: a scientific fact or a factual opinion? A critique of the veracity of attention deficit hyperactivity disorder', *Emotional and Behavioural Difficulties*, 14(2): 127–40.

Volkow, N. and Swanson, J. (2003) 'Variables that affect the clinical use and abuse of methylphenidate in the treatment of ADHD', *American Journal of Psychiatry*, 160(23): 1909–18.

Wahl, K. and Metzner, C. (2012) 'Parental influences on the prevalance and development of child aggressiveness', *Journal of Child and Family Studies*, 21: 344–55.

Wainwright, M. (2011) 'Almost 900 pupils suspended from school each day for violence', *The Guardian*, 29 July 2011. Available HTTP: http://www.guardian.co.uk/education/2011/jul/28/pupils-suspended-exclusions-violence (accessed 30 July 2012).

Wakefield, J., Pottick, K. and Kirk, S. (2002) 'Should the DSM-IV diagnostic criteria for social conduct include social context?', *American Journal of Psychiatry*, 159(3): 380–6.

Walker, D. (2006) 'ADHD as the new "feeblemindedness"', in G. Lloyd, J. Stead and D. Cohen (eds) *Critical New Perspectives on ADHD*, London: Routledge.

Walker, H., Ramsey, E. and Gresham, F. (undated) 'Heading off disruptive behavior: how early intervention can reduce defiant behavior—and win back teaching time. Available HTTP: http://www.aft.org/newspubs/periodicals/ae/winter0304/walker.cfm (accessed 12 June 2013)

Walker, R. and Sonn, C. (2010) 'Working as a culturally competent mental health practitioner', in N. Purdie, P. Dudgeon and R. Walker (eds) *Working Together: Aboriginal and Torres Strait Islander mental health and wellbeing principles and practice*, Perth: Commonwealth of Australia.

Walkerdine, V. (1984) 'Developmental psychology and the child-centered pedagogy: the insertion of Piaget into early education', in J.Henriques, W.Holloway, C.Urwin, C.Venn and V.Walkerdine (eds) *Changing the Subject, Psychology, Social Regulation and Subjectivity*, London: Methuen.

Wall, G. (2004) 'Is your child's brain maximized?', *Atlantis*, 28(2): 41–50.

Wallin, J.E.W. (1914) *The Mental Health of the School Child. The psycho-educational clinic in relation to child welfare. Contributions to a new science of orthophrenics and orthosomatics*, New Haven: Yale University Press.

Wallin, J.E.W. (1927) *Clinical and Abnormal Psychology. A textbook for educators, psychologists and mental hygiene workers*, London: George G. Harrap & Company.

Wallis, C. (1994) 'Life in overdrive', *Time*, 18 July 1994. Available HTTP: http://www.mentalhealth.com/mag1/p51-adhd.html (accessed 4 July 2012)

Ware, L. (2005) 'The politics of ideology: a pedagogy of critical hope', in L. Ware (ed.) *Ideology and the politics of (in)exclusion*, New York: Peter Lang.

Warner, F. (1890) *A Course of Lectures on the Growth and Means of Training the Mental Faculty. Delivered in the University of Cambridge*. Cambridge: At the University Press (Cambridge).

Wastell, D. and White, S. (2012) 'Blinded by neuroscience: social policy, the family and the infant brain', *Families, Relationships and Societies*, 1(3): 397–414.

Watson, G.B. (1933) 'A critical note on two attitude studies', *Mental Hygiene*, 17(1): 59–64.

Weller, S. (2009) 'You need to have a mixed school: exploring the complexity of diversity in young people's social networks', in J. Allan, J. Ozga and G. Smyth (eds) *Social Capital, Professionalism and Diversity*, Rotterdam/Taipei: Sense.

Wheeler, L. (2010) 'Critique of the article by Visser and Jehan (2009): "ADHD: A scientific fact or a factual opinion? A critique of the veracity of Attention Deficit Hyperactivity Disorder"', *Emotional and Behavioural Difficulties*, 15(3): 257–67.

Wickman, E.K. (1928) *Children's Behaviour and Teachers' Attitudes*, New York: The Commonwealth Fund, Division of Publication.

Wigal, T.I.M., Greenhill, L., Chuang, S., McGough, J., Vitiello, B., Skrobala, A., Swanson, J., Wigal, S., Abikoff, H., Kollins, S., McCracken, J., Riddle, M., Posner, K., Ghuman, J., Davies, M., Throp, B. and Stehli, A. (2006) 'Safety and tolerability of methylphenidate in preschool children with ADHD', *Journal of the American Academy of Child and Adolescent Psychiatry*, 45(11): 1294–1303.

Wile, I.S. (1932) 'Mental health of the preschool child', *American Journal of Public Health and the Nation's Health*, 23(3): 191–7.

Williams, P. (writer) (2007). 'Doses of reality' [television broadcast], in P. Williams (producer), *Insight*, 22 May 2007, Special Broadcasting Service.

Williamson, A.B., Raphael, B., Redman, S., Daniels, J, Eades, S.J and Mayers, N. (2010) 'Emerging themes in Aboriginal child and adolescent mental health: findings from a qualitative study in Sydney, New South Wales', *Medical Journal of Australia*, 192(10): 603–5.

Williamson, B. (2008) 'The gunslinger to the ivory tower came: should universities have a duty to prevent rampage killings?', *Florida Law Review*, 60: 895–914.

Willis, R. (2005) *The Struggle for the General Teaching Council*, Abingdon: RoutledgeFalmer.

Willis, T. (1672) *De anima brutorum*, Oxford: Impensis Ric. Davis.

Willis, T. (1683) *Two Discourses Concerning the Souls of Brutes* (English trans. of *De anima brutorum*), London: Thomas Dring.

Wolff, J. and De-Shalit, A. (2007) *Disadvantage*, Oxford: Oxford University Press.

Wolnick, E. (2007) 'Depression discrimination: are suicidal college students protected by the Americans with Disabilities Act?', *Arizona Law Review*, 4: 989–1016.

World Health Organization. (2003) *International Statistical Classification of Diseases and Related Health Problems*, 10th Revision. Available HTTP: http://apps.who.int/classifications/apps/icd/icd10online2003/fr-icd.htm (accessed 18 December 2013).

Wright, J. and Harwood, V. (eds) (2009) *Biopolitics and the Obesity Epidemic*, New York: Routledge.

Youdell, D. (2011) *School Trouble: identity, power and politics*, London: Routledge.

Young, I. (2000) 'Five faces of oppression', in M. Adams, W. Blumenfield, R. Castañeda, H. Hackman, M. Peters and X. Zúñiga (eds) *Readings for Diversity and Social Justice: an anthology on racisim, anti-semitism, sexism, heterosexism, ableism and classism*, New York/London: Routledge.

Yurduşen, S., Erol, N. and Gençöz, T. (2013) 'The effects of parental attitudes and mothers' psychological well-being on the emotional and behavioral problems of their preschool children', *Maternal and Child Health Journal*, 17(1): 68–75.

Zachary, C.B. (1929) *Personality Adjustments of School Children*, London: Charles Scribner's Sons.

Zeanah, C.H. (2000) *Handbook of Infant Mental Health*, New York: Guildford Press.

Zerilli, L. (2006) 'Truth and politics', *Theory and Event*, 9: 4.

Zero to Three. (2013) 'Early experiences matter'. Available HTTP: http://main.zerotothree.org/site/PageServer?pagename=key_mental&AddInterest=1144 - 2 (accessed 25 April 2013).

Zito, J.M., Safer, D.J., Valluri, S., Gardner, J.F., Korelitz, J.J. and Mattison, D.R. (2007) 'Psychotherapeutic medication prevalence in medicaid-insured preschoolers', *Journal of Child and Adolescent Psychopharmacology*, 17(2): 195–203.

Zubrick, S.R., Silburn, S.R., Lawrence, D.M., Mitrou, F.G., Dalby, R.B., Blair, E.M., Griffin, J., Milroy, H., De Maio, J.A., Cox, A. and Li, J. (2005) *The Western Australian Aboriginal Child Health Survey: the social and emotional wellbeing of Aboriginal children and young people*, Perth: Curtin University of Technology and Telethon Institute for Child Health Research.

# Index

ABA *see* Applied Behavioural Analysis
abjection 86
Achenbach, T.M. 76
achievement gap 52
ADDISS (Attention Deficit Disorder Information and Support Service) 64
Adelman, A. 138
ADHD (attention deficit hyperactivity disorder) 5–6, 145; danger and risk 108–14; diagnosis 93–4, 104, 107, 148–9; and gender 62–4, 160; in early childhood 77, 78; in primary school 90–1, 93–4, 102; in secondary school 104, 105–9, 168–9; medication 3–4, 110; pharmaceutical arousal 94; prevalence of 2; and race and ethnicity 50–1; racialized naming practices 51; and school exclusion 64; and schools 8–9, 159; and social class 9, 53, 54; *see also* Scotland
adolescence *see* secondary school
affective aspects of *medicus interruptus* 152–5
Aljazeera 123
Alkon, A. *et al.* 76
Allan, J. 84
Allin, M.P.G. *et al.* 71
Amini Virmani, E. *et al.* 72, 81
Andre, L. 71
anorexia nervosa 78
anti-social behaviour 107–8, 109
anxiety disorders 128
Appadurai, A. 5, 12
Applied Behavioural Analysis (ABA) 114, 115
Arendt, H.: on critique and political action 12, 165–6; on education 168; on factual and rational truths 122, 126, 127, 131, 136, 140, 142, 165
Armstrong, D. 96

arousal *see* pharmaceutical arousal; points of arousal
Artiles, A. 51, 66
Ashley, M. 62
Asperger's syndrome 6, 43, 107
attachment 81, 148–9, 154
attention 60; *see also* ADHD
Attention Deficit Disorder Information and Support Service (ADDISS) 64
Australia 13, 14; ADHD 50, 54, 62, 63, 168–9; colleges and universities 121; Imagining University Education (IUE) 1, 14; Indigenous Australians 157–9, 160, 162, 171; National Health and Medical Research Council (NHMRC) 63; The New Outsiders project (TNO) 13, 14; peer discrimination 113–14; Positive Behaviour Support (PBS) 114; positive learning centres 118; Queensland Teachers Union 112, 118; Royal Australasian College of Physicians 50; Schools for Specific Purposes (SSPs) 158, 162; social class/disadvantage 53, 54; training systems 20, 100–1
autistic spectrum disorder 6, 43, 107
Averill, L.A. 36, 38

Baby Brain Box 80–1
backwardness 32, 33
Baker, B. 92, 96, 170
Baldwin, S. 95
Ball, S. 86
Bamford, R.W. 20–1, 159
Banhatti, R.G. 50–1
Barkley, R.A. 93
Barnes, J. 72
Baumeister, A.A. 93
Bayram, N. 120

Beach, D. 163
Bean, P.T. *et al.* 49
behaviour: anti-social behaviour 107–8,
    109; assemblages 61, 150; attitudes
    towards 39; criminalization of child
    behaviour 107, 109–10, 112–13;
    psychopathologization of 8; *see also*
    ADHD; medicalization: of children;
    *medicus interruptus*
behavioural disorders 6; in preschool 72–3,
    76; in secondary school 110–12, 115,
    118–19; prevalence of 2, 112; and race
    and ethnicity 49–50; and social class 9,
    53; *see also* ADHD; gender
behavioural units 118
Bennett, J. 155–6
Bernstein, B. 163, 170
Berrios, G.E. 130
Berubé, M. 65
Biesta, G. 168
Bilgel, N. 120
Bilkey, T. 110
biopower 86–7, 92, 96, 102, 103–4, 105–6
bipolar disorder 3, 6, 107, 123
birth (time of year) 68
birth weight 78
Bowlby, J. 81
brain development 79–81
Brantlinger, P. 29, 65
Brazil: ADHD 50, 51, 62; social class/
    disadvantage 54
Breggin, P.R. 95
Bronfenbrenner, U. 87
Brooks, R.A. 47
Brown, P. 42
Bruer, J. 79–80, 84
Burnham, W.M. 35, 36, 38
Burt, C. 32
Burton, R. 124, 130
Bussing, R. *et al.* 50

Cantwell, D. 62
Caplan, P. 42–3
caregivers of young children 69; *see also*
    fathers; parents; pregnant women
Carr, E.G. *et al.* 114
Carter, A.S. *et al.* 77
cartography 52
Centre for the Developing
    Brain 79, 80
Charach, A. *et al.* 110
charity schools 28–9
Chilcott, T. 112

Child Behavioral Checklist 77
child development theories 87–8
child guidance clinics 39–41
child psychiatry 35–6
childcare 69, 72, 73, 83–4
Cho, S.H. 124, 125, 126, 127–8, 134, 134*f*,
    135, 136
Clarizio, H.F. 43, 77
Clark, A. 3, 4
Clark, C. 138
Clarke, A.M. *et al.* 32, 34
classification of children 18–20, 19*f*
Clausing, J. 113
Cohen, E. 83
Coldstream, J. 32, 34
colleges and universities 120–2, 162;
    depression 120–2, 124–5, 127, 128, 133,
    140, 162; desired consequences 140–2;
    disorders of interest 128–33; modes of
    practice 133–40; points of arousal
    122–6; relations of power 126–8;
    student as threat 121–2, 123–6, 127–8;
    threat assessment 125–6, 133–4,
    137–9, 140; violence 121, 122,
    123–4, 127, 134–5, 137, 139, 140,
    141–2
colonialism 52
Comber, B. 158, 171
concentration 38
Concerto 94–5
conduct disorder (CD) 6
Connell, D. 137
Conrad, P. 7
Continuous Performance Test 51
Cooksey, E. 42
corporal punishment 20–1
creative ontology 165
Crenshaw, K. 65
criminal profiling 137
criminality and criminalization of child
    behaviour 107, 109–10, 112–13
Critchley, J. 169
critical periods 80
critique 12, 163, 165
Crone, D. 101
cultural competency 8, 51

danger and risk *see* risk
    factors; violence
Daniels, H. 63
Davies, G.K. 136
Davis, L. 64–5
De Landa, M. 146

defining mental illness 31–4, 47–9, 76–8; *see also* diagnosis of mental disorders
dejection 130
Del Giudice, M. 70–1, 78
Deleuze, G. 147, 170
Deleuze, G. and F. Guattari 12, 55, 144–5, 146, 155, 166–7, 169
Demotes-Mainard, J. 135
DeNoon, D. 124
D'Entrèves, M.P. 127
depression: impotency of 129–33; in early childhood 78; in the *DSM* 132–3; in tertiary students 120–2, 124–5, 127, 128, 133, 140, 162; and melancholia 128–30, 129f, 132; and violence 121, 122, 124–5, 127, 128, 134–5, 137, 139, 140, 141–2
depressive disorders 6
deterritorialization 12, 144–5, 146–7, 155, 166–7; *see also medicus interruptus*
developmentalism 2–3
Dewey, J. 52
diagnosis of mental disorders 6, 11; and biopower 105–6; definitions of disorders 48; diagnostic qualifiers 90, 92–4; expectations of medicalization 149–52, 153; in secondary school 104, 107; inter-rater reliability 88; *medicus interruptus* 148–9, 152–3; and network of services 7; and social class/disadvantage 55–7, 149, 153, 160
*Diagnostic and Statistical Manual of Mental Disorders (DSM)*: depression 132–3; diagnostic criteria 20, 88–9; *DSM-5* 41, 43, 77, 89, 106–7; history of 41–4, 77; inter-rater reliability 88; psychiatric disorders 6
Dickens, C. 28–9
disability 64–5
disability benefits 89, 91, 107, 149, 153–4
disposition 130
Dodge, K.A. 141
Donnelly, K. 63
Doyle, L.W. 78
*DSM see Diagnostic and Statistical Manual of Mental Disorders*
Dukes, C. 22–3
Duncan Smith, I. 53
Durand-Fardel, M. 25
Dürer, A. 129f, 130, 135
Dwivedi, K. 50–1
dyslexia 56
dysphoric mania 123

early childhood 67–8, 161; desired consequences/outcomes 84–5; disorders of interest 6, 76–8; focal points of experience 67–8, 84–5; modes of practice 78–84, 82t; points of arousal 69–73; relations of power 73–6
education: compulsory education 29; educational failure 2; special education 34, 49–51, 160, 162; teacher education 20, 100–1, 112, 163–4, 170; *see also* pedagogy
educational interventions 98
Egan, M. 34
Egger, H.L. 68, 76, 77–8, 82t
Eisenberg, D. 120
elementary school *see* primary school
Elias, M. 139
emotional difficulties/disorders 6; and *medicus interruptus* 150; in preschool 76; prevalence of 112; and race and ethnicity 49–50; and social class 53; *see also* affective aspects of *medicus interruptus*
England 13; anti-social behaviour 107–8; behaviour disorders 111, 115; crime 109–10; diagnosis 104; race and special educational needs 49–50; school exclusion 64; secondary school 104, 107–8, 109–10, 111, 115; social class/disadvantage 54–5
Erevelles, N. 88
Erikson, E. 87
Errington, M. 47
Eryigit-Madzwamuse, S. 72
ethnicity *see* race and ethnicity

facts 122, 126–7, 136, 137, 140
Fair, B. 155
family 71, 83, 96
fathers 71
feeblemindedness 32, 33, 34
Ferri, B. 65
focal points of experience 10, 67–8, 84–5
foetal programming 70–1
Fontana, A. 90
Forain, J.L. 57–8, 58f
Foucault, M. 9–12, 164–5, 167; on class 53; on critique 12; on diagnosis 90, 92; on educational interventions 98; focal points of experience 10, 67, 84–5; on governmentality 106, 111; grid of analysis 12–13, 74, 78–9; on health 100–1; on madness 10, 17, 44,

90, 121, 122, 130; on melancholy 130, 131–2; on power 9–11, 46, 48, 73–4, 86, 87, 89, 90, 92–3, 103, 104, 164; on psychopharmaceuticals 43–4; on scholastic criteria 34; on separation 96, 119; on specification of danger and risk 108, 165; on the structure of perception 121, 122, 128, 132, 133, 136, 141; on the subject 9, 10, 11, 88; on technologies of security 117–18, 119; on truth 9, 17, 48, 75, 89, 121, 141
Fox, C. 135
Fox, N.J. 61
Frances, A. 89
Fraser, K. 118
Freud, S. 87

Galton, F. 86
Garth, T. 51
gender: ADHD 62–4, 160; boys 61–2, 73, 160; naming the gender danger 62–3; and school exclusion 64
Gentschel, D. 115
ghettos 52
Gillborn, D. 52, 53, 65
Gillies, V. 54–5
Goode, E. *et al.* 123
Goodley, D. 154
Goodman, A. 54
Goto, Y. 78
Gove, M. 100
governmentality 106, 111
Graham, L.J. 158, 162
Gregg, P. 54
grid of analysis 12–13, 74, 78–9
Gros, F. 10
Grotius, H. 126
Guattari, F. *see* Deleuze, G. and F. Guattari

Hack, M. *et al.* 71
Hackett, L. 50
Hackett, R.J. 50
Hacking, I. 165
Harwood, V. 13, 84
Hawkins, M.F. 93
health and schooling 22–3, 100–1
Heinemann, H.A. 21–2
Henry, C. 135
Hickey-Moody, A. 170
high school *see* secondary school
history of mental disorders in school 17–18; classification of children 18–20, 19*f*;

problems caused by schooling 20–6; psycho-educational concerns 26–31; worrying about mental problems 31–5; mental health and mental hygiene in schools 35–41, 37*f*; *DSM* 41–4
Hoffman, H. 62–3
holidays 3–5
Holmes, J.E. 123
Horner, R. 101
Howard, J. 146
Hunt, J. 120
Hyman, S. 88

ICD (International Classification of Diseases) 6
idiocy 33, 34
imbecility 33, 34
inclusion 8, 105, 111–12, 160
infant mental health 67, 68
infant psychiatry 68
Infant-Toddler Social Emotional Assessment 77
information sharing 139–40
intensity 12–13, 160–1
International Classification of Diseases (ICD) 6
intersectionality 47, 54, 64–6, 160
Ireland, W. 24–5
Irvin, R. 124
Isaacs, D. 9, 54

Jacob, J.I. 71, 72
James, R. 131–2
Jastrow, J. 130
Jehan, Z. 93, 95
Jenkins, R.L. 43
Johnston, J. *et al.* 114, 115
Jones, D. *et al.* 73

Kaine, T.M. 125
Kaiser, S. 71
Kamler, B. 158, 171
Kaufman, R. 83
Kimmins, C.W. 38
King, M.L. 172
Kirk, S.A. 43
Kurtz, Z. *et al.* 84
Kutchins, H. 43

Ladson-Billings, G. 52
Lancaster, J. 29
*Lancet* 89

Land, N. 155
language: discourse demos-tration
    168–9; labelling 34, 105, 113–14, 152;
    in *medicus interruptus* 147–9; terminology
    6–7, 31–4
Lapage, C.P. 32
Lareau, A. 55
Latour, B. 163, 164
Latuff, C. 134, 134*f*, 135
Laurence, J. 48
learning disabilities 114
learning disorders 6
Lee, S. *et al.* 110
Lee, Y.A. 78
Leger, M.C. 42, 95
Levy, D.M. 30
looked-after children 107
Lorry, A.-C. 131–2
Lyotard, J. 163

McCallum, D. 48
McCartney, K. *et al.* 71
McCoy, G.F. 43
McDowell, L. 62
McGrath, P. *et al.* 71
McKay, R. 103
Mackie, D. 111–12
McKinney, F. 36–8, 37*f*
McLaughlin, J. 154
McLaughlin, T. 115
McMahon, S. 6
MacNaughton, G. 86
madness 10, 17, 44, 90, 121, 122, 123, 130
maladjusted children 88
Malins, P. 156
Mandel, S. 35–6, 44
Marcus, J. 137, 138
Martin, J. 113
Marwick, H. *et al.* 77
Maslow, A. 87
Masschelein, J. 164–5
maternal stress 70–1, 78
medicalization: of children 1–2, 3–5, 7,
    83–4, 110, 151, 154; expectations of
    149–52, 153; of poverty 53–4, 61; *see
    also medicus interruptus*
*medicus interruptus* 145, 146, 147, 155–6,
    162–3; affective 152–5; linguistic 147–9;
    visual 149–52
melancholia 129*f*; and depression 128–30,
    132; impotency of 129–32
Meltzer, H. *et al.* 122
mental deficiency 32–4

mental disorders: defining mental
    illness 31–4, 47–9, 76–8; descriptive
    approaches 76; diagnostic approaches
    77; dimensional approaches 76–7; in
    early childhood 76–8; in primary school
    90–1; in secondary school 104, 105–8;
    in colleges and universities 128–33;
    prevalence in children 2–3; terminology
    6–7, 31–4; *see also* diagnosis of mental
    disorders; history of mental disorders in
    school
mental handicap 34
mental health consultations 81–3, 82*t*
mental health services 7, 136–7, 139
mental hygiene 35–41, 37*f*
mental retardation 34
Miller, R. 111
Miller, T. 42, 95
modes of action 167–8; discourse demos-
    tration 168–9; privileging pedagogy over
    pathology 168; professional training that
    is educational 170
modes of practice: connecting the dots
    135–7, 139; diagnostic qualifiers 92–4;
    grid of analysis 78–9; in early childhood
    78–84, 82*t*; in primary school 92–101; in
    secondary school 108–19; in colleges and
    universities 133–40; information sharing
    139–40; moral treatment 114–16;
    pharmaceutical arousal 94–5; potency
    as a mode of practice 134–5; separation
    95–6, 117–19; specification of danger
    and risk 103, 108–14, 165; supporting
    parents 116–19; threat assessment 125–6,
    133–4, 137–9, 140; training parents to
    be 'good' 96–8; training
    systems 98–101
moral treatment 114–16
morality 29
mothers *see* maternal stress; parents;
    pregnant women
Multimodal Treatment Study for
    Attention-Deficit Hyperactivity Disorder
    (MTA) 102
Mundasad, S. 80
Murthy, R.S. 49

Nature 70
Naylor, R. 122
Nealon, J. 12–13, 86–7, 96, 103, 160–1
neuroimaging studies 79, 93–4
neuroscience 79–81
Newman, K. 135

Newman, L 53
Nietzsche, F. 164

O'Brien Caughy, M. *et al.* 72
O'Dowd, C. 62
oppositional defiant disorder (ODD) 6
O'Regan, F. 63
orthophrenics 30–1
Osmond, A. 48–9
Osterwell, N. 125
O'Toole, M.E. 124
Owens, P. 126

Paperson, L. 52
parenting contracts 117
Parenting Orders 117
parents: of adolescents 104–5, 116–19;
    behaviours and attitudes 69–71; maternal
    stress 70–1, 78; personality 71; and
    racism 72; training parents to be 'good'
    96–8; 'Triple P' approach 97–8, 117
Paton, G. 62
Patton, P. 155
PBS (Positive Behaviour Support)
    programmes 114–15
pedagogy 92; *vs.* pathology 168; of
    reconnection 157–8, 159; the thrill of
    pedagogy 170–2
peer discrimination 1, 109, 113–14
Pelham, W. *et al.* 113
perception, structure of 121, 122, 128, 132,
    133, 136, 141
Perry, D. *et al.* 81
personality: of children 78; of parents 71; of
    teachers 26
personality disorders 6
Peterson, S. 79
pharmaceutical arousal 94–5
pharmaceutical sales 3–4
Phillips, D.I.W. 70
physical exercise 73
Piaget, J. 87
points of arousal: in early childhood 69–73;
    in primary school 87–9; in secondary
    school 104–5; in tertiary students 122–6
political action 12, 165–6, 169
Porter, J. 63
Positive Behaviour Support (PBS)
    programmes 114–15
Positive Parenting Programme (Triple P)
    97–8, 117
poverty 9, 11; medicalization of 53–4, 61;
    *see also* social class/disadvantage

power relations 9–11, 12, 46, 48, 73–4,
    164; analysis of power 74–5; biopower
    86–7, 92, 96, 102, 103–4, 105–6;
    governmentality 106, 111; in early
    childhood 73–6; in primary school
    89–90, 92–3; in secondary school 105–6;
    in colleges and universities 126–8;
    surplus-power 87, 89, 92, 94
pregnant women 69–71
prenatal life 69–72
preschool/kindergarten *see* early childhood
preterm babies 69, 78
primary school 86–7, 161; desired
    consequences/outcomes 101–2; disorders
    of interest 90–1; modes of practice
    92–101; point of arousal 87–9; relations
    of power 89–90, 92–3
professionals' practices: deterritorialization
    144–5, 146–7, 155; territorialization
    145–6; *see also medicus interruptus*
Pruitt, D. 108–9
psychiatric disorders 6
psychiatrists' attitudes to children's
    behaviour 39
psychiatry 89, 90
psychopathologization of
    children 7–8, 11
psychopathology 1–2; diagnosis 6; and
    educational failure 2; and schools 8–9,
    11, 159–63; and social
    disadvantage 9, 11
psychopharmaceuticals 43–4
punishment 20–1

quiet corners 118–19

race and ethnicity: achievement gap
    52–3; and ADHD 50–1; and emotional
    and behavioural difficulties 49–50;
    intersectionality 54, 64–5; parents and
    racism 72; racialized naming practices
    51; spatializing 'race' 52–3; and special
    educational needs 49–51, 160, 162
Radden, J. 128
Rancière, J. 169
Rappley, M.D. 93
reading disorders 6
Ream, R.K. *et al.* 52
Reavis, W.C. 27–8
Reid, M.J. *et al.* 73
Rescorla, L.A. 77
reterritorialization 155
Reti, I.M. *et al.* 71

risk factors 11, 46–7; intersectionality 47, 54, 64–6, 160; specification of danger and risk 103, 108–14, 165; *see also* depression: and violence; gender; race and ethnicity; social class/disadvantage
Ritalin 94–5, 110
Rivlin, H.N. 39
Roberts, S. 62
Robinson, K. 60
Rohde, A.L. 50, 51, 62
Roithmayr, D. 52
Rose, N. 48, 67, 86
Roy, K. 167
Runswick-Cole, K. 154
Rushmann, A. 133
Rutgers Newark 138
Ryan, C.W. 25–6, 35, 38

Sachser, N. 71
Said, E. 53
Saigal, S. 78
Sameroff, A.J. *et al.* 68
Sandiford, P. 22, 31, 32–3
Sanon, K. 133, 137
Scheffler, R.M. *et al.* 5
schizophrenia 6, 78
Schlotz, W. 70
Schmidt, J. 131
scholastic criteria 34
school exclusion 9, 64, 72
school medical inspections 29–30
schools and psychopathology 8–9, 11, 159–63
Schram, S.F. 12, 46, 54, 61
Science Daily 2
Scotland 14; primary school 91, 93–4, 95, 96–7; secondary school 104, 105, 107, 110, 115–16, 118–19; behaviour disorders 110, 115, 118–19; diagnosis 104; Medicalization of Child Behaviour (MCB) 14, 113, 145; *medicus interruptus* 145, 146, 147–56, 162–3; social class/disadvantage 54–7, 59–60, 61
secondary school 103–4, 161–2; adjustment of students 27–8; desired consequences/outcomes 119; disorders of interest 106–8; mechanisms of security 117–19; modes of practice 108–19; point of arousal 104–5; relations of power 105–6; supporting parents 116–19
security 117–19, 121–2; *see also* threat assessment

selective serotonin uptake inhibitors (SSRIs) 135
self-control 60
Senellart, M. 106
separation: primary school 95–6; secondary school 117–19
Sharpe, M. 126, 127
Sibley, M. *et al.* 107
Siegler, M. 48–9
silences 12
Simmons, T. *et al.* 51
Simons, M. 164–5
Skounti, M. *et al.* 62
Slee, R. 90, 98
Smith, D. 146
Smith, G. 39–40
Smith, J. (1857) 34
Smith, J. (2001) 122
Smith, J. (2011) 2
social class/disadvantage: and ADHD 9, 53, 54; and diagnosis 55–7, 149, 153, 160; and higher education 122–3; intersectionality 54, 65; *medicus interruptus* 146, 149–50, 151–5; naming chaos and lack 57–60; and psychopathology 9, 11; and social, emotional, behavioural difficulties 9, 11, 13, 53; territorializing the home 60–1
Soja, E. 47
Solórzano, D.G. 65
Sonuga-Barke, E.J.S. *et al.* 83
spatialization: of mental disorder 47, 49; of race 52–3; and social class/disadvantage 55
special educational needs 34; and race and ethnicity 49–51, 160, 162
Sroufe, L.A. 2
SSRIs (selective serotonin uptake inhibitors) 135
Stein, A. *et al.* 71
Stevenson, G.S. 39–40
Still, G. 60, 63
Stoughton, E. 96, 98
Strahan, S.A.K. 24
Strand, S. 55
structure of this book 14–16
student as threat 121–2, 123–6, 127–8
studies discussed in this book 13–14
the subject 9, 10, 11, 88
subnormality 34
suicide of children 24–5
Swanson, J. 94

Symonds, B. 49
synapses 79, 80, 84

Tavistock Clinic 95
Taylor, C. 98–100
Taylor, E. 50
teacher education 20, 100–1, 112, 163–4, 170
teachers: attitudes to children's behaviour 39, 111–12; confidence 151, 155; in preschool 72–3; in primary school 87–8, 95; in secondary school 104, 111–12; and medicalization of children 83–4, 151; personality of 26
territorialization 12, 60–1, 145–6, 155, 166; see also deterritorialization
Thehumanteacher 170–1
theoretical perspective: Foucault 9–12; key arguments 11–12; possibilities for action 167–70; use of theory 163–7; see also Arendt, H.; Deleuze, G. and F. Guattari; Foucault, M.
Thomas, G. 88
threat assessment 125–6, 133–4, 137–9, 140
Thwing, C.F. 4
Timimi, S. 50
Tomlinson, S. 53, 118
Torrance, H. 163
training: training parents to be 'good' 96–8; training systems 98–101
trauma 148–9, 150, 151
Triple P see Positive Parenting Programme
Troyna, B. 65
truth 9, 10, 11, 17, 48, 75, 89, 121, 122, 126; factual truths 122, 126–8, 140, 141, 165; rational truths 122, 126, 127–8, 131, 132, 136, 141, 142, 165
Turkey: university students 120
Tyre, P. 62

United Kingdom: Association of Teachers and Lecturers 61, 63, 112; behaviour disorders 117; Cabinet Office 53; CAMHS (Child and Adolescent Mental Health Service) 84; Child Guidance Council 34–5, 40; colleges and universities 120, 121; Department for Education 98–9, 100, 104; medicalization of children 83–4; Mental Health Foundation 2;

Ministry of Education 86, 88, 95; National Association of Schoolmasters and Union of Women Teachers 112; National Collaborating Centre for Mental Health 50; National Council for Special Education 110; National Union of Teachers 112; parenting contracts 117; Parenting Orders 117; preschool mental disorders 76; Royal College of Preceptors 21; Royal College of Psychiatrists 120, 122; secondary school 117; social class/disadvantage 53, 54–5; training systems 98–100; see also England; Scotland
United States 13; ADHD 50, 51, 54, 62; American Journal of Public Health 69; American Psychiatric Association 88, 89; colleges and universities 120, 121; criminalization of child behaviour 112–13; Federal Bureau of Investigation 124; Federation of Teachers 112; FERPA (Family Educational Rights and Privacy Act 139–40; National Institute of Mental Health 120; Positive Behaviour Support (PBS) 114–15; social class/disadvantage 54; threat assessment 125–6, 133–4, 137–9, 140; training systems 101; see also Diagnostic and Statistical Manual of Mental Disorders (DSM); Virginia Tech Massacre
universities see colleges and universities
Unwin, C. 32
Upshur, C. et al. 73

Van Acker, R. 63
Vaughan, B. et al. 101
Vincent, C. et al. 55, 96
violence 121, 122, 123–5, 127, 128, 134–5, 137, 139, 140, 141–2
Virginia Tech Massacre 121, 124, 125–6, 133–4, 136–7
Visser, J. 93, 95
visual aspects of medicus interruptus 149–52
Voisin, F. 30
Volkow, N. 94
voluntary sector organizations 116

Walker, D. 51
Walker, H. et al. 112
Walkerdine, V. 3, 68
Wall, G. 80

Wallin, J.E.W. 29–31, 40–1, 41*f*
Ward, K.J. 61
Warner, F. 18
Warnock Committee (1978) 88
Wastell, D. 67, 69, 79, 80, 84
Watson, G.B. 39
Wheeler, L. 95
White, S. 67, 69, 79, 80, 84
Wickman, E.K. 39
Wig, N.N. 49
Wile, I.S. 69

Willis, R. 21
Willis, T. 131

Yosso, T.J. 65
Youdell, D. 110
Young, I. 65

Zachary, C.B. 40
Zerilli, L. 141
Zero to Three 68
Zito, J.M. *et al.* 83